This book is to be returned on
or before the date stamped below

UNIVERSITY OF PLYMOUTH

EXMOUTH LIBRARY

Tel: (01395) 255331
This book is subject to recall if required by another reade
Books may be renewed by phone
CHARGES WILL BE MADE FOR OVERDUE BOOKS

The Passion to Learn

This is the first book to provide a detailed overview and analysis of auto-didactism, or self-education. Autodidacts' strong preference for teaching themselves is likely to manifest itself, in childhood, as a pronounced resistance to formal schooling. However, in later life, an autodidact's passion for learning will emerge as they participate in open or distance learning or even take responsibility for devising, structuring and following their own programme of education.

Beginning and ending with comprehensive and stimulating discussions of learning theories, *The Passion to Learn* includes fourteen case studies of autodidactism in informal learning situations, all written by authors with specialised knowledge. These wide-ranging case studies reflect the inherent diversity of autodidactism, yet four common themes emerge: emotional/cognitive balance; learning environment; life mission; and ownership of learning. The final chapter addresses the implications of autodidactism for educational theory, research, philosophy and psychology.

This inquiry into autodidactism provides fresh insight into the motivation to learn. It shows how closely cognition, emotion and sensory perception act together in learning processes and draws upon memory studies, neurobiology, complexity theory and philosophy to illuminate the findings. At a time when such issues as participation in education, lifelong learning and alternative, non-formal modes of teaching and learning are at the forefront of international educational discourse, this fascinating, inspiring and timely book will be of great interest to anyone involved in the practice or policy of teaching and learning.

Joan Solomon is currently Senior Research Fellow and Visiting Professor at the Open University, King's College London and the University of Plymouth. She has researched and published widely on science education and vocational education.

The Passion to Learn

An inquiry into autodidactism

Edited by Joan Solomon

RoutledgeFalmer
Taylor & Francis Group

LONDON AND NEW YORK

First published 2003
by RoutledgeFalmer
11 New Fetter Lane, London EC4P 4EE

Simultaneously published in the USA and Canada
by RoutledgeFalmer
29 West 35th Street, New York, NY 10001

RoutledgeFalmer is an imprint of the Taylor & Francis Group

© 2003 Joan Solomon

Typeset in Palatino and Gill by BC Typesetting, Bristol
Printed and bound in Great Britain by
MPG Books Ltd, Bodmin, Cornwall

British Library Cataloguing in Publication Data
A catalogue record for this book is available from the British Library

Library of Congress Cataloging in Publication Data
A catalog record for this book has been requested

ISBN 0–415–30418–0

Contents

Illustrations

Figures

Tables

Contributors

Joan Solomon During more than 25 years teaching Physics and the Social relations of Science (STS) in a variety of secondary schools she became deeply interested in the learning of students of all abilities. After moving to Oxford University she taught student teachers and delivered professional in-service education. She carried out several research projects for the government on the new vocational courses once again making detailed observations of the students. More recently she has become Visiting Professor at the Open University and the University of Plymouth. She has run a small 'hands-on' Interactive Science Centre for research on primary pupils, taught adult classes, and carried out research on learning through practical work, as well as writing widely on students' learning, publishing four substantial books and many articles in international journals.

Margaret Boden is Research Professor of Cognitive Science at the University of Sussex. She is an elected Fellow of the British Academy, and of the American Association for Artificial Intelligence (and its British and European equivalents). Her work is highly interdisciplinary, since she holds degrees in medical sciences, philosophy, and psychology. Among her books are 'The Creative Mind' and 'Dimensions of Creativity' (ed.) which have been translated into 17 languages, and she has given lectures and media-interviews around the world. She has two children and one grandchild, and lives in Brighton.

Helen Brooke lived and worked in France for 13 years, teaching Health Education to varied groups. Her own children grew up to be bilingual there, and her interest in different ways of learning originates from this time. On returning to Great Britain she worked as research assistant at the small Interactive Science Centre run by Professor Joan Solomon. Helen is currently team leader of a language resource base for pupils with speech and language difficulties attached to a mainstream secondary school. She is working towards a PhD based on her research at the science centre, which focuses on the extent to which this environment allows young people with severe learning difficulties to be autonomous learners.

Paul Howard is an education and training consultant and a partner in Dreyfus Training & Development. Having formerly worked as a youth and community worker, teacher, lecturer, he was for eleven years the Headteacher of the behaviour Support Service in the London Borough of Newham, where he was at the forefront of that Authority's Inclusive Education strategy. His continuing commitment to social inclusion is reinforced by an interest in Multiple Intelligences theory as a basis for placing learning differences rather than learning difficulties at the centre of education thinking and practice.

Robin Hodgkin has been an eminent mountaineer climbing in Skye and the Alps as well as an active Quaker and spent many years teaching in Kenya and the Sudan. On his return to England he became a Tutor in Geographical Education at the Department of Educational Studies at Oxford University. He read constantly into many branches of philosophy and about the various paths of creativity. He has published many articles such as *The Seriousness of Play,* and two notable books on similar themes *Born Curious. New perspectives in Educational Theory* (1976) and *Playing and Exploring* (1985).

Vivian Leyser da Rosa is a lecturer in Human Genetics at Federal University of Santa Catarina (Florianópolis, SC). Teaching and researching in her field for over 15 years, she became increasingly involved with the education of future health sciences professionals, including medical students. The training of such future Brazilian professionals in the field of Genetics, given its present ethical, social and cultural implications and the need of professionals to act as mediators between science and the public, became a theme for her doctoral thesis, part of which she developed with Joan Solomon at Oxford University. Besides teaching Human Genetics, she organises seminars in Genetics and Ethics and provides genetic counselling services.

Richard Edwards is Professor of Education at the University of Stirling, Scotland. Prior to this he worked in Adult Education in Kent and London and at the Open University, UK. His interest in self-directed learning derives from his own experience of learning philosophy as an undergraduate and postgraduate, as his attendance at lectures and seminars was minimal. Books and friends have been the source of much of his learning in both personal and professional contexts. It is not surprising therefore that he has researched and written extensively on adult education and lifelong learning.

Stephen Lunn is a Research Fellow at the Open University, specialising in learning and pedagogy in primary and secondary education. Subject emphases are science and design technology; particular foci are the cross-curricular themes of creative problem-solving and sustainability. The theoretical perspective is broadly socio-cultural, with concerns for the relationships between models of learning, knowledge, and pedagogy; and relationships between individuals and communities of practice. His interest in autodidactism is centred on the latter, particularly where the communities are more or less remote from the learning individual.

John Ziman is Emeritus Professor of Physics at the University of Bristol and a Fellow of the Royal Society. During his career as a theoretical physicist he became interested in the social and personal aspects of science, on which he has written a number of books, including Public Knowledge (1968), Reliable Knowledge (1978) and Real Science (2000). He might be tempted to describe himself as an autodidact in the sociology and philosophy of science, except that all scientists and scholars have to go on teaching themselves new things all their lives.

Paul Caro is a former 'Directeur de Recherche' at CNRS. He is an inorganic chemist specialising in lanthanides. He became involved by chance (1980) in science popularisation in the form of newspaper articles, radio and TV broadcasts on a variety of topics across the scientific world. Appointed Délégué aux Affaires Scientifiques of la Cité des Sciences et de l'Industrie in Paris in 1989 he became more involved in the ways and means of public understanding of science and scientific literacy both from the practical and theoretical point of views, especially in the Science Museum framework. Besides articles in specialised literature he has published five books on science popularisation and the science–society relationship and was also involved in European programmes assessing the diffusion of scientific knowledge especially through education and pedagogical experiments.

Tim Hunkin trained as an engineer, but then became a cartoonist (drawing a strip for the *Observer* called 'The Rudiments for Wisdom' for 15 years). His next career was in television (writing and presenting three series called 'The Secret Life of Machines' for Channel 4). He now works mainly for museums, building interactive exhibits and curating and designing exhibitions (most recently the Visitor Centre for the Eden Project in Cornwall).

Anita Rampal is Professor of Elementary and Social Education at Delhi University (India). Trained initially as a Physicist, her involvement as a voluntary resource person for the Hoshangabad Science Teaching Programme caused her to change track. The engagement with school science, especially for the disadvantaged majority, who struggled with irrelevant and poor educational programmes in dilapidated rural schools gradually grew into a lifelong commitment. She has co-authored books such as *Numeracy Counts* (1998), the *Public Report on Basic Education* (1999) and others written in Hindi, in addition to several other research articles and reports.

Eileen Scanlon has worked with science learners at the Open University, UK for the past 28 years. Before this she worked as a schoolteacher with secondary school pupils, teaching general science, physics and mathematics. At the OU she has been involved with design and evaluation of a wide range of science courses and is now a Professor of educational technology. She is particularly interested in the uses of information technology in education and directs the Computers and Learning Research Group working on a range of projects including remote access to laboratory work. Her publications about science teaching include Open Science: the distance teaching and open learning of science subjects. Recently her research has included work on communicating science.

Albert Paulsen has for the last 25 years been a senior lecturer at the University of Roskilde in Denmark, which is recognised for its alternative studies based on problem centred, participatory project work. His main research interests are in learning science through practical work and in Science for Citizenship. Besides being a teacher and supervisor in Physics and Science Education at the university, he has participated in and carried out several research projects in a national and European context as well as been involved in national evaluation and curriculumm work. During the years he has edited, contributed to and been the author of several books on science education and teaching material. Recently he has retired from his post and now holds a part-time senior affiliation to the university.

Jack Diamond was born and brought up in a poor part of Leeds, where he attended Grammar School and later trained to be a chartered accountant. The lack of opportunity for young people from poor backgrounds influenced him to join the Labour Party. He took a practical approach to learning about politics serving as a governor of a hospital and of a school in the East End of London, and using his business training to probe their management. He entered Parliament in 1945 and was First Secretary to the Treasury from 1962–68. He was given a life peerage and served in the House of Lords as Leader of the new Social Democratic Party and Chairman of many committees. In his early nineties he embarked on an extensive reading programme to read and explore religious literature of the Abrahamic tradition in the original languages.

Acknowledgements

Figure 3.1 from Helen Brooke and Joan Solomon 'From playing to investigating: research in an Interactive Science Centre for primary pupils' in *International Journal of Science Education*, 1998, Vol 20, No 8, 959–971. Reprinted with permission of Taylor & Francis Journals. www.tandf.co.uk

Figure 6.1(a) from *Patterns of Discovery* by N.R. Hansen. Copyright 1958 by N.R. Hansen, reprinted with permission of Cambridge University Press.

Figure 6.1(b) From *American Journal of Psychology* LXVII (1954) 550. Copyright 1954 by Board of Trustees of the University of Illinois. Reprinted by permission of the University of Illinois Press.

Figure 17.7 is from *Adult Education and the Postmodern Challenge* by R. Usher, I. Bryant and R. Johnston (1997). Reprinted by permission of Routledge.

Introduction

Joan Solomon

As the title suggests, this book is an inquiry into an area which is little charted. There are fifteen central chapters written by those who know something valuable about autodidacts. Their contributions are first-hand stories about children or adults in different but autonomous learning circumstances. To collate these chapters and relate them to what is known about learning, the book needed an opening chapter to present an overview of the learning theories that might be applicable, so that was added. A handyman attempt was made to compress the multitude of words written on the subject into one readable and useful chunk.

Then it needed at least two more chapters at the end to pursue and round off the investigation, however incomplete. One was to collect and draw attention to any common features which were emerging under the very different circumstances of the fifteen central chapters. These were drawn out from the process of reading and rereading the contributions of my colleagues, who had little or no communication with each other. Then what was thought to be a final chapter was written from the different perspective of some important and controversial contemporary social theories. Like most finalities this one also lost its place and was shunted backwards when the publisher and reviewers suggested that yet another chapter was needed. This became an epilogue where I started the process of finding out how insights into the nature of autodidactism might be used within the many worlds of education. It could only be very incomplete at this stage.

This study and book forms a part of the programme of The Epistemology Group. All their work has addressed the theme of the evolution of knowledge and invention – with publications on *Technological Invention as an Evolutionary Process* (ed. Ziman 2000) and *The Evolution of Cultural Entities* (ed. Wheeler, Ziman and Boden in press). They funded the original seminar for the present project, 'Autodidactism and Creativity' which was held jointly by the Royal Society of Arts and the Open University, and from which this book drew for many of its contributors. For all of this it is a pleasure to express my gratitude to the Epistemology Group, the Open University, and to the contributors who made the work possible. After the opening seminar I badgered some of my other colleagues to add a few more contributions for which I am equally grateful. I also need to thank numerous friends for useful comments and informal information.

Finally my thanks and love go to John Ziman, who encouraged me in this excursion into a new field of knowledge by judicious administrations of acclaim and the reverse, as appropriate, during the writing of this book.

May 2002

Chapter 1

Theories of learning and the range of autodidactism

Joan Solomon

Who is an autodidact?

From its etymology, an autodidact seems to be one who teaches her or himself. Indeed a Greek friend of mine, on learning of my interest, said 'Why use a Greek word? Why not "self-taught"?'

But at once there is a problem. None of us could possibly be anywhere near to being completely self-taught. From the moment our mothers put a spoonful of food to our lips so that we could suck at the spoon's edge, we were being taught, although it must be added that quite a few babies spit out the food and seize the spoon themselves! Is that autodidactism? Every time someone speaks, or points out a bird doing something strange on the lawn, or reconfigures the computer slowly enough for us to follow – if we want to, we are being taught. Perhaps we might say, in retrospect, that we were *allowing ourselves* to be taught. That puts autodidacts in a new light. Why do such people, and indeed it may be nearly all of us, sometimes react in such a difficult 'ornery' way to being taught? This is close to some of the central problems that this book will address in trying to describe the range of autodidacts. These do not occur because autodidacts don't want to learn. They do.

Not all children enjoy school, but we are all 'born curious', as Hodgkin wrote (1976). This wonderful quality, curiosity about *new* things, is so well established by experiment that it is used to study small babies' recollections of music even from the time they were still in the womb, understanding of gravity, or the cadences of their mother's voice. Even babes just a few days old will turn to look at something new and ignore effects that are old and well-known. This is the beginning of learning from experience, which is concerned with delight as well as knowledge and is the background to almost all the accounts in this book.

So 'self-taught' will not quite do as a complete description of the autodidact. We need a word to describe a range of people who prefer to teach themselves or to pick up knowledge from non-teaching situations, in one way or another. The state of being such a person is our title word –

autodidactism. We can also tap into neighbouring and more familiar words, such as 'autonomous', which bring with them a whiff of independence if not rebellion. They may get angry when someone tries to teach them instead of letting them find out for themselves. It is a familiar human reaction. All two-year-olds go through this process intensively, we call it 'the tantrums' and it shows a perfectly healthy development of independence. Supporting comment comes from Howard Gardner. He wrote, from the results of his study Creators of the Modern World (1994), that he had found some psychological features common to all these very autonomous people. Not only were they energetic and demanding, but they also retained some of the features of childhood such as going on asking questions and ignoring the conventions, and were themselves fascinated by the exuberant, inquisitive and emotional traits of children.

Most of us have some tendencies towards autodidactism, but that does not mean that we are great creative geniuses (see Chapter 2). At one time or another we all want the freedom to choose. The wish of auto-didacts *not* to be taught in certain ways is coupled with a great wish to learn for and by themselves. The awkwardness of these two conflicting drives can sometimes cause trouble for them at school, but may be rewarded in later life by the achievement of original outcomes and fluent personal ways of learning. Those who display these features span a great range of people. We may all have felt, from time to time, their kind of anger at being over-instructed, and their kind of exhilaration when finding out something new for themselves. Autodidacts also come, as we shall see, in a range of emotive and cognitive colours.

People sometimes think that in the days before schools and plentiful books everyone was, perforce, an autodidact. However, learning without a teacher is not necessarily the same as teaching oneself in solitude. There are many other possibilities. One is that a bank of knowledge is picked up by physical imitation. Young predators like fox and lion cubs learn to use their bodies more skilfully for hunting through play. Arthur Koestler (1966) in his book about creativity called this 'ludic learning', although that may well be nearer to sports training than to how autonomous learners cherish new ideas. Apprenticeship for the learning of practical skills can take place through a method of authoritative imposition, which the autonomous amongst us might find insupportable. But it could also take place in a more acceptable way, where apprentices pick up what to do by unpressured imitation. I knew one autodidact who had regularly truanted from secondary school, was unhappy at university, and only started enjoying learning in a research laboratory. Here, she told me, you were expected to pick up skills in a relaxed 'hands-off' way as a part of an established group. We shall also see how this method may be applied to training in a modern industrial workshop (Richard Edwards in Chapter 7).

If what we learn comes only through our bodies then the acquired knowledge may well continue to reside permanently *in our bodies* in a very local sense (see Polanyi's [1958] discussion of such 'in-dwelling' knowledge quoted in Chapter 5). Knowledge so acquired may be essential for instinctive life-saving, and other primitive reactions over which we have little control. Swimming and judging by eye as carpenters do, and other more advanced practical skills are also largely learnt by this ancient method. However we humans learn a great deal more by our gift of speech with others, and our internal reflection about what we do, and once this happens in tandem with actions and skills that our hands have already learnt, it becomes powerful for all kinds of learning.

The start of human learning

During the 1920s Wolfgang Köhler (1925) carried out some famous experiments with chimpanzees to find out if and how they could teach themselves to solve problems. In every case a banana or other fruit was placed out of reach, and various lengths of stick and rope, and sometimes boxes, were supplied. The apes seemed to have different degrees of persistence, and different rates of success just as humans have. Köhler was able to show that the apes, some more quickly than others, were able to make simple implements from ropes and one or two sticks, or from two boxes stacked on top of each other, and use them to reach the objective. One of his interesting conclusions was that once the solution was 'seen', the two actions required to reach the fruit were done sequentially without pause. It is as though the ape has constructed an image of the complete solution in his mind, and then simply carried out the required actions. They seemed to learn from their own imaginative efforts. Sometimes they also learnt by imitation but they never tried to instruct each other (1925: 193). Köhler was quite clear about this. Autodidactism might be a very early contribution to learning.

Very soon after news of these investigations had reached the Soviet Union, one of the colleagues of Lev Vygotsky, the famous cognitive psychologist, started some similar research in which Köhler-like problems were set to groups of four- and five-year-old children. Vygotsky and Alexander watched this with great interest and were struck not by the similarity but by the contrast with the apes' behaviour. They commented on the 'planful' character of the speech which accompanied the children's action and concluded that:

> Children solve practical tasks with the help of their speech, as well as their hands and their eyes. This unity of perception, speech, and action, which ultimately produces internalisation of the visual field,

constitutes the central subject matter for any analysis of the uniquely human forms of behaviour.

(Vygotsky and Alexander 1930)

This 'internalisation of the visual field' is richer than what the apes may have achieved, but similar. Then talk helps it to become socially shared, and this is also fundamental to making sense of learning. Vygotsky's internalisation of the visual field is similar to Hodgkin's 'conceptual space', an idea which turns up at several points in this book, especially in Chapter 5 which is about two boys playing a new building game with wet sand on a slightly dangerous beach. Like Köhler's apes, Vygotsky's children had to imagine their proposed procedure before carrying out the actions. Out of this prepared space came their planning. In some respects this was like the babbling talk of toddlers as they face up to a new game which later 'turns inward', in Vygotsky's words, to become the basis of silent adult thinking.

If we watch two-year-olds we can often catch them talking out aloud, even if no one else is there, as they prepare to do something interesting with their toys. (And some of us adults still talk aloud to ourselves when no one else is around!). So reflecting when alone on some problem, which might have seemed to be the very prototype of isolated behaviour, can become a kind of internal theatre for the re-enactment of play or problem-solving in the playhouse of our minds. There it draws on earlier social learning situations and becomes quite similar to them. Learning by reflection may take place alone or in a group, sometimes it is intentionally taught and learnt, sometimes it is picked up by silent imitation. Often it is almost impossible to distinguish the one from the other.

Tales of autodidacts

Peter was about 15 when the following event took place. He was a very intelligent and confident boy, taller than average, and he slouched slightly in a casual way. One day after teaching about the transformation of energy I had set the school's model steam engine going. The solid fuel pellets burnt, the water boiled and hissed out of places where the fit of the pistons in the cylinders was not too good. The piston rods punched in and out and the flywheel spun so fast as to be reduced to a blur. That and the noise and the smell was very exciting and most of the pupils pushed eagerly round the engine and shouted comments to each other. Not so Peter. With his hands in his pockets he drew away from the commotion and commented to me that he had always thought about engines and that they only worked because there was a difference of conditions. Either it was hotter inside than out, or there was less pressure outside than in, and that made it work. But, he said, as it worked it seemed like this difference got less, so that it gradually stopped working. I was amazed! This, for any reader who does not know, is a home-made version of the famous second law of thermodynamics, which seemed to have been worked out by Peter on his own.

You need to know two more things about Peter. First, he frequently truanted from school. I had not realised this until a staff meeting was called to debate 'What shall we do about Peter?' and as I could not remember him missing physics lessons, I put it to him soon after the steam engine episode. I said something like 'What is this I hear about you playing truant?', to which he answered 'You don't need to worry Miss, I'm always here for physics lessons on Tuesdays and Thursdays'. We may deduce from this that Peter's truanting was quite deliberate, allowing him to learn only what and when he wanted to. There were other subjects that he did not want to learn, or some types of teacher instruction that he did not like.

The last thing to tell you is that Peter was killed soon after this. He and his friends had stolen a car and in the resulting police chase the car went out of control and the group were all injured or died. Peter did not just dislike being taught at school, he also quite enjoyed breaking regulations of other kinds. (I am *not* suggesting that other autodidacts are equally 'defiant' as Margaret Boden describes them in Chapter 2, but there *might* be some kind of connection in some cases, which we shall explore at the end of this book.)

The next story is about Gillian. At the time I first met her she was about 16, although to me she looked no more than nine or ten because she had Down's syndrome. She did not talk at all during her visit, but she did seem to understand speech and probably could use words and a few simple signs in Makadon – a simplified sign language for those with learning difficulties – that she had been taught at the special school she attended. (I should add that when I saw her the following year she had learnt to read very simple work-cards, and could talk more. She also appeared to have a boyfriend from the college which she attended, to whom she called loudly across the room whenever she wanted to show him what she had done.)

On both occasions Gillian was visiting a simple Interactive Science Centre where I and my colleague Helen Brooke (see Chapter 3) had set up some simple hands-on exhibits. In the first case her teacher was with the class and I was just watching and video recording what happened. The teacher tried hard to draw Gillian's attention to a skeleton which was lying on a table with a deflated balloon in its mouth. With her arm round Gillian's shoulders the teacher talked trying to explain how the skeleton was breathing by pushing the plastic diaphragm in and out. She talked and taught, trying to get Gillian to take part, and to blow up the balloon, but Gillian was clearly set on escape. By ducking out of reach she finally got free and arrived at the electricity table. Here she saw two wires, which she seemed to know needed to be joined together. She also seemed to know that this might have something to do with turning on the light; but she still had some thinking to do and confidence to gain. She took the wires, one in each hand, and approached them together very hesitantly. Then she looked up at the lamp. Was she wondering whether you had to touch the lamp with the wires to make it light up? Very slowly the wires approached both each other and also the lamp. In the end I could not tell if the wires made direct contact, or if they completed the circuit through the brass housing of the lamp. But it did light up, to Gillian's great pleasure.

It was Gillian's body language as she tried to make her escape from the teacher's instruction which is my abiding memory from this episode. She seemed to have just one thing in common with the gifted Peter – neither of them liked being taught. Later we found other Down's syndrome youngsters who turned their heads and looked obstinately away while their teacher was talking, only to start work again once the teacher had gone. One might guess that the outing to the Interactive Centre was understood as a challenge to find out for themselves – that was indeed what the organiser had said to them when they arrived. It was an opportunity they did not want to lose. Another possible explanation is that the speed of their thinking was so much slower than the speech of their teachers, that it made understanding more difficult.

Elaboration of theories

Educational research, whether empirical or theoretical, has been very busy during the last fifty years. Piaget (1972) had written that 'The attribute of intelligence is not to contemplate but to transform'. The prototypical Greek thinker, with head in hand, was now definitely out of date, but Piaget was using the verb 'to transform' in his own technical sense, as the reversal of perceived operations in the theatre of the mind. Similarly the 'conservation' of properties which was fundamental to his whole stage development theory of genetic epistemology also required mental transformations. Despite his important contribution to educational theory Piaget never did see teaching as a real contribution to the development of learning. On one occasion he claimed trenchantly, in the preface to a book by colleagues, *'bits of learning are not development'* (Inhelder, Sinclair and Bovet 1974). Never a very tactful man!

For Piaget learning was an increasingly logical process that we grow into by an internal maturation. The autonomous striving to learn could find no place in this predetermined scheme. Vygotsky emphasised the two-way nature of the teaching/learning process. It seems that he thought of all learners as taking an active part in the process, not accepting taught ideas in the passive way that had previously been assumed. He called this autonomous process of reflection and change 'elaboration'. 'Pedagogy has usually operated on the supposition that children are *receivers* of instruction and not, as they certainly are, *elaborators* of the contents presented to them' (Vygotsky 1978).

This might have been a focal moment in the understanding of autonomous learning, but, sadly, it was not. Neither Vygotsky nor others who used the word tried to pin down what they meant by the elaboration of instruction. No doubt this frustrating omission was partly due to the difficulty in communication between the Soviet Union and America during Vygotsky's short lifetime, or to a contemporary concentration on changing the curriculum in the USA (a common reaction to any or all educational problems). So when a new theory of meaningful learning did arrive (Ausubel 1963, *et al.* 1968) it received comparatively little attention, even though it presented the fertile idea of a connected structure of knowledge in the mind to which, under favourable conditions, new knowledge could be attached. However an aspect of Ausubel's theory known as 'concept mapping' (Novak and Gowan 1984), in which the pupils explore their own learning by drawing out on paper how they see the connections between the concepts they have been taught, has achieved permanent and widespread use. It may also have been the first classroom method which could be said to be based on pupil autonomy and, when it has been used by the pupils as their own research rather than as a method of yet more teaching, it has been very promising. (In Chapter 17 of this book we describe complexity theory, which has some resemblance to Ausubel's theory and can be used to think about the autonomous elaboration of learning in quite a new way.)

Research into student learning

In 1976 two landmark papers were published by a pair of Swedish researchers, Ference Marten and Roger Säljö. These were attempts 'to identify different levels of processing of information' used by Swedish university students who had been given substantial passages to read about economics. At one level, called 'surface learning' the students focused on memorising what they expected to have to face later as test questions. There was no elaboration and, unsurprisingly, they did not much enjoy this pressure to learn.

> 'Well I just concentrated on trying to remember as much as possible.'
> 'I'd sort of memorised everything I'd read. . . . No, not everything, but more or less.'

> 'It would have been more interesting if I'd known that I wasn't going to have a test on it . . . instead of all the time trying to think now I must remember this, and now I must remember that.'
>
> (Marten and Säljö 1976)

But the deeper kind of learning was quite different. Students who learnt in this way were concerned about the meaning of the passage and often looked to see how the new ideas linked with ones already existing in their minds.

> 'I tried to look for . . . the principal ideas . . . '
> 'and what you think about then, well it's you know – "what was the point of the article?"'
> 'I thought about how he had built up the whole thing.'
>
> (Marten and Säljö 1976)

This last comment, and others in the research, suggests that these deep learners might be thinking about the knowledge as a connected structure, as Ausubel had done.

Similar results were reported from research carried out in England by Noel Entwistle and Judith Ramsden (1983) and from Australia by John Biggs (1980). Biggs had become impressed by the evidence that some months after any teaching/learning process the student's understanding could be found to have gone either up or down. Going down could be explained easily enough by forgetting, but what could increased understanding, improvement without any teaching, mean? Was this autodidacticism?

> The individual then . . . thinks it over, sees some personal relevance he or she had not noticed before, relates this new material to previous material – and so the stored version is now at a higher level than at encoding. *Studying is to elaboration as teaching is to encoding.*
>
> (Biggs 1980)

This research into what students said about their own methods of learning showed, unsurprisingly, that being pressured into learning for examinations was not at all well liked: but contributing to the learning for themselves, 'elaborating' as Vygotsky had called it, was both more effective and somehow self organising. This last finding by Biggs – the autonomous reorganisation of learning – suggested that either students keep on reflecting about what they have learnt, or that some neural activity had the power to move, change, or possibly link up the learning in their minds. This exciting new approach will be discussed in Chapter 17.

John Biggs had at least one more piece of information which might con-
nect the way students learn to the concept of autodidactism. Using his
large database from the thousands of university students who had filled
in the questionnaire about their characteristic methods of study he was
able to show which statistical variables were most strongly associated
with a 'deep' approach to learning. For our purposes, it is only marginally
interesting to note that intelligence as measured by IQ tests was a more
significant characteristic of deep learners than of surface learners; whether
as a cause or an effect, or both, we cannot know. However there was
another factor showing an even stronger statistical correlation with the
factors that identified deep learning. This was having an internal locus of
control (wanting to be in control of one's own activities). It is perhaps
the strongest evidence yet that our investigation into learning is on the
track of autodidacts.

Constructivism and conceptual change

At about the same time as John Biggs' work, a lot of research was going on
into school students' own naive ideas about natural phenomena. This was
called constructivism in educational circles (the term is differently used in
sociology). It is included here because the method was based on experiential learning, which could be called the lived learning of people who,
for example, note the appearance of rainbows with curiosity as well as
aesthetic delight. In science education this worked both with and against
the autonomous ideas of pupils, and it is now possible to look back on
this research, which was so plentiful during the 1980s and 1990s, in the
light of this difficult mixture of educational goals.

The contributions to constructivist research by Rosalind Driver, who is
so sorely missed in the educational world, was mostly about thinking in
the classroom which used stored ideas from experiential learning to
answer questions about science (1978, 1983). At this time my own
research was on the social influences on how pupils constructed explanations for what they observed in the world, and then discussed with
others (Solomon 1987, 1991). There were also some contributions from
von Glasersfeld, which were different again, although on the same general
topic, being severely internalist and solipsistic (1989). (This differentiation
between the social and the personal aspects of learning will arise again in
the discussion of sociological controversies in Chapter 17.)

The educational world, with its interest in assessment, is always very
focused on conceptual change – how to *change* students' ideas into the
scientifically correct ones. First Driver's team of gifted teachers set about
eliciting the pupils' own ideas about phemomena in a classroom situation.
Sometimes they had the pupils write diaries about their ideas, and from

these we can often see autodidacts of different kinds not only putting forward their ideas but subsequently defending them very persistently. Any autodidacts worth their salt would stick to their own notions as long as possible. The constructivist classroom process could be quite uncomfortable for both such pupils and their teachers. Explaining your own ideas to others might be satisfying, but being forced to change at the teachers' behest in front of the whole class could well be humiliating. Some of the students fought to show that the teacher's arguments and demonstrations did *not* refute their idea, even if they seemed to do so. In my own experience this method was, at the very least, difficult to manage in the classroom. By the 1990s, careful longitudinal evaluation had shown that this way of teaching, which some autodidacts might have enjoyed in parts, was not any more effective for learning science than the more usual one which was administered to the control group (Johnston 1990).

There was another more complicated problem that was often ignored. If, as Johnston reported, the pupils were highly motivated by sharing their own ideas with others rather than being taught by a teacher, why didn't this increase their interest in science and so their learning achievement? This seemingly simple question has two *negative* answers. In the first place the constructivist way of teaching, as we have seen, does *not* improve achievement. Second, in a surprisingly large number of other studies of motivation the correlation between interest and achievement has always been low, variable, and sometimes *even negative* (Gardener 1975). There was a serious anomaly here which seemed to run contrary to common sense (see page 194 Chapter 16).

Educational psychologists began to wonder if these apparently rogue results were due to student anxiety being aggravated during tests. They introduced more supportive teaching, only to find that, in some cases, this actually decreased achievement further still (Weinart and Helmke 1987). Very curious! Eventually some further results from Helmke (1988), Valås and Søvik (1993) and others suggested that it was the teaching process itself which was the cause of the problem. If teaching produces something like anxiety or demotivation which reduces learning efficiency, there are at least two quite different ways we can deal with the problem.

> In the first place we can try and change the students to fit the instructional provisions. That means, that an attempt must be made to decrease their fear of failure and increase their self-efficacy, task orientation and intrinsic orientation. However we know from experience that changing personality traits is notoriously difficult . . . An alternative solution is to modify the level and type of instruction.
>
> (Boekaerts 1994: 6)

So the research project began to investigate what happened when 'the density of instructional input' was reduced. Like the special needs student Gillian, mentioned earlier, students *did* learn better without too much instruction. When such research was backed up by interviews with the students there was not just verbal corroboration but also identification of particular teachers who were seen as having had oppressive 'controlling tactics'. For the researchers this pinpointed the very lessons where controlling words like 'should' and 'ought' were most frequently used. This seemed to show that intensive teaching was simply counterproductive – more teaching but less learning. These are vital findings for the education of all our students, not just for those we identify, always rather uncertainly, as some kind of autodidact.

The wish of students to be autonomous also arises with respect to environmental action. In a review article about issues in environmental education Peter Posch (1993) told the story of a Swedish school where students had taken the initiative in treating a local lake with lime in order to neutralise its acidified water. When the treatment was found to be successful, several other local teachers were inspired by it and tried to get their students to do the same. However, now that the action was no longer an initiative by the students, they seemed to have lost heart. If done at the behest of the teacher it became little more than the mechanical carrying of buckets of lime on to the ice, and students were not enthusiastic. They no longer held the locus of control; they were not autonomous.

From liberty to logic?

Being in control of their own education is very rare for children. Not only do they *have* to go to school until the stipulated age; they also *have* to submit to the ways in which teachers instruct them. In the education given to our children in schools over the ages there have been centuries of beating, together with an absence of liberty of any kind. Even in the Enlightenment the philosopher John Locke, who wrote so eloquently and passionately about freedom, justice and the civil society, could see no use at all for liberty in the context of school education. 'Liberty and indulgence can do no good to children: their want of judgement makes them stand in need of restraint and discipline' (1693).

There had been just one outstanding exception to this rejection of freedom for the learning youngsters, and that was from the inspirational educational philosopher Jan Amos Comenius. About thirty years before the above quotation was written, and in good time for Locke to have read it, had he cared to do so, this great European teacher had summed up his life's work on education in just three main principles. The second and third of these might almost be called the first charter for autodidacts:

1   Proceed by (small) stages.
2   Examine everything yourself without submitting to authority (which Comenius, rather unfortunately, called 'autopsy').
3   Act on your own impulsion: (Comenius' term was 'autopraxy'). This requires, with reference to all that is presented to the intellect, the memory, the tongue and the hand, that pupils shall themselves seek, discover, discuss, do and repeat, without slacking, by their own efforts.

There is much more that could be written about Comenius – his admiration for Francis Bacon's New Atlantis where all of science would be discovered and verified by open experiment, his strong opposition to any form of corporal punishment, his inclusion of girls and also of those whom we would now call students with special needs like Gillian, and his insistence that education must continue throughout life. Comenius' views on sensual intelligence, mostly residing in the hands, led him to recommend 'learning through doing' so that the students could practise autonomy while learning the practical arts and crafts.

The Age of Revolutions which followed was largely inspired by the stern non-humanistic views of the French Enlightenment philosophers, like Voltaire and Condorcet. Only J.-J. Rousseau (1968 [1762]) was an exception to this. He began his book *The Social Contract*, with the famously phrased dilemma, as he saw it, 'Man is born free, and yet everywhere he is in chains'.

Very little of what Rousseau taught was put into practice at that time, perhaps fortunately, since it reads to us now as a sadly isolated sort of education in a natural but empty environment. (It is also revisited in Chapter 17.)

In the new United States of America the exhilaration of liberty echoed around a society which did not primarily aim to reproduce the education of the old Europe, nor deliberately to reform it. Their hero, Benjamin Franklin, was a far more practical man – an inventor, and patently some kind of autodidact himself. He was apprenticed to a printer because his parents could not afford to send him to school, so while he was setting up the print, he self-educated himself by reading the books. When still only 25 he recognised his debt to this process and set up the earliest American subscription library in Philadelphia. Twenty years later Franklin wrote a paper entitled 'Proposals for the Education of Youth in Pennsylvania' which was to be in the 'useful arts and sciences'. To this day there is a subject in American high schools called industrial arts which in England might be called design-technology (see also Hunkin's comments about the Useful Arts in Chapter 11). There was no snobbism in the new USA about being an engineer or an inventor rather than an arts person. Quite the contrary.

A successful inventor is likely to be an autodidact. Ideas form in the students' heads when they design and make their own inventions, and there is a huge emphasis on being original (Solomon 1998, Roth 1995). As Margaret Boden says in Chapter 2, 'Most artists, musicians, and scientists earn their living by relying on exploratory creativity. Many of their new ideas are novel to everyone, not only to themselves'.

Inventors fit perfectly into this class, and Benjamin Franklin, who was successfully inventing bifocal spectacles at the age of seventy, never stopped having combinational creative ideas with useful applications, and sometimes with amusing ones like the ladies' parasols which carried a lightning conductor connected to a trailing earth wire! From time to time Franklin had real top-class 'transformational' ideas (see page 26), like those which completely changed our understanding of the nature of electricity.

There is another point to include here. Franklin characteristically mixed humour with his work. For example, there is an account of an 'electric picnic' which he set up with his scientific colleagues. They ate a turkey which had been electrocuted, lit the fire with an electric spark, and even gave their wives electric kisses by holding on to a charged Leyden jar at the same time. (What did their long-suffering wives think of that?) Tim Hunkin's work in Chapter 11 may fit into the same behaviour pattern. In Chapter 12 we see Indian folk-mathematics, which was born in the marketplace, also being turned into riddles and jokes. This surprising aspect of the psychological side of autodidactism will be examined further in Chapters 16 and 17.

Critical political education

The nineteenth century saw adult education emerging in Britain. There was pressure from workers who wanted to know why it was that they seemed destined to live in conditions of such poverty with no hope of betterment. By the early decades of the nineteenth century there was also growing anger. No longer was there to be sentimental and patronising poetry like that of Thomas Gray from the previous century.

> Some village-Hampden, that with dauntless breast
> The little tyrant of his fields withstood;
> Some mute inglorious Milton here may rest,
> Some Cromwell guiltless of his country's blood,

The nineteenth century's Hampdens, Miltons and Cromwells had no intention of being mute. They had a thirst for learning, especially those in the Chartist movement who were seeking what we could now call their human rights. While the bloody and glorious revolution in France had made little change to the workers' social conditions, this angry British movement did. Slowly by our measurements but rapidly by those of previous centuries, workers seized upon every opportunity to make learning more accessible. The workers were certainly novices in education but they knew what knowledge they wanted. A new shift in autonomous learning was about to take place.

Chartism was founded in 1838, the first specifically working class movement in Britain. In addition to universal male suffrage its members had dreams of a new social order, and its numbers grew stronger every time unemployment increased, or there was an increase in the price of corn. As Richard Johnson (1993) has eloquently written, what the Chartists wanted was 'really useful knowledge' in a political sense. What they wrote about the light-hearted antics of the British Association makes uncomfortable reading in these days of colourful promotions for the public understanding of science. 'A man may be amused and instructed by scientific literature but the language which describes his wrongs clings to his mind with unparalleled pertinacity.' Poor Man's Guardian, 25 October 1834 quoted in Johnson (1993).

The Chartist movement withered away in the second half of the nineteenth and the early twentieth century under the influence of increasing affluence, and before all of its educational objectives had been achieved. Other political movements which also looked forward to a new social order were to follow. Whether it was anarchism in Germany, or Marxism in Europe, or post-colonial emancipation in South America there were always educators who wanted to go beyond the occasional reductionist comments of John Dewey (1916) that the second grand aim of all education was social efficiency and industrial competency. Dewey did himself realise the danger that this aim might pose in the hands of an autocratic commercial regime, and wrote that the truly democratic path was to pursue the development of practical skills only up to the minimum age of individual career choice.

Meanwhile revolutionary authors like Illich (1963) and Freire (1970) argued that education needed to be both individually liberating and socially and politically emancipatory. They argued against schooling and they preached their doctrine with such vehemence that, in some cases, it began to transgress the bounds of individual judgement which are always so precious to autodidacts. Freire was explaining cultural choice as 'action which was to become a preoccupation to the masses'. Was there any room within that definition for the individuals who did not want to follow the general preoccupation? By the 1990s Henry Giroux (1997) had begun to critique the whole idea of autonomous choice in learning. His 'pedagogy of hope', promoted a process by which the teacher could bring relevant topics closer to the students and then encourage them to 'make their voices heard'. This echoed a new approach to autonomy and hence to democracy itself.

Throughout the centuries, from Comenius to the present day, there have always been a few alternative voices in education who argued on behalf of autonomy. Wherever alternative schooling became popular or even possible during the nineteenth and twentieth centuries, there was an argument for freedom for young people to learn from experience as and when they wanted. Once again the question of informal lived-learning was discussed, along with the old and difficult question of teaching as indoctrination.

Education in the working group

The idea of a lone, self-actualising person teaching themselves in some isolated space seemed far too individualistic for modern sociological thinking. Could a child or adult really profit from such an empty environment if learning was going to depend on experience? Vygotsky's work, as has already been discussed, went some way towards suggesting that reflection was at least in part a social process. We may imagine the friend we will be meeting and try to rehearse what they are going to say. The engine for this is our memory of previous social encounters. So it is our social life that not only teaches us how to reflect and learn, but also lives on in our reflections, and even in the constructions of ourselves.

The concept of the self is slippery because of our surprising capacity to take on different roles whenever needed. In conversation we are always anxious about whether we are properly understood. So we continually ask others if they 'know what I mean?' These points were made many years ago by the sociologist G.H. Mead (1937).

> The individual is continually adjusting himself in advance to the situation to which he belongs and reacting back upon it. The self is not something that exists first and then enters into a relationship with others, but is so to speak, an eddy in the social current and so still a part of the current.
>
> (p. 182)

It is obviously vital to understand the operation of self in the context of autodidactism, and this will be a substantial part of Chapter 17.

Almost all learning situations are social, but if the learner can almost disappear into the setting, as new apprentices on the periphery of a loose apprenticeship group may do, or by being with a gang of friends discussing a project, then any learning which takes place may seem experiential rather than formal. The more realistic and exciting environment of the work place has always been popular with students from school and further education, which is backed up by numerous reports from students on sandwich courses, and their tutors. All of this may well make it easier for an uncomfortable autodidact to learn without conflict with the institution and its teachers. In addition the situation will provide the social comfort of being with others.

But this method can also have drawbacks. As Hudson (1976) and others have pointed out, the apprentice master has always had tight control over his apprentices, to whom he may have passed on blind prejudices along with technical or academic skills. In the present time of rapidly changing technologies such fossilised apprenticeship practices could prove a disaster in personal and economic senses. New types of extended apprenticeships have been introduced which require more part-time study along with a specified range of certificated qualifications.

The first of two interesting books on this general theme of work and learning was written by Jean Lave. She set out to study how people did arithmetic in practical situations, like the supermarket, and after several years concluded that 'The same people differ in their arithmetic activities in different settings in ways that challenge theoretical boundaries between activity and its settings' (Lave 1988: 3). In Chapter 12 of this book we examine a new study of practical mathematics as exhibited by Indian women market traders who have taught themselves mathematical methods and extend this to a wide cultural context.

Recently a consensus emerged among anthropologists that our culture consists less in the way we behave, or even in our social meanings, than our very identity. By this they mean no less than who we believe we are. For people who were learning in the social setting of an apprenticeship it clearly meant enculturation into the community of plumbers or carpet weavers or estate agents. This produced 'situated learning', Lave and Wengen's (1991) title for their next and famous book. The learning/training process may have worked not just because it was simple, nor because there were others present to give comfort and help if things got difficult, but because it was about a central feature of our being – identification with our employment. Ask someone who they are, and they will almost always answer by naming their employment: I am a teacher, a consultant, or a car salesman.

Lave and Wengen claim that this sort of situated learning is different from learning in school from a teacher. Apprentices pick up what it is like to be a trained worker in their field. In some ways it is more akin to the body learning by imitation than formal learning. Lave and Wengen agree that apprenticeship and similar communities of learning rarely set out to involve 'the whole person' complete with affective and reflective cognitive activities. So although we can appreciate the balm of situated learning for any autodidacts who feel they have to hide from the teacher's interference by being in a crowd, others might well find these structured training situations too confined to slake their interest in wider learning and problem solving.

Lave and Wengen attempted a Marxist analysis of knowledge itself, which

> [T]urns the apparently 'natural' categories and forms of social life into our understanding of how they are (culturally and historically) produced and reproduced. The goal, in Marx's memorable phrase, is to 'ascend from (both the particular and the abstract) to the concrete'.
> (Lave and Wengen 1991: 38)

These authors, inspired by Marxist doctrine, have attributed a higher place in the cognitive scheme of things to practical situated learning than to analytical, reflective, or any other kind of learning. It is rather like a class system being extended to knowledge. Why should one kind of learning be higher or lower in importance than another? Clearly we need all kinds. I was working in Cambodia at the time of reading Lave and Wengen's book, and did not feel willing to make any allowances at all for Marxist thinking and the awful acts of cruelty that were carried out in its name. The thinking behind the appallingly brutal treatment of the gentle Cambodian people in the 'Killing fields' derived directly from this hierarchical approach to education. Every teacher and lecturer, even the uneducated whose only crime was to wear glasses, were summarily shot down, or worse, for having been contaminated by 'the wrong sort of knowledge'. The Cultural Revolution in China was very similar. Auto-didactism, as we shall see, includes emotional and ethical reactions, along with the cooler effects of cognition, in almost every chapter in this book. This chapter can be no exception.

First approaches to adult learning in 'the learning society'

Before the 1950s there were very few attempts to teach adults, except in higher education. Teaching was what happened to children, and only some 5 per cent of young European adults went on to university. Those who had fought in the 1939–45 war were heroes when they came home, and a hollow promise was made in many countries that all who wanted to could enter university. At first it was largely ignored on the grounds that an entry level of talent was necessary. In Britain new red-brick universities were built during the 1960s, but there were never enough places to satisfy demand. In France and Germany students rioted in the streets demanding more and better education. In the UK students had to work for entry against an urgent elitist chorus from old time lecturers in favour of 'maintaining standards' at all costs. For the majority of young people this seemed to mean perpetually closed doors.

At the same time a very few voices were heard in several countries (e.g. Michael Young (1961) from the UK, and Torsten Husén from Sweden) speaking about the future, and trying to promote a different and more appropriate approach to mass education beyond the school. Both foresaw how a society saturated by a uniform flow of education, monitored at the gates to higher education by stout entrance qualifications, would be left with a sizeable residue of the less talented. Those who never achieved a higher level of education might face a life of menial work and intermittent unemployment. Equal opportunity, for so long the basis of democratic education was not enough. This is how Husén, writing in 1974, described his view of the future.

> By the year 2000 society [will have] become so highly rationalised and machine-controlled that there are no jobs left for those with IQs below the average, the idea will be to make these unskilled individuals useful by giving them tasks that the unskilled should not have to waste their time on, such as charring.
>
> (p. 93)

Now that the year 2000 has come and gone we can see Husén's vision becoming horribly realised. Worse still, but in the path he had foreseen, there is a growing workless underclass perpetuating its lack of achievement so that in some inner-city areas families can be found where all adults have been unemployed for three generations. Ours is now a meritocratic democracy, but certainly not a liberal one.

At least two basic questions needed to be asked about learning then and now. First, does older people's learning capacity remain stationary throughout life? and second, what is the point in learning work skills, when technologies change so fast?

These questions are not completely separate. If the answer to the first is affirmative, then there is the chance that the workers mentioned in the second, caught out by technological change, could learn new skills for new jobs (see Chapter 7). Indeed it seemed that the learning capacity of the post-16 cohort, about which educational research had very little to tell, was now the key to our democratic future.

There are few research-based theories of adult learning, but they will be discussed in Chapter 17. More troubling still, it had been shown by the psychologist Liam Hudson and others, that there was almost no correlation between academic success in school or college, and what the same people achieve in their lives outside these institutions. Some research scientists who became Fellows of the Royal Society, and legal practitioners who became eminent and successful High Court judges, may have such low class degrees that they might be precluded from postgraduate work in any British university by today's standards. It did begin to seem that these eminent people, when students, were not being taught the appropriate subject matter – content and skills – that would be of use in their life work. They may have been autonomous learners, part of the brigade of autodidacts who found, as Winston Churchill did, that being taught in school was a constraint to learning, which evaporated in the wider world of work.

The economic rewards of learning, to the individual and society, have been the government's prime target during the last decade, producing vocational qualifications parallel to academic ones, education summed up by lists of outcomes and competences, methods of formative assessment, skills relating to Information Technology, teaching students how to plan their own learning, and attempts to widen access to Higher Education.

Most of these innovations might claim to have had learning autonomy in mind. Those who learn practical skills, as we have argued, may do so through non-verbal, more autonomous methods. But to achieve parity with academic degree courses the proponents of these courses felt a need to increase the quantity of familiar 'knowledge' components. Teaching to lists of prescribed outcomes and competences was supposed to leave room for a choice of learning method. Transparent formative assessment in which students had their say was also, some said, a way to increase autonomy. It was hoped that the Internet would enable students to acquire knowledge without teaching, and might also facilitate working for a degree in Higher Education. My own experience during several years of research projects carried out for the Employment Department and then the DfEE, showed the new teaching methods were being skilfully aimed at containing and training post-compulsory students who might have preferred to learn through employment, if only it had been available. There was no 'space' (a word much used in later chapters) for almost any of the learning freedom that a Comenius or a Rousseau would have recommended.

What of the more defiant autodidacts? Every new vocational course was tightly prescribed in all its outcomes, and extended the period of insti-tutionalised study yet further into adult life. No learning inducement for autodidacts there. But information computer technology (ICT) and distance learning was about to introduce other ways of learning for those prepared to enrol in a course and plan their own learning, with or without a tutor, to a fixed schedule of assignments and examinations. Was that enough, or were there other places for these dissenting learners to 'hang out'?

References

Ausubel, D. (1963) *The Psychology of Meaningful Learning*. New York: Grune and Stratton.

Ausubel, D., Novak, J. and Hanesian, H. (1968) *Educational Psychology: A Cognitive View*. New York: Holt Rinehart and Winston.

Biggs, J. (1980) 'Developmental processes and learning outcomes', in J. Kirby and J. Biggs (eds) *Cognition, Development and Instruction*. New York: Academic Press, 91–118.

Boekaerts, M. (1994) *Motivation in Education*. London: British Psychological Society.

Dewey, J. (1916) *Democracy and Education*. New York: Free Press.

Driver, R. (1978) 'Pupils and paradigms: a review of literature related to concept development in adolescent science students', *Studies in Science Education* 5: 61–84.

Driver, R. (1983) *The Pupil as Scientist?* Milton Keynes: Open University Press.

Entwistle, N. and Ramsden, P. (1983) *Understanding Student Learning*. London: Croom-Helm.

Freire, P. (1970) *Pedagogy of the Oppressed*. London: Penguin.

Gardener, P. (1975) 'Attitudes to science: a review', *Studies in Science Education* 2: 1–41.

Gardner, H. (1994) 'The Creators' Patterns', *Dimensions of Creativity*. Cambridge, Mass.: MIT Press, 143–158.

Giroux, H. (1997) *Pedagogy and the Politics of Hope*. Oxford: Westview.

Glasersfeld, E. v. (1989) 'Constructivism reconstructed: a reply to Suchting', *Science and Education* 1(4): 379–384.

Helmke, A. (1988) 'The role of classroom context factors for the achievement–impairment effect of test anxiety', *Anxiety Research* 1: 327–352.

Hodgkin, R. (1976) *Born Curious*. London: John Wiley and Sons.

Hudson, L. (1976) 'Singularity of Talent', in S. Messick (ed.) *Individuality in Learning*. San Francisco: Jossey-Bass, 211–221.

Husén, T. (1974) *The Learning Society*. London: Methuen.

Illich, I. (1963) 'The deschooled society', in P. Buckman (ed.) *Education Without Schools*. London: Souvenir Press.

Inhelder, B., Sinclair, H. and Bovet, M. (1974) *Learning and the Development of Cognition*. London: Routledge and Kegan Paul.

Johnson, R. (1993) 'Really useful knowledge 1790–1850', in M. Thorpe, R. Edwards and A. Hanson (eds) *Culture and the Processes of Adult Learning*. London: Routedge, 17–29.

Johnston, K. (1990) Students' response to an active learning approach to teaching the particulate nature of matter, in P. Lijnse (ed.) *Relating Macroscopic Phenomena to Microscopic Particles*. Utrecht: CD-B Press.

Karmiloff-Smith, A. (1992) *Beyond Modularity: A Developmental Perspective on Cognitive Science*. Cambridge, Mass.: MIT Press.

Koestler, A. (1966) *The Act of Creation*. London: Hutchinson.

Köhler, W. (1925) *The Mentality of Apes*. Harmondsworth: Penguin.

Lave, J. (1988) *Cognition in Practice*. Cambridge: Cambridge University Press.

Lave, J. and Wengen, E. (1991) *Situated Knowledge: Legitimate Peripheral Participation*. Cambridge: Cambridge University Press.

Locke, J. (1693) *Some Thoughts Concerning Education*, quoted in *Thinkers on Education* (1995) UNESCO.

Marten, F. and Säljö, R. (1976) 'On qualitative differences in learning I: outcome and process', *British Journal of Educational Psychology* 46: 4–11.

Mead, G. H. (1937) *Mind, Self and Society*. Chicago: University of Chicago Press.

Novak, J. and Gowan, D. (1984) *Learning How to Learn*. Cambridge: Cambridge University Press.

Piaget, J. (1972) *Psychology and Epistemology*. Harmondsworth: Penguin.

Polanyi, M. (1958) *Personal Knowledge*. London: Routledge and Kegan Paul.

Posch, P. (1993) 'Research issues in environmental education', *Studies in Science Education* 21: 21–48.

Roth, W.-M. (1995) 'Inventors, copycats and everyone else', *Science Education* 79: 475–502.

Rousseau, J.-J. (1968) *The Social Contract*. London: Penguin.

Shweder, R. (1984) 'Preview: a colloquy of culture theorists', in R. LeVine and R. Shweder (eds) *Culture Theory*. Cambridge: Cambridge University Press, 1–24.

Solomon, J. (1987) 'Social influences on the construction of pupils' understanding of science', *Studies in Science Education* 14: 63–82.

Solomon, J. (1991) 'Group discussions in the classroom', *School Science Review* 72(261): 29–34.

Solomon, J. (1998) 'Technology in elementary school: blind variation and selective retention', *Research in Science Education* 28(1): 153–167.

Valås, H. and Søvik, N. (1993) 'Variables affecting students' intrinsic motivation for school mathematics. Two empirical studies based on Deci and Ryan's theory on motivation', *Learning and Instruction* 3(4): 281–298.

Vygotsky, L. (1978) (trans.) *Mind in Society*. Cambridge, Mass.: Harvard University Press.

Vygotsky, L. and Alexander, L. (1930) 'Tool and symbol in child development', in R. and V. Van der Veer, J. (eds) *The Vygotsky Reader*. Oxford: Blackwell: 99–174.

Weinart, F., and Helmke, A. (1987) 'Compensatory effects of student self concept and instructional quality on academic achievement', in F. Hallisch J. Kuhl (eds) *Motivation, Intention and Volition*. Berlin: Springer, 233–247.

Wightman, T. (1987) *The Particulate Nature of Matter*. Leeds: CLIS University of Leeds.

Young, M. (1961) *The Rise of the Meritocracy*. Harmondsworth: Penguin.

Chapter 2

Are autodidacts creative?

Margaret Boden

How nice it would be to be able to answer the question 'Are autodidacts creative?' with a simple 'Yes' or 'No' – or even a judicious 'Some are, some aren't.' We could all go home happy, and concentrate on other things.

But it's not so straightforward. The reason is that both crucial terms cover significantly different cases. In principle, one could compose a many-dimensional 'matrix' of all the combinations, wherein each one was marked, 'Yes' or 'No' – or more likely, 'Probably' or 'Probably not' – but without somehow distinguishing the various subclasses of both concepts, one simply cannot answer the question.

Or rather, one can – but not in an especially informative way. One might answer 'Yes' on the grounds that all normal human adults are creative, therefore all autodidacts are creative. In other words, creativity is not a special talent possessed only by a fortunate elite. On the contrary, it is an unavoidable aspect of normal intelligence, and rests on psychological processes – such as perception, reminding, recognition, and associative memory – that are the essential basis of our everyday thinking (Perkins 1981). This answer is certainly worth giving if any reader thinks that creativity is a special faculty (a Romantic belief that has horrendous educational implications). Otherwise, it doesn't get us very far.

First, then, let's consider the different types of creativity. There are three, the last two of which are closely related: combinational, exploratory and transformational creativity (Boden 1990, 1994). In general, a creative idea or artefact is one that is novel, surprising and valuable. The three types of creativity differ in the psychological processes involved in generating the novel ideas – and, for that matter, in understanding or appreciating them once they have arisen.

Novelty here, may be understood psychologically or historically, defining P-creativity and H-creativity, respectively. Each of these exists in all three forms: combinational, exploratory, and transformational. P-creativity is the ability to generate ideas that are *new with respect to the mind of individual concerned*. H-creativity is the ability to generate ideas that are, so far as is known, *novel with respect to the whole of human history*. Clearly, H-creativity is a special case of P-creativity. People sometimes restrict the term 'creative' to the historical sense. That's not helpful here, for we want to know both whether autodidacts are likely to be more P-creative than other people and, if so, whether they are also likely to be more H-creative. As we'll see, high P-creativity need not go along with high H-creativity.

Combinational creativity involves making unfamiliar connections between familiar ideas. Comparing one's lover to a summer's day is one example, comparing the atom to a solar system is another – and putting an unmade bed into an art exhibition is yet another. Most psychologists who study creativity focus on this type. But there are two more, which are related in that they both arise out of some accepted style of thinking, or structured conceptual space. These conceptual spaces include styles of dance, painting, cookery, chemistry, mathematics, carving . . . in short, any culturally recognised way of doing things in a particular domain of activity.

In exploratory creativity, the space is explored: the person (artist, scientist, cook, choreographer) asks what ideas/artefacts can and cannot be reached within the space, what are the limits of the space – and maybe how the space could be expanded by being superficially tweaked. For example, the basic ingredient of ice cream can be altered: will water, or yoghurt, do as well as cream? Or one can tweak by addition: perhaps putting nuts on top of the finished ice cream, or adding them while it's being made. The first nutty ice cream (in both senses) was a pleasant surprise, even a lasting contribution to the gaiety of nations. It may have made a good living for the inventor. But it wasn't a radical change, either for the intellect or eaters.

It's important to realise that exploratory creativity can generate surprising and valuable novelties even *without* tweaking. The reason is that we're typically unaware of all the possibilities within a reasonably complex conceptual space. It took over a century to exhaust the space of aromatic molecules in chemistry, and the space of possible sonatas – even if restricted to a particular composer's style – is infinite. Possible chess games are finite, but the number is so astronomical that for all practical purposes it's infinite. This is why chess will always offer surprises. (Noughts and crosses, no: the space is so tiny that only beginners can be surprised.)

Most artists, musicians, and scientists earn their living by relying on exploratory creativity. Many of their new ideas are novel to everyone, not only to themselves. No-one would employ a workaday research chemist to tell them textbook facts, or pay a dress-designer or song-writer who never came up with anything new. That is, ideas produced by exploratory creativity can be *historically* new; when they are, they are, by definition, examples of H-creativity. However, immediately the H-novel idea is generated, people familiar with the style can see that, in a sense, it was there all along. The relevant rules of thinking had already defined a place for it in the conceptual space concerned. It just so happened that Jo Bloggs was the first person ever to reach that particular point. Good for Jo Bloggs! But although this form of H-creativity may earn him a living wage, it won't earn him a place in the history books.

Transformational creativity, on the other hand, might. For most examples of creativity recorded in the history books are transformational ones. (Most, but not all: poets, in particular, are remembered largely because of their exceptional ability to generate H-novel ideas by combinational creativity.) Here, the tweaking of one or more boundaries (rules) of the space is more radical, more daring – and more surprising.

Specifically, transformational creativity enables ideas to be generated which, with respect to the previously accepted style of thinking, simply *could not* have arisen before. Compare this with exploratory creativity: Jo Bloggs discovered the new idea on Tuesday, but John Doe might well have discovered it on Monday; after all, it was already potentially 'there'. Some dimension of the pre-existing space is not just slightly tweaked, but radically transformed – inverted, for example. So for a chef to try freezing milk instead of heating it is to do something radically different – and histories of cooking celebrate the people who did this first.

Cooking is a relatively easy case, not in the sense that it's any easier to have a 'new' idea, but in the sense that it is relatively easy to evaluate the previously-impossible result once it's there. Admittedly, different cultures have different culinary tastes, but within a certain culture, and given our shared human physiology, it's fairly easy to be sure that a good number of people will – or won't – savour the new concoction. It's more difficult to evaluate a new theory in chemistry or palaeontology: it took years of argument and experiment – not to mention personal and nationalist rivalries – to replace phlogiston by oxygen, and to decide who 'discovered' dinosaurs (Schaffer 1994). It's even more difficult to be sure of one's ground in art. Even within one country, the accepted styles and criteria of art can shift with the century, or even the decade. Difficult or not, evaluation is crucial: creative ideas were defined above as being not only novel, but *valuable*.

It's all very well for someone to come up with new ideas, but these must be recognised as valuable if they are to be called creative. We all know of famous cases where virtually no one but the individual concerned found the novelty valuable at the time. There are even cases where the creator himself didn't do so (Kepler, on first thinking that planetary orbits might be non-circular, dismissed this idea as 'a cartload of dung' [Koestler

1975]). But such cases are necessarily rare, because someone who was virtually incapable of judging the worth (or worthlessness) of their own new ideas wouldn't normally be regarded as creative. They might be a useful member of a creative team where the evaluative judgements were made by other team-members. Even so, they'd probably lead their colleagues to waste a lot of time.

What has all this got to do with autodidacts? Well, it shows us that there can be no straightforward 'Yes or No' answer to the question of whether autodidacts are creative. For we must ask whether *this* type of creativity, or *that* one, is more likely in autodidacts. What's more, if there are several different types of autodidact, then the very same queries must be raised about each of them. It might turn out that a certain kind of self-taught person was likely to show a relatively high – or low – degree of one kind of creativity, but not of the others. In general, this will depend on two things:

1   Whether any of the three relevant kinds of psychological process is more likely in (some type of) autodidacts than in other people, and
2   Whether the necessary mental resources (scattered ideas and/or structured conceptual spaces) are more likely to be available.

As for the types of autodidact, the other chapters in this book may indicate how many, and various, these are. For instance, one can distinguish what I'll call the unschooled and defiant groups (Chapters 4 and 12). Unschooled autodidacts never had the opportunity of formal education. Maybe their society simply didn't provide it, except perhaps to a favoured few. Or maybe their place – class, caste, gender, income, urban/rural location – in that society made it unavailable to them. Or maybe ill-health (their own and/or their parents') prevented them from getting the education that they'd otherwise have had. Probably, these different reasons for their lack of schooling tend to have different psychological effects. Certainly, there will be variations in the extent to which their elders made an effort to educate them informally, in a more or less diverse range of skills. Strictly, one should bear these differences carefully in mind when considering individual life-histories. For present purposes, however, I'll (crudely) ignore them, and speak of unschooled autodidacts as though they were a single group.

These people may have a relatively high degree of self-confidence and determination, which they will need to educate themselves without the support (*pace* Ivan Illich 1963) or the stimulus of school. Otherwise, because their lack of education was independent of their wishes, they will be a normal cross-section of their community, in terms of intelligence and adventurousness.

Defiant autodidacts by contrast have, for varying psychological reasons, a distrust of and resistance to authority of any sort. They may undergo many years of formal education, but they respond to it in highly non-receptive ways. At the extreme, they switch off, opt out, and turn their attention to unrelated pursuits – in which case, they may come close to being unschooled in the sense defined above. But if they stay in school, and pay attention at least sometimes (perhaps to only one subject), they are likely to use their intelligence so as deliberately to transgress accepted ways of thinking. Similarly, in later life they will challenge or ignore the accepted canons and conventions of their chosen occupation.

A subclass of these (let's call them 'diverse defiants') will deliberately foster interests in non-school, unfashionable, and perhaps even disreputable subject domains – such as (in twenty-first century Britain) pigeon fancying, archery, computer games, or Internet pornography. They may put just as much effort and self-discipline, and even reading time, into studying their chosen area(s) as the most demanding school-teacher could wish. By all the usual standards of the accepted academic curriculum, however, their schoolwork may be a disaster.

Because combinational creativity is the least constrained of the three types, lack of education is no great barrier. Certainly, a person who has encountered relatively more and/or diverse ideas is in a better position to come up with unfamiliar combinations. One might infer that an unschooled autodidact will be less capable of combinational creativity; but this doesn't follow. If their out of school experience has been comparably rich, then they can freely combine ideas just as everyone else can. The results will differ in content (someone with no education simply couldn't write the multiply allusive poem *The Waste Land*). But they need not be inferior in creativity – or in value, unless one values classical allusion above every other aspect of poetry. Indeed, one could say that the unschooled autodidact has an advantage, precisely because their novel combinations are likely to be relatively unexpected and so valued more highly.

Diverse defiants, too, are in a good position here. Since they have made themselves expert in one or more unusual areas, their experience is wider than – or different from – that of their peers. Someone who knows about the practice and history of archery is equipped to generate certain unfamiliar combinations that just aren't possible for the rest of us. The more deviant and the more diverse their interests, the more this is so. Educated people may be just as adventurous in their combinational processing, but they use more conventional idea-banks as their resources.

Exploratory creativity is more problematic for autodidacts. Specifically, it depends on how easy it is, given the person's life situation, to pick up the relevant styles of thinking. This involves both accessibility and motivation. It took even Mozart a good twelve years of unrelenting effort to master the music of the day well enough to do something creative with it, as opposed to something merely competent. In general, it takes self-discipline to master a discipline and some disciplines are accessible only through certain routes, which may be all but inaccessible outside the usual educational institutions. Modern chemistry, for instance, can't be done creatively with a chemistry set in one's back bedroom. Whereas William Perkin could discover the first aniline dyes in his study, using a few chemical crocks he'd brought home from his university laboratory (Garfield 2000), the next breakthrough in chemical dyes is unlikely to be made by exploring chemical space in that way.

Moreover, the space of chemistry changes, and changes fast. A friend of mine, a potter, had an unschooled father. Having heard her mention chemistry as being important for glazes, he bought a textbook of chemistry on a market stall, and put hours of effort into reading it. On her next visit home he proudly said he'd like to discuss chemistry with her – only to regale her with talk about phlogiston. This is a true story, as well as a sad one. Her father not only didn't know that phlogiston was passé, but he also didn't know that any chemistry textbook published long ago was likely to be unreliable.

Today, a few such changes in chemical space hit the headlines, occasionally even featuring in the tabloids. Buckyballs, for instance, were so strange and, in essence, so readily intelligible, that they were widely featured in the media. But other changes are reported only in the specialist journals and, sometimes, magazines of popular science. The autodidact, by definition, is not part of the commonly-accepted scientific network. If he manages to break into the network, he'll very likely be ignored or disparaged – this is even more likely, if he is a she. Even highly-educated professional people may experience this sort of rejection, if they try to discuss (meddle with?) issues relating to a different discipline. In short, autodidacts of any sort will find it very difficult, even impossible, to access the conceptual spaces of modern science and to learn their way around them.

If someone cannot access or explore these culturally-given spaces, then they cannot fruitfully transform them either; for this requires both appreciating the limits of the old space and evaluating the still unexplored potential of the new one. These are subtle judgements, requiring years of work (and usually of discussion with one's peers) behind them. Nor can the novice rely on the cognoscenti to make these evaluations on their behalf. For suppose that an imaginative autodidact had said 'Perhaps carbon atoms can join up into hollow balls?' The only people who might have listened to him would have been those (few) experts with the confidence and imagination to consider such an idea seriously – which is to say, creative individuals highly educated in chemistry, like Sir Harry Kroto himself.

The reference to confidence, here, raises a further way in which distinct types of autodidact are differently placed. The deviant autodidact is, by definition, rebellious. Such people have the self-assurance and the courage (two different things), not to mention the motivation, required to swim against the cultural stream. They are relatively unlikely to be discouraged by others' disapproval, for they meet it – maybe even savour it – every day. If they come up with a novel idea which they think is valuable, they will be less put off by indifference, or even criticism, from the accepted experts. By contrast, unschooled autodidacts may retain a lifelong sense of inferiority and diffidence, especially if they have internalised any negative cultural expectations of their entire class, caste, or gender. It will be much easier for critics to take the wind out of their creative sails.

I've made two potentially misleading simplifications so far. First, I've mentioned only two broad types of autodidact, even though I've also hinted at further psychological diversities that should not be ignored. Second, I've tacitly implied that the different types of creativity are never conjoined.

In defining the three forms of creativity, I was making analytical distinctions between psychological processes that are different in principle. In practice, something normally regarded as a single case of creativity may involve more than one of these types. T. S. Eliot's *The Waste Land*, for example, is not only a glorious profusion of combinational creativity, full of unexpected mythical and literary allusions, including private jokes accessible only to those who share his own classical education. It also explores (sic) a new poetic form, Eliot having transformed (sic) some of the existing conventions of poetry to make a new poem possible which simply could not have been written in the pre-transformational days. So one shouldn't assume that every example of creativity, originality, or imagination can be neatly slotted into one, and only one, of the three categories. Human thinking, whether in autodidacts or anyone else, is often much richer than that. That is just one of many reasons why one shouldn't ask 'Is this idea creative, *Yes* or *No*?' but rather 'Is it creative in any respect(s) – and if so, *which* and *how*?'

In sum, one may be able to decide whether the fresh thinking and originality of a particular self-educated person is *relatively* strong or weak in one type of creativity rather than another. One may be able to do this for psychologically distinct groups of autodidact and one may even be able to explain why one such group comes up trumps, or falls down, on one sort of creativity rather than another. But to claim that autodidacts in general are, or are not, more creative than the rest of us is to be guilty of sloppy thinking. We need to look at things much more closely.

References

Boden, M. A. (1990) *The Creative Mind: Myths and Mechanisms.* London: Abacus.

Boden, M. A. (1994) *What is Creativity?*, in M. A. Boden (ed.) *Dimensions of Creativity.* Cambridge, Mass.: MIT Press, 75–119.

Garfield, S. (2000) *Mauve: How One Man Invented a Colour that Changed the World.* London: Faber & Faber.

Illich, I. (1963) 'The deschooled society', in P. Buckman (ed.) *Education Without Schools.* London: Souvenir Press, 9–19.

Koestler, A. (1975) *The Act of Creation.* London: Picador. (First published 1964).

Perkins, D. N. (1981) *The Mind's Best Work.* Cambridge, Mass.: Harvard University Press.

Schaffer, S. (1994) 'Making up discovery', in M. A. Boden (ed.) *Dimensions of Creativity.* Cambridge, Mass.: MIT Press, 13–52.

Chapter 3

Children in an interactive science centre

Helen Brooke and Joan Solomon

What is play?

The great educational reformers of the eighteenth and early-nineteenth centuries – Rousseau, Pestalozzi and Froebel – all stressed the importance of play for learning, but made very little attempt to describe it. They knew that teaching formed no part of play, and valued it highly for its freedom and autonomy.

Later reformers often used Darwinian theory to assign a more serious role to play in the evolution of the species. One early idea was that play is a recuperation from work, while Herbert Spencer, on the other hand, saw it only as the 'aimless expression of surplus energy'. Play, he thought, evolved in the higher animals because 'with their greater range of skills they needed to spend less time on keeping themselves alive' (quoted in Millar 1968). By the end of the nineteenth century Karl Groos had put forward the explicit theory of play as the practice of survival skills. Thus play-fighting or hunting or love-play were for the autonomous development of skills.

In the early twentieth century Freud saw children's play as roughly equivalent to the dreams and fantasies of adults. Play, he argued, was the child's means of expressing feelings that would otherwise be repressed, or of acting out wishes which could not otherwise be fulfilled. This view did not account for the extent to which children will also act out experiences which they have obviously *not* enjoyed. So Freud later came to the conclusion that play might also be a means for the child to come to terms with unpleasant happenings. Melanie Klein, who began the psychoanalysis of children in 1919, used spontaneous autonomous play in her therapy in much the same way as Freud used free associations with his adult patients.

Jean Piaget saw play as an early part of learning development. Play was for him the predominance of assimilation – the process by which ideas or experiences are adapted to existing schemas – over accommodation – the adjustment of mental schemas in the light of new experiences. Play only used existing mental structures, and the young child could only use activities in this way while still egocentric enough to 'distort' the phenomena to fit into his or her private reality. After that, Piaget claimed, the child does not play but uses logical thought in its place. Despite this characteristic position on the superiority of logic, Piaget provides one of the first convincing descriptions of play and the sheer happiness it brings.

> After learning to grasp, swing, throw etc., which involve both an effort of accommodation to the new situations, . . . the child sooner or later (even during the learning period) grasps for the pleasure of grasping, swings for the pleasure of swinging. In a word he repeats his behaviour . . . *for the mere joy of mastering it,* and of showing off to himself his own power of subduing reality.
>
> (Piaget 1951)

We have probably all seen this kind of play that Piaget so beautifully describes.

Bruner's ideas on play and problem-solving

In his book *Play: Its role in Development and Evolution* (Bruner *et al.* 1974) Jerome Bruner reported his research on 3–5 year old children. He made the following points about play.

1   The process is more important than the ends
2   The risk of failure is lessened by this de-emphasising of the end
3   There is less frustration because of the precedence of process over product
4   There is freedom to notice seemingly irrelevant details
5   Play *is voluntary and self-initiated.*

The first three points are important in freeing the child from imposed goals and outside pressure. The last two points illustrate important aspects of autodidactism. Bruner thought that play provided an opportunity to try out combinations of behaviours. Using one of Margaret Boden's definitions of creativity (Boden 1994) as the *combination* of different possibilities, we can see a valuable link between play as a kind of autodidactism and creativity. Both children and inventors use the process of combining different ways of using the parts of the equipment, to find out what can be done with it (see Vincenti 1990). 'What appears to be at stake in play is the opportunity for assembling and reassembling behaviour sequences for skilled action. That, at least is one function of play' (Bruner 1972).

Play is concerned with learning, not in the sense of amassing facts, but of mastering the components of complex skills whether physical or cognitive. The beauty of this view of play-as-learning, through the exploration of new combinations of behaviour with the pressure switched off, is that it can be applied to so many different types of learning. One important characteristic, which Bruner somehow failed to mention, is that all young animals derive pleasure from such activities!

- It may be sensory motor play which permits the exploration of physical capabilities.
- It may be exploratory play which tries out the operation of objects and mechanisms. (This can lead to classic problem-solving, as we shall see below.)
- It may lead to the exploration of language through babbling and the repetition of amusing nonsense syllables.
- Through make-believe it explores the social order and so may reduce anxiety about authority figures and other bogies.

The literature of primates at play provides more corroborative detail. Jane Goodall (1968) describes the termite-fishing skills of a group of free-ranging chimpanzees in Tanzania. She observed the young animals playing at more and more complex features of this technique as they got older and more adept. On the other hand the chimpanzee which was brought up by Cathy Hayes (1952) with her own child, showed a fundamental difference in language-play: the chimp experimented very little with sounds and by the age of four months the young primate gave up all kinds of 'babbling'. This became a barrier to further creative aspects of language development. In the make-believe play of small children we frequently see the use of a single prop to symbolise a character known but not fully experienced in society. Cathy Hayes reported how, for several days, the young chimp she brought up appeared to be pulling a toy behind her wherever she went. But the human child soon left the ape far behind.

To explore the connection between play and problem-solving Bruner, Sylva and Genova carried out a very interesting experiment with children between the age of three and five, somewhat similar to Köhler's experiments with chimpanzees (Chapter 1).

(The children) had the task of fishing a prize from a latched box out of reach. To do so they had to extend two sticks by clamping them together. The children were given various 'training' procedures beforehand, including demonstrations of the principle of clamping two sticks together, or practice in fastening clamps on a single stick, or an opportunity to watch the experimenter carry out the task. One group was simply allowed to play with the materials. (It was found that this group) did just as well in solving the problem as the ones who had been given a demonstration of clamping sticks together *and better than any of the other groups.*

(Bruner, Sylva and Genova 1974)

This surprising result seems to indicate that autonomous uninstructed play is more effective in learning to solve practical problems than almost any other kind of instruction.

Learning without words

When a human or an animal learns to use some object which fits into the hand, it is as though the hand is itself modified to become a part of it. We can see this very clearly in the case of a hammer being used to knock in a nail. Although the bodily contact is with the handle end of the hammer, the user's attention is focused on the far end to ensure that it hits the nail on the head. It is in this sense that we can say that the hammer has become, as it were, an extension of the human arm. Learning becomes 'indwelling' in the body, as Michael Polanyi (1958) put it. We see this even more clearly in the experienced driver who inches the car forward between concrete bollards, cringing slightly and pulling his shoulders inwards, for all the world as if the human body extended outwards to the chassis of the car and might be hurt or scratched. This kind of learning is body/tool centred, and it is also tacit. It can neither be learnt or taught through words. In that sense it is only available to autodidacts.

Certain other kinds of knowing, such as how to swim, are essentially body-centred and difficult, though not impossible, to articulate. Coaching this sort of activity shows that it can profit from spoken teaching. The complete learning process may require an interplay between the two modes of teaching, one tacit and one articulated in words. Polanyi saw this as a holistic gestalt process which he compared with a medical student learning to interpret an X-ray photograph (see Chapters 5 and 17).

The body also has other indwelling memories which makes this kind of memory our oldest and deepest. Almost all animals can be trained to do some task in the manner of Skinner's operant conditioning. With time this can become so independent of thought and reflection that dishabituation, the unlearning of routines, becomes almost impossibly difficult. So fish, like carp on whom the first operant conditioning was practised by Pavlov, never *unlearn* the taught habit of coming to the surface for food at the sound of a bell. In humans these habits become indwelling within a library of learnt motor representations of the world that could be used later in dancing or miming. Here the teaching agent is simple experience received by the body's autonomous neural system.

Susanna Millar (1968), who has written widely about play, suggested that adults may translate visual events into speech *before* storing them in the mind. They are therefore likely to recall them in words. This allows ready access to the higher order semantic memory which is the usual goal of science and language education. For children without this association with language the recoding process may be much more difficult. Retrieval and recall may then require physical re-enactment for which, once again, play becomes very important.

Playing in an Interactive Science Centre (ISC)

Carrying out research in ISCs has not been uncommon in recent years, but the intentions of the researchers have covered a multitude of objectives. Many want to find out how much science the child visitors have learnt. That does not exhaust the possibilities but it is enough to show how little interest there is in how, or even if, young visitors play at the ISC. Curators of museums want to know what scientific concepts have been learnt, what behaviour to expect, and which kind of exhibit was the most memorable. We have yet to see any research which sees autonomous play with the equipment as the real objective. Is this because the public think of activities as experiments, and as John Ziman (1984) wrote, 'Scientific experiment is never *playful*'.

Our ISC is very small and very poor in resources by comparison with most, but our objectives have always been clear. We had two questions.

How do groups of children play together at the exhibits?

This meant that the equipment had to be designed, like all the best toys would be, so that there are many playful actions that can be performed with it. It also meant that we would *not* expect the children to read notices (which they rarely do even when the labels are provided).

If and when do they move on to their own intentional investigations?

In some ISCs it is possible to press a button and see an illuminated transparent wind tunnel with streamers to show where the speed of airflow is at its fastest and where it is slowest. Almost always there is a printed notice which states Bernouilli's Principle and tells you where the air moves fastest and the pressure is least, so that the air flow will cause the aeroplane to lift up and fly. The action of visitors consists in no more than pressing a button, and reading the notice. The visual effect may be remarkable, but is this learning through active play?

A variant of this exhibit is one where the visitors are provided with two toy cars of different shapes. This time the instructions tell them to place the cars on a ramp leading down into the wind in order to find out which one travels fastest. There is still very little activity and still less thinking or modelling. The answer is either 'car A' or 'car B'. In our own ISC the child visitors are presented with two identical cars, a heap of card, scissors and sellotape, and asked to construct a shape for the car to run fast into the wind. This time there is a lot of activity and no either/or right answer. The children usually have a real plan for their activities, although they often had to change it. We know that they are playing from the laughter coming from the direction of the wind tunnel (Brooke and Solomon 1998, 2001).

We characterised play, as Bruner had done, in terms of action which was more important and enjoyable in itself than in its ends. There was, at this early stage, no specific goal to be reached, so the children could be imaginative in a sense that was sometimes humorous and sometimes pure make-believe.

- *Make-believe* – a pair of girls playing at the wind tunnel drew a face on the cardboard windscreen they had fashioned for the car which was running down into the wind, and crashing into the barrier at the end.
- *Humour* – a boy sits in front of a barrel from which a vortex of air can move forward if the barrel is thumped. His quiff of hair is pushed up by the moving vortex, so he stands up and then laughs as it hits him in the tummy! The rest of the group run forward to take part, some of them also raising their T-shirts to feel the air on their skin.

We wanted to watch for the emergence of a new phase in which the children began to investigate something which had caught their interest. We had simply said at the beginning of the visit that their job was 'to make discoveries like real scientists', adding 'see what you can find out'. At the end of the visit, we asked everyone what *they* had discovered. That was our Scientists Conference which took place instead of written accounts, much to the relief of the children!

From play to investigation

Because play is essentially *not* goal orientated, there is licence to indulge in jokes. If and when the activity became an investigation we would expect to see far more intentional behaviour since by then they have a goal to pursue.

For children who were habitually autodidactic we might also hear about further reflection or private activity carried out after the visit was over. But

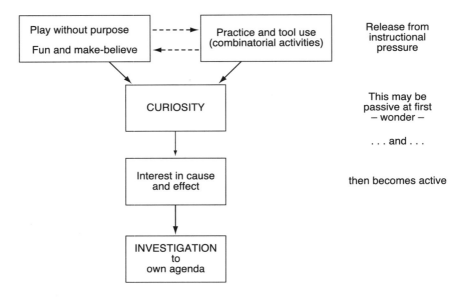

Figure 3.1 From play to investigation.

because the actual research was carried out with groups of three or four children at each exhibit, we also expected differences in social behaviour such as:

• Collaboration about how to use the equipment,
• Social or single decisions over the direction the investigation should take, and
• Explanation and/or argument about cause and effect.

Some twenty primary pupils from six different classes were followed in their activities being observed and recorded, and interviewed a week or two later back at their school.

Use of the equipment

In the first playful stage the children took turns at using the equipment. In other cases there was enough for all the children to take an equal part at the same time. From our earlier discussion of tool use, we knew there had to be enough practice to acquire a body-centred familiarity with the apparatus as this is essential.

Here is Tim, aged 7, who had been using a long cardboard tube to listen through, talking about it all a week later (this is an abbreviated version).

Tim: Well first thing I listened to, I went to the window and all I could
    hear was the birds going 'chirp' . . . And then I went to the cushion
    and when I moved it, it went 'sh, sh'. . . and when Sally talked through
    the um tube . . . it sounded really funny in my ear.
Interviewer: Did it? Did it sound loud in your ear?
Tim: Yeah, cos it didn't escape.

It seems here that the period of trying things out has cumulated in the first
formulation of an explanation – that the sound was loud because it was
confined to the tube.

There were a few groups who held a firm belief in dividing up the tasks
from the beginning so that one child was responsible for turning on and
off the wind, while the others made different car shapes. This sadly mis-
taken idea of team-work prevented some of the children from gaining
any first-hand experience.

On the other hand there were groups, like this one with three boys,
who worked so closely together that even their reporting was 'in chorus':

John: Well, we went over and tried . . .
Grant: we turned all the lights on . . .
John: . . . turned all the lights on and see what we got
Grant: We started with turning the um
Dave: . . . the yellow on
John: No the red
Dave: . . . leaving the red and blue on and got purple.

Negotiating about the investigation

Serious investigation began only when something surprising happened
which called for repetition, and testing out under different conditions.
You could say it was a puzzle. Gradually the activities become more intentional, the jokes stopped and the results were noted and compared.

Four boys are playing at the colour table – Sam, Pete, Kelvin and Jim –
all aged between nine and ten, and the following transcript shows just
how difficult it was for all four boys to collaborate and to repeat the right
combinations of coloured light in order to check what they had seen
before.

Sam: Mix all the colours
Jim: There, it's purple (a pale purple colour which Kelvin later calls pink).
Kelvin: Purple.
Pete (American accent): 'Purple'
Jim: What colours does it mix into?
Sam: Take the red out. Mix blue and green.

Jim: Turquoise (Then they go back to all three colours)
Sam: Take this back a bit (Moves one light backwards)
Kelvin: (Trying it out) It still makes purple (a pale colour that he later calls pink)
Jim: Move the red, Sam. (Sam moves in the red light, and takes away the blue)
Pete: Yellow.
Sam: Yellow! So if we do all those . . . (Jim puts the blue light back)
Kelvin: Pink! Pink! Pink!
Sam: Pink. Shall we do those colours? (Indicating red and green)
Pete: Orange? (Guessing)
Sam: OK. Like red and green, red and green . . .
Jim: *All* the colours.
Sam (taking no notice of Jim): Move the blue out.
Jim: No (still wanting all the colours) Red and green make yellow. Look!

So the four boys argue their way to a fairly successful repetition of the results that they had noticed. Throughout all the suggestions, commands, and counter commands, we can still recognise the different roles that the boys had taken on – Sam as self-appointed manager and organiser of the lights, Jim as thinker, and would-be designer, Kelvin and Pete as colour recorders. The puzzle consisted in finding out just how the different colours mix together. No boy acts completely on his own, and none really disrupts the investigation. However it is hard to read this record without wondering whether Jim might not have found it more satisfying on his own.

Another kind of investigation was more conducive to collaboration. In this the problem was set. First the children played with the skeleton-on-the-bicycle exhibit which had balloons to represent the pairs of 'antagonistic' muscles on the legs. These were to be measured as the wheels turned round, with most children trying to open and close the skeleton's mouth to superimposed speech! There was also a leg hanging down over the edge of a table with a verbal challenge – 'You have string and scissors to make muscles. Try to work the leg and make it kick!' It seemed that having a defined challenge cut out the difficult stage of all the group having to agree about the investigation. The question had been set for the pupils so this was no longer a completely autonomous activity.

Finding an enigma

In the extract below we see that one boy, Aeron, has noticed something very puzzling which does not seem to interest the other two – Steve and

Daniel – at all. All three coloured lights are on and the object casts three brightly coloured shadows – yellow, turquoise and magenta – none of which correspond to the colours of the lights (see diagram p. 42). The extract begins with the slow identification of Aeron's *enigma*.

Steve: That's pink there, fluorescent pink.
Daniel: They're just really bright lights and they've used . . . (explaining that the coloured filters make the light coloured).
Aeron: Why does it change colour? How does it (the shadow) change colour?
Steve: Put them (the coloured spectacles) there. They're fluorescent pink.
Aeron: Yeah, but if you put it like . . . how come it's (the spectacles) that colour, and it (the shadow) changes to that colour?
Daniel: (Ignoring Aeron and reading) 'What can you find out about coloured lights and shadows?'
Aeron: (still looking at the coloured shadows with amazement). *That's crazy!*

This emphatic comment identifies the enigmatic nature of Aeron's observation. The other two pay no attention and go on playing with the coloured spectacles.

Steve: If we put something on here and then put it under there, see what it does!
Daniel: Yeah.
Steve: Oh that's nice isn't it?

While Steve and Daniel continue to giggle and play with the coloured spectacles Aeron puzzles on, speaking out of kilter with the others. He has discovered another way of making coloured shadows which, eventually, is going to help him.

Aeron: Now put your hand under (the lights) and look. It's (the shadow has) got all different colours.

About a week later all three boys were interviewed in their school. The enigma of the coloured shadows was still on Aeron's mind. He brought it up even before they reached the interview room. Then the interviewer spoke directly to him.

Interviewer: I think you noticed something a bit strange about the shadows, didn't you Aeron?
Aeron: They were different colours from the lights.

Figure 3.2 Three 'coloured' lights producing three 'coloured' shadows. (From left to right, the lights are Red, Green and Blue. The shadows below, also from left to right, are Yellow, Magenta and Turquoise.)

The two other boys now joined in the discussion for the first time. Finally Aeron expressed his idea about how shadows are usually formed, and articulated the question again.

Aeron: It (the object) is blocking out the light.
Interviewer: Yeah . . . and?
Aeron: Why did it change colour though?

Gesturing to the other two lights he says 'There might be light going down there (from the unblocked lights) to make it a different colour.' Aeron had now formulated his enigma in words and almost resolved it.

In 1981 John Ziman wrote about *Puzzles, Problems and Enigmas*. He concluded by defining them in reverse order.

It is often said that scientists are full of natural curiosity . . . Without *individual curiosity* there could have been no notion of an enigma; without an interest in the enigmatic there would be no scientific problems; only by the solution of problems have we acquired the technical power to solve the puzzles of our complex civilisation.

(1981: 8, our emphasis)

The first two of these were mirrored for us in the autonomous play of many of our young visitors. But when the wish to solve an enigma becomes something of a passion, as it seems to have done for Aeron, we are seeing the qualities of a promising autodidact at work on ideas which then spread to his friends.

References

Boden, M. (1994) 'What is creativity?', in M. Boden (ed.) *Dimensions of Creativity*. Cambridge Mass.: MIT Press.

Brooke, H. and Solomon, J. (1998) 'From playing to investigating: research in an Interactive Science Centre for primary pupils', *International Journal of Science Education* 20(8): 959–971.

Brooke, H. and Solomon, J. (2001) 'Passive visitors or independent explorers: responses of pupils with severe learning difficulties at an Interactive Science Centre', *International Journal of Science Education* 23(9): 941–953.

Bruner, J. S. (1972) 'Nature and the uses of immaturity', in J. S. Bruner, A. Jolly and K. Sylva (eds) *Play: its Role in Development and Evolution.* Harmondsworth: Penguin.

Bruner, J. S., Sylva, K. and Genova, P. (1974) 'The role of play in problem-solving of children 3–5 years old', in J. S. Bruner, A. Jolly and K. Sylva (eds) *Play: its Role in Development and Evolution.* Harmondsworth: Penguin.

Goodall, J. (1968) *The Behaviour of free-living Chimpanzees of the Gombe Stream area*. Animal Monographs. Bailliere: Tindall and Casell.

Hayes, C. (1952) *The Ape in our House*. London: Gollancz.

Millar, S. (1968) *The Psychology of Play*. Harmondsworth: Penguin.

Piaget, J. (1951) *Play Dreams and Imitation in Childhood.* London: Routledge and Kegan Paul.

Polanyi, M. (1958) *Personal Knowledge*. London: Routledge and Kegan Paul.

Solomon, J. (1980) *Teaching Children in the Laboratory*. London: Croom Helm.

Vincenti, W. (1990) *What Engineers Know and how they Know it. Analytical Studies from Aeronautical History*. Baltimore: Johns Hopkins University Press.

Ziman, J. (1981) *Puzzles, Problems and Enigmas*. Cambridge: Cambridge University Press.

Ziman, J. (1984) *An Introduction to Science Studies.* Cambridge: Cambridge University Press.

Chapter 4

Do autodidacts have EBD?

Paul Howard

When I was invited to contribute this chapter, I leapt at the chance to examine the links between emotional and behavioural difficulties (EBD) and autodidactism. Subconsciously, perhaps, I hoped to demonstrate that many of the children and young people, whom we label as *having* EBD, or sometimes ungrammatically as *being* EBD, are misunderstood autodidacts. Apart from some anecdotal evidence, there is as yet no body of research to support this degree of relationship. However, there are some clear connections between pupils 'with' EBD and those who relish teaching themselves, not least in the ways in which they are perceived by others and in terms of the learning conditions in which they are most likely to thrive. I will explore this common ground through reflection on inclusive education.

The lesson

I open with a description of a familiar scene. It is the last Friday of the summer half-term in a comprehensive school in an inner city setting. The teacher is tired and the pupils in her Year 9 science class are excited. Just five minutes into the lesson and the noise level is high, most of the pupils are in animated conversation and a few are raising their voices in heated argument. A student, who has been assessed as having emotional and behavioural difficulties, is at the centre of one of the more heated debates. Several members of the class are out of their seats and moving around the room. A few students are singing and dancing. Only a handful of the pupils are not engaging with the noise and action, but looking at books and writing.

Standing at the front of the room, the teacher looks at the class, but makes no effort to quieten them as a whole group. Instead, she approaches knots of students, homing in on a pair arguing or an individual cavorting about. Invariably, she is greeted with a similar response. 'It's OK, we don't need your help', says one student briefly breaking off from a dispute with a peer before returning to the fray. 'Could you leave us, please?' says another as she dances to the accompaniment of her peers who are rapping on the table and making whooping noises. After a tour of the room, having had no impact on the decibel level or the amount of movement, she sits down at her desk and . . .

> Before reading on, spend a few minutes visualising the scene. If it helps, close your eyes and try to hear the sounds of that science class. Put yourself in the teacher's shoes and try to feel what she might be feeling. Ask yourself questions about the scene, perhaps 'Who is in control?', 'What would I do in this situation?' and 'What *does* the teacher do next?'

. . . she smiles.

Of course, had you already suspected that this was a class out of control with an ineffective teacher and students neither learning nor achieving anything, those two words 'she smiles' will not only have confirmed your suspicion but also suggested that the teacher was cracking up.

A few years ago, the *Guardian* newspaper ran a television ad, which depicted a long-shot of an aggressive-looking skinhead running towards a bowler-hatted, briefcase-carrying city gent. The initial impression, that something untoward and unpleasant was about to happen, was confirmed when the youth grabbed hold of the businessman and pushed him. Only in the third scene, which revealed a heavy object falling from scaffolding around a building, did the full meaning of the action become revealed. The young 'assailant' had saved the other's life.

Without possessing the eloquence of the makers of that advertisement, I have attempted a similar deception in my portrayal of the Year 9 science class. For, far from being an example of the supposed demise of schooling in our inner cities, this lesson was a beautiful illustration of education at its best. What I omitted from the first picture of this advertisement for education were the antecedents and purpose of the action I described. These are revealing.

> With the Key Stage 3 SATs and the narrowness of the preparation for them behind her, this teacher had given her class notice of some of the themes they would be studying in Year 10. Having split the class into groups, she randomly allocated themes to the groups and set them the task of finding out what they could about the subject. At the end of a two week period, each group was to give a presentation to the rest of the class, using a range of media, one of which had to be large sheets of paper.

Revisiting my opening description of the scene, you are now entitled to the qualification, which I previously withheld. The noise levels were appropriate to the task, with many students eagerly engaged in discussion of how to develop the presentations or in debriefing their peers on specific data they had unearthed. As for the arguments, these were also focused upon the task in hand, as the adversaries sought to convince each other and their colleagues in the group that they had seen a smarter way of putting their presentation together. During three-quarters of an hour in this cauldron of action, not one word was uttered which had no bearing on the task.

Moving around the room was crucial to the completion of tasks, as students consulted available resources on book shelves and on noticeboards, while the singing and dancing was by way of rehearsal for the diverse and imaginative presentations which were to follow . . . and how diverse and how imaginative they were! A panel game, a studio discussion with phone-in, a spoof of the Ricky Lake Show, a secondary school lesson and an Open University style of TV presentation all featured among the group's responses to the task. Presentations included music, dance, visual material, social interaction, oral material, personal reflection (in the form of a poem about one student's concerns over environmental pollution) and, lest I lose sight of what appeared on the school timetable, a great deal of scientific fact!

Anyone familiar with the theory of multiple intelligence, developed by Howard Gardner (1993) and applied by others, will recognise it in this science lesson. It shows all the hallmarks of an enlightened model of education, in which the diverse range of skills and aptitudes possessed by a class of students is acknowledged, valued and given expression.

Apart from shedding light on how diversity can be accommodated and encouraged in the course of an 'ordinary' lesson, this anecdote challenges assumptions about the control of learning. Without knowing the background, it is possible that you may have concluded that this was a class out of (the teacher's) control. Indeed, someone walking into the room unannounced may not have been pleased by their initial impression. In itself, that is a sad indictment of the superficiality of much of the official scrutiny of contemporary education. However, with the benefit of the full picture, it becomes clear that both the teacher and her class were in control of key elements. This lesson was one of those modified vehicles, used by driving or flying instructors, in which the teacher had control of the general context and direction of the task, while the students had control over the specifics of their own learning. In short, this was the teaching/learning dynamic at its best.

But what, you may be wondering, of the pupil with EBD? What of special note needs to be said about her involvement? In fairness, I must admit that the specific reference I made to her at the start of this chapter was a mischievous red herring, designed to add to the illusion that this was a class in disarray! However, no further comment on her participation is necessary, because it was not extraordinary. In common with her peers, her contribution to her group was from areas in which she felt most confident and competent. The context for learning, which the teacher had facilitated, was one in which the pupil's perceived emotional and behavioural difficulties became imperceptible or invisible. The corollary to this vanishing act is that students' EBD may be compounded by, or even created by the classroom context.

Who is the autodidact? Who has EBD?

What behavioural consequences are likely to follow from this? Often those who prefer to be more in control of their own learning – we might call them autodidacts – play truant from school, as Peter in Chapter 1 had done. This might provide a valuable cooling off period for them, but the law stipulates that the schools may not allow it. Schooling is compulsory, a word which is anathema to such youngsters, so it feels like some sort of prison and that alone may be enough to make them angry and quarrelsome. Anecdote and informal history often provide evidence that such students may return later to education, perhaps when they have learnt through experiences as we mentioned in Chapter 1, in 'the school of hard knocks', as Mark Twain and many other less famous people have done. It is instructive to speculate about which of the children in the classroom described in the opening section were autodidacts. Could the assessed EBD of the girl, who might have been in the middle of some noisy group, be her way of expressing frustration at being constrained to learn and behave in a largely prescribed way? Were the much quieter children who were writing or reading autonomous learners trying to create an oasis of quiet where they could learn in their own way? Or were the autodidacts simply not there in the classroom at all, having slipped out to escape from even the threat of being caught in a learning situation devised by someone else? Perhaps, as I have already confessed, there were no such individual labelled pupils, but a classroom full of children who were all keen on learning if it was under their own control.

This raises important questions about the process by which pupils are identified and assessed as having particular learning difficulties, in this case EBD, since there is no category labelled autodidact. While the thinking behind the Code of Practice for the Identification and Assessment of Special Educational Needs is no doubt benign, its application can have negative consequences. The Code is, after all, principally a medium for assessing difficulties, not addressing them. As such, it tends to compound the notion of difficulties being located within the pupil. So, the girl referred to in this chapter is regarded as having EBD, in much the same way that someone might have measles, albeit with one important qualification. Whereas the diagnosis of measles brings with it an expectation of healing after a relatively short period, the conclusion that a pupil has EBD is much more enduring. Consequently, a pupil can be consistently described as having EBD (or even as *being an EBD pupil!*), regardless of whether he or she is experiencing or presenting such difficulties in a particular setting at a particular time. Having acquired the epithet, the student is stuck with it.

The problems of inclusion

In the least sophisticated models of inclusion their mere location in mainstream schools of pupils with EBD is taken to be beneficial. Here, the assumption appears to be that the children and young people are normalised by the simple act of placing them in a particular context. I would suggest that this falls so far short of the mark that we should consider excluding it as an interpretation of inclusion. Apart from being over simplistic, it is predicated upon the pupil having to change, reflecting the fact that many definitions of EBD imply in-child pathologies as the main source of difficulty and ignore contextual factors. As the science class demonstrates, the process of inclusion is as much about changing the context as it is about changing the individual through direct and special intervention. Moreover, it is concerned with *all* pupils (and the teacher!), not just the special minority. If one accepts that the process of inclusion has universal implications, then the response of schools and teachers to autodidactic learners has to be in the same frame. Again, the key concern is whether systems and curricula are flexible and diverse enough to accommodate significant variations in learning style. Besides this general common ground between the two groups of pupils, in individual cases, autodidacts may express their frustration with being taught through behaviours comparable to those assessed as having EBD.

Gardner's work on multiple intelligences provides a very strong rationale for approaching inclusion as a universal interest rather than a minority pastime. As Armstrong (1987) indicates, if we use the term 'learning differences' instead of 'learning disabilities' or 'learning difficulties', we immediately shift the emphasis away from deficiencies to possible strengths, from what the child *cannot* do, to what it *can* do, and from particular individuals to all learners. In so doing, we start to bridge the gap between the *rhetoric* of a positive approach, to which nearly all educators subscribe, to the *practice* of a positive approach, which relatively few feel able to adopt within the prevailing orthodoxy of the expectations upon them.

Given the pressure on schools and teachers to achieve a particular and narrow type of result and to cover a particular and narrow syllabus within an inflexible time frame, we should not underestimate how difficult it is to create inclusive conditions for learning, as the science teacher did in my example. (It is worth recalling that she and her class too had previously been confined to the uninspiring slog which characterises much preparation for SATs.) However, nor can we afford to ignore the damaging consequences of not trying to create these inclusive conditions. As Elkind (1981) points out in *The Hurried Child*, a preoccupation with equipping children, especially young ones, with the tools of academic attainment frequently leads directly to learning and behavioural difficulties . . . and so to *teaching* problems. In order to create conditions in which children's learning can be maximised, we must surely remove some of the burdens on them and on the hurried and hustled teacher.

While there is no disputing that education in the UK continues to be under-funded, when they articulate the need for more resources teachers seldom refer to time for them and their pupils. Yet time is unquestionably one of the vital organs in a healthy educational body. Unfortunately, successive governments have framed their espousal of increased attainment and school improvement in such a way as to marginalise the significance of time. Thus 'failing' (*sic*) schools and Local Education Authorities are expected to be turned around within ludicrously simplistic time scales, while improving, but in terms of *learning* largely meaningless, SATs results are claimed as evidence of a quick fix. Needless to say, pupils with unrecognised learning differences are the most at risk when insufficient time is allowed for learning to evolve in diverse forms.

Of course, time is not the only constraint imposed upon teachers and learners in a way that impedes both teaching and learning. A testing culture ought also to feature in a contemporary table of learning impediments. At a time when educationalists in the United States are questioning that country's historical reliance on standardised tests (Lambert and McCombs 1998, Hart 1994), in the UK such tests have recently become the predominant feature on the educational landscape.

At a general level, the testing culture holds little appeal or relevance to most children, many of whom happily retain the sort of 'crap detectors' advocated by Postman and Weingartner (1973). In a letter to the *Times Educational Supplement* in 1999, one ten-year-old neatly summed up the fallacy of a reliance on tests: 'If school is supposed to be a place where we go to learn, why is so much of the teachers' and pupils' time spent on tests and getting ready for them?'

If there are distinct disincentives and disadvantages for all pupils in a test regime, the difficulties are compounded for those with unrecognised learning differences (including those with EBD who may be crypto-autodidacts), who are invariably both failed by the tests and then subjected to yet more tests and assessments. To make matters worse, the second round of testing seldom impacts on the pupils' perceived difficulties. As Armstrong (1987) observes:

If they don't locate a disability after two or three tests, they administer up to fifteen or twenty other tests until they either find a disability or exhaust their entire battery. This way of working with children encourages fault-finding and minimizes the chances of discovering strengths and abilities.

He goes on to cite research on tests 'which may have looked good but failed to provide any useful information about how children actually learn'.

Styles of thinking

Our understanding of how children (and adults) learn has increased greatly during the last twenty years with the proliferation of research into the workings of the brain. Meier (2000) suggests that traditional approaches to learning

> [T]ended to emphasise the Reptilian functions: rote learning, repeat-after-me, the teacher as power centre, the learner as passive obedient servant following a routine and precedent established by the hierarchy, a system driven by survival (the fear of failure).

Such approaches have little regard for new discoveries about how the brain works. They ignore the huge consumption of energy in new learning processes, the social, emotional and long-term cognitive memory functions, and the implications of these for both behaviour and learning. New theories of learning, like new models of the brain, supplant older ones but the criticism remains exactly the same. Emotional and behavioural difficulties may be compounded or even generated by narrow, restrictive methods of teaching, as Hall (1977) indicates: 'The way children are treated in schools is sheer madness. Those who can't sit still are stuck with the hyperactive label and are treated as anomalies and frequently drugged'.

Many children and young people who are assessed as having EBD are reported as wanting to move around a lot or to adopt a hands-on approach, and invariably these descriptions are couched in negative terms. Similar observations may be made about autodidactic learners, whose need to move outside the constraints of the conventional classroom are often not only physical but also emotional and cognitive. However, whether through Gardner's plurality of intelligences (1993), Armstrong's notion of learning differences (1987) or the general rebuttal of the traditional separation of body and mind in learning (Meier 2000), we would be better placed by regarding these behavioural characteristics as positive features of learning.

Models of teaching that are based upon a partial view of learning not only exclude emotional elements of understanding but also exclude people. Where a pupil's preferred learning styles are not recognised, accommodated and celebrated, he or she is likely to be perceived as either an outlaw or an outcast. In this respect the experience of autonomous pupils with EBD is sad not only for them but also for the community at large, which may be missing creative contributions. Clearly, the narrower the model of teaching and the understanding of learning, the greater is the resultant degree of exclusion. According to Rogers and Freiberg (1994), in order to establish an inclusive context, we need to devote less attention to direct teaching and more to creating conditions in which children will want to learn. This requires considerably less intervention than inheres in most established models of Western teaching and parenting. Therefore, it is perhaps fitting that an eloquent description of a less intrusive model can be found in the writings of Lao-tse (cited in Ginnis 1992):

If I keep from meddling with people, they take care of themselves.
If I keep from commanding people, they behave themselves.
If I keep from preaching at people, they improve themselves.
If I keep from imposing on people, they become themselves.

Postscript

As a corollary to the model of inclusion, which I have presented in this chapter, we need to review our view of pupils with EBD or autodidacts as minority groups. Once we define particular individuals as having emotional and behavioural difficulties, we run the risk of cutting those individuals loose, of denying the links between their emotions or behaviours and ours, as similar constituents in the single universal set of emotions and behaviours. Likewise, if we regard autonomous learners, those who prefer to teach themselves, as an unusual minority group, we may compound any feelings of alienation which they experience. In the process, we may also fail to recognise that autodidactism is a characteristic of all our informal learning in early childhood. Were we to preserve and encourage this characteristic in formal education settings, it is arguable that this could significantly reduce the incidence of learning difficulty and associated emotional and behavioural difficulty.

Bibliography

Armstrong, T. (1987) *In Their Own Way*. New York: Tarcher Putnam.
Elkind, D. (1981) *The Hurried Child*. Reading, MA: Addison-Wesley.

Gardner, H. (1993) *Multiple Intelligences: The Theory in Practice*. New York: Basic Books.

Ginnis, P. (ed.) (1992) *Learner-centred Learning*. Ticknall: Education Now.

Hall, E. T. (1977) *Beyond Culture*. New York: Anchor Books/Doubleday.

Hart, D. (1994) *Authentic Assessment*. New York: Addison-Wesley.

Lambert, N. M. and McCombs, B. L. (eds) (1998) *How Students Learn*. Washington DC: APA.

Meier, D. (2000) *The Accelerated Learning Handbook*. New York: McGraw-Hill.

Postman, N. and Weingartner, M. (1973) *Teaching as a Subversive Activity*. Harmondsworth: Penguin.

Rogers, C. and Freiberg, H. J. (1994) *Freedom To Learn*. Upper Saddle River, NJ: Merrill.

Chapter 5

Homo Ludens

Robin Hodgkin

Stuart Kauffman, in *At Home in the Universe*, his book on complexity and order, writes about the essentially playful nature of humankind.

> We call ourselves by many names: *Homo Sapiens*, man the wise, *Homo Habilis*, man the able, the tool maker and, perhaps most appropriate, *Homo Ludens*, man the playful . . . It is this, the science of *Homo Ludens* that expresses the most creative case of humanity. Here science is art. What honour and what joy to seek its laws.
>
> (Kauffman 1995: 131)

In this chapter, which has grown into a collection of disparate notes, I shall reflect on *Homo Ludens* and his children, on that creative core of knowing which it is the task of parents and sensible teachers to cultivate and to guide. Play is the starting point of much good science and of all good making. It can, at times, blaze into an autodidactic flame. It cannot be compelled or instrumentalised in the curriculum. Like a Zen joke or 'koan', it disappears if you try too hard to describe it. And there is a further paradox: play can be the precursor of practice (e.g. in a child repeating a mnemonic jingle) and it can also be an extension of creativeness – the pushing out of a skill to a new limit. That is the meaning of my learning frontier in Figure 5.1 on p. 59: a place where novelty is encountered and new things are made – the place of P-creativity in Margaret Boden's chapter, and of curiosity in Helen Brooke's Interactive Science Centre in Chapter 3. Play consolidates what is becoming familiar and probes what may be emerging. This two-directional nature of play is suggested by the figure of eight shaped arrow in Figure 5.1.

It is said that Beethoven – deaf and prematurely old – would in a mood of depression, retire to his piano and thump out a therapeutic improvisation until the black mood began to lift. Sometimes he would find in those random rhythms the seed of a new composition. A new creation would begin to emerge in that only partly constrained chaos of his improvising. This story about Beethoven is a good starting point:

- Because it is about *musical playing* and that points in a less trivial direction than is suggested by children playing, and
- Because it exemplifies an experienced craftsman (the musician with his 'tool') on the look out for new emergent patterns. 'Every kind of human knowing', writes Michael Polanyi; 'ranging from perception to scientific observation includes an appreciation both of order contrasted to randomness and of the degree of order' (Polanyi 1958: 38).

Conceptual space, 'a world of suckable things'

Margaret Boden, in her book on Piaget, observes that 'a baby sucking is constructing a world of suckable things and not merely finding things that he (or she) can do' (Boden 1979: 30). Boden is not being patronising to that infant; she sees it as taking first, early steps in the furnishing of its own conceptual space with meaningful objects. This is what the young Helen Keller achieves in a rare, all-embracing vision in an episode quoted later in this chapter.

I don't find Boden's term 'conceptual space' adequate, and prefer the more extensive and dynamic terms used by Polanyi and Winnicott. The former speaks of a heuristic or discovery field in which an infant or a scientist presses her enquiry. But discovery is not only a finding; it often involves making too. This was realised by Donald Winnicott who, writing in 1970, was asking readers to accept an extension of their terms when he developed his vocabulary of potential space and of the very earliest toys, tools and probes. These objects emerge in such play space and are often jointly created by the interaction of parent and infant. The Winnicott pattern or paradigm has an advantage if we are considering self-directed exploring as being applicable to all the main modes of competence. It helps us to understand the various practices and technologies that can emerge.

The rest of this chapter consists of three parts: some autobiographical fragments from a family of slightly adventurous, scientifically inclined children, and quotations from the philosopher Suzanne Langer and the rather eccentric chemist Michael Polanyi. All concern special 'aha!' moments when children or students experienced a crucial breakthrough in understanding. The quotations are also a small salutation to those two important thinkers who, in the middle of the twentieth century, were attempting to swing our Western world-view away from the mechanistic and narrowly reductive tendencies which had been dominant for so long. Finally there are some comments on the main diagram. This 'ideas map' was central to my book about education – *Playing and Exploring* – written in the 1980s when my aim was to nudge our educational thinking and practise into a better direction for the twenty-first century. We still need to be nudging in the same direction.

On the beach: where play can get serious

Much of my own family's teenage and pre-teenage self-initiated learning happened on the beach among the sandhills below Bamburgh Castle in Northumberland during the 1920s. We three children were, I think, particularly fortunate in enjoying a direct experience of that environment. Electronic representations of nature certainly have their uses but they also get in the way and muffle our close, sensory encounters with our environment. Children draw a very special benefit from experiencing the real texture, the detailed challenge and sometimes the wearisome slog of making their way in uncrowded hills and on wild shores. My brother, Alan, claimed that his first feeling for serious, scientifically organised enquiry was under the aegis of Aunt Katie – planning a campaign to locate a stonechat's nest in the gorse above the sandhills. But that was a bit too systematic for my tastes and for those of my younger brother, Keith, so we stayed together on the beach.

A good beach is certainly an ideal place for any self-directed exploring. Why? Because a beach is a place of movement and incipient chaos, a zone where the land is crumbling away and where new transient forms are emerging, so it is well suited for metaphor, for poetry and for the overlapping of meanings. It is fairly chaotic but not quite beyond human influence or control. Other places, where the bones of the world stick through, or where civilisation and propriety crumble, share this quality. The rocky ridge with gendarmes and frost-shattered spikes above the *bergschrund*, the creeks and lagoons where small boats can wander and not be too quickly committed, the caves and potholes of old miners or of ancestors, or even the bottom of your garden, where the fence is broken and there are the remains of a rusting air raid shelter – all of these are the environments of chaos and movement. Of course such places may be luring you to danger. But a little danger is an essential part of the package for those with passion for self-directed exploration, and must be coped with.

So, Keith and I opted for the less disciplined ploys of the sandy shore and left the stonechats to the More Serious Ornithologists. We were going to build a city which would last to the next high tide: an extremely rococo city using our newly invented drip-technology where the turrets and statues emerge from the half dry forms which harden as the sandy slush drips off our fingertips.

First you dig a slush mine – six inches down into the water table and you pull up handfuls of liquid sand. Then you judiciously drip the suspension from the ends of your fingers. The drops harden into fantastic blobs or lenticels of drying sand. Statues, minarets, towers and gargoyles begin to emerge almost miraculously and decorate the skylines for a while. Of course, you keep your head down; at Lilliput level, to get the best view. Until the next high tide comes.

You develop a language too: for describing the technique – terms partly borrowed from architectures that you already know for some of these new creations – flying buttress, gargoyle, minaret. Some of what you handle and observe will leave conceptual gaps for when you learn a bit more science – capillarity, seepage, and meniscus. Suspended grains of mica, shell and quartz – floating and moving in a phase space between liquid and solid. But these words come later. The whole technology itself is mobile and open-ended; partly understood and partly waiting for better explanations. The challenge of this kind of play is to find and develop just such a slightly chaotic context, and as you live within it, experience may perhaps help you to recognise when some new patterns begin to emerge.

If, at a later stage, you should (perhaps rashly?) carry your exploring play over on to the steep and rocky cliffs of reality you may find yourself facing and coping with the sharp edges of real risk – the risk of loose rock, of inadequate foothold, avalanche or storm. There are always serious contingencies waiting down the road. But it is of the nature of all true 'play space' to be open-ended and not quite predictable. Exploring isn't safe. On that Bamburgh coast the more serious scientists, the ornithologists, did find the stonechats' nest and also, using similar systematic methods, a rare golden plovers' nest on Belford Moor (Hodgkin 1992: 223).

From play to autodidactism

Playfulness is certainly one of the conditions for self-teaching and form-finding. Play is, as we have seen, Janus-faced and a notoriously difficult concept to clarify. This is because it is an activity in part defined by absences. It is activity within light restraints, or in much reduced ones. It is, in short, an aspect of what John Holland calls a CGT – a constrained generating procedure (Holland 1998: 126). In most forms of play the constraints are not entirely absent, but they can be reduced to a fine minimum to suit those who want to be autonomous. That means submitting to *some* rules and yet hoping also for the unexpected gifts of freedom from rules. In rock climbing, for example, and in many forms of creative artistry such as poetry the rules, like other tools of the trade, cannot be totally dispensed with, but they must be kept to an optimal level of simplicity.

As suggested above, autonomous play has a double purpose for perfecting a skilled intelligent practice and regular habits. For example: I might be repeating a manual movement, on a piano keyboard – over and over again. This could be because I am trying to improve and speed up a special skill, which I am in the process of acquiring, or because I feel that I am about to take off on an experimental flight of creativity.

Suzanne Langer and Michael Polanyi – on getting to know

Below are two extracts from writers of great importance and profundity who have been largely neglected recently, especially by those who write about education. The first quotation is from Suzanne Langer's *Philosophy in a New Key* (1957). For some of us it was the first radical and clear statement about what signs and symbols are and what a key role *feelings* and sensory involvement play in the generation of meaning. In Langer's quotation from Helen Keller it is important to remember that this child was born into normal sight and hearing but lost both in an illness before she was a year old. In both of these experiences there is a carer or teacher in the background. The 'aha!' experience, called an emergence in Chapter 17, is so central that the helper is more of a midwife than instructor.

This is a famous passage in the autobiography of the deaf-blind Helen Keller, in which she describes the dawn of language. Of course she had used signs before, formed associations, learned to expect things and identify people or places; but there came a great day when all sign meaning was eclipsed and dwarfed by the discovery that a particular act of her fingers constituted a word. This event had required a long preparation; the child had learned many finger acts, but they were as yet a meaningless play. Then, one day, her teacher took her out to walk – and there the great advent of language occurred.

> She brought me my hat, [*the memoir reads*] and I knew I was going out into the warm sunshine. This thought, if a wordless sensation may be called a thought, made me hop and skip with pleasure.
>
> We walked down the path to the well-house, attracted by the fragrance of the honeysuckle with which it was covered. Someone was drawing water and my teacher placed my hand under the spout. As the cool stream gushed over my hand she spelled into the other the word water, first slowly, then rapidly. I stood still, my whole attention fixed upon the motion of her fingers. Suddenly I felt a misty consciousness as of something forgotten – a thrill of returning thought; and somehow I knew then that w-a-t-e-r meant the wonderful cool something that was flowing over my hand. That living word awakened my soul, gave it light, hope, joy, set it free! There were barriers still, it is true, but barriers that in time could be swept away.

I left the well-house eager to learn. Everything had a name, and each name gave birth to a new thought. As we returned to the house every object which I touched seemed to quiver with life. That was because I saw everything with the strange, new sight that had come to me.

(Langer 1957)

Michael Polanyi was a medical doctor who became a well-known physical chemist. He was born into an intellectual Jewish and Catholic family in Hungary. He turned from medicine to chemistry during the First World War and later left Berlin under pressure from the Nazis, for a Chair in Manchester. He realised more clearly than almost anyone else the dangers of all totalitarian regimes and was one of the first to speak against the folly of the USSR's aim of centrally controlling science so that it could 'serve society'. By 1958 Polanyi had switched to philosophy and wrote his great work – *Personal Knowledge*. It stresses the importance of personal skills and perception as well as of the personal commitment to a search for truth as being the essential spring of science.

Here he remembers a moment of dawning insight.

Think of a medical student attending a course in the X-ray diagnosis of pulmonary diseases. He watches in a darkened room shadowy traces on a fluorescent screen placed against a patient's chest, and hears the radiologist commenting to his assistants, in technical language, on the significant features of these shadows. At first the student is completely puzzled. For he can see in the X-ray picture of a chest only the shadows of the heart and ribs, with a few spidery blotches between them. The experts seem to be romancing about figments of their imagination; he can see nothing that they are talking about. Then as he goes on listening for a few weeks, looking carefully at ever-new pictures of different cases, a tentative understanding will dawn on him; he will gradually forget about the ribs and begin to see the lungs. And eventually, if he perseveres intelligently, a rich panorama of significant details will be revealed to him: of physiological variations and pathological changes, of scars, of chronic infections and signs of acute disease. He has entered a new world. He is about to grasp what he is being taught. Thus, at the very moment when he has learned the language of pulmonary radiology, the student will also have learned to understand pulmonary radiograms. The two can only happen together. Both halves of the problem set to us by an unintelligible text, referring to an unintelligible subject, jointly guide our efforts to solve them, and they are solved eventually together by discovering a conception, which comprises a joint understanding of both the words and the things.

(Polanyi 1958)

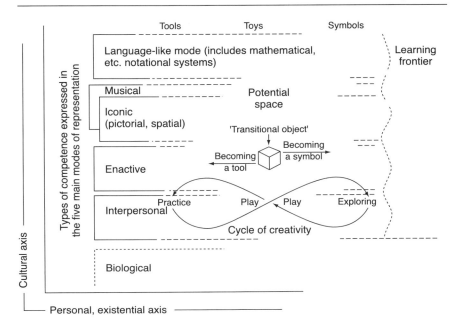

Figure 5.1 The space of play, exploring and learning.

The joint understanding of the picture, *and the language* about it, is implied by the curving arrow which links frontier imagery with the language mode above – top right hand corner in Figure 5.1. What it has in common with the understanding by Helen Keller that water could be signified by a word, will be discussed in the section on complexity theory in Chapter 17.

Cultural and personal dimensions of learning

The central concept in my diagram is of a human being – child or adult – exploring. Her or his inherited powers are nurtured at first through play by interaction with maternal influences. Children grow through mastery of human competence to become still-exploring adults – at least they *should* so develop, for we are all born to be self-teaching autodidacts and discoverers.

Taken together, these ideas might be seen to be pointing to some radical changes in our educational pattern but they do not just imply soft liberal, child-knows-best policies. They point specifically to a rethinking of apprenticeship and of craft learning; a greater use and understanding of early systematic practices in an area of incipient chaos, and of the importance of adventurous habits in learning. All of these are necessary for the emergence of autonomous and competent adults.

Competence

Education is about developing our competences: not just one, but several which complement each other. Competence, rather like the 'Talent' in our Christian parable, is not meant to be buried, but to be developed, and if we are competent in some field of action we will be motivated to do more with it.

A competence does not consist of just one skill but of several, inter-related ones. In his important book, *Frames of Mind* (1983) Howard Gardner takes a similar approach. He uses the word intelligence with a wider than usual meaning where I use competence. Gardner's collection of seven intelligences closely parallels my five competences. But he squeezes in an extra one called *intra*personal intelligence. Gardner also, rightly, separates off a distinct mathematical intelligence, which I had included under the language-like mode – a serious oversimplification.

Synergy

Most of these competences are probably controlled and patterned by different parts of the brain. But there is close neural communication between its different parts and a complex sharing of tasks. I use the analogy of a small, conductor-less, musical ensemble, where the players must not only share a script but also watch each other (Hodgkin 1983: 206). Teachers will often have had the experience of a student who seemed blocked in some areas of learning and was then helped by a *sudden breakthrough* (an emergence, in complexity theory) elsewhere in his or her repertoire. The Polanyi quotation gives a vivid example of how a student's visual competence can suddenly be enriched by learning to work within the linguistic mode as well as in the iconic or visual mode. That move upwards is represented by the branching arrow at the frontier in the diagram. Researchers have often described such moments of enlightenment, and technologists call it the 'eureka moment'. Visual diagrams and enactive experiments seem to cry out for articulate representation, either numerically or in an exchangeable hypothetical prediction that can be checked through the intersubjectivity that we all share.

There is another dimension operating through all human competence. Essentially it concerns the developing and deepening of human action throughout the lifespan of an individual. Very little children use pieces of cloth for comfort as they go to bed, and also sometimes during the day, and these are the forerunners of all toys, tools and probes. Polanyi's idea about using probes to find out about a shared reality, and MacIntyre's ideas about how virtues are distilled from shared practice (MacIntyre 1987) are of the greatest value because they too remind us of the social sharing out of which new creativity can often grow, as it did for my brother and myself on that rather harsh Northumberland beach.

The frontier

The idea of an attractive frontier applies to the development of all competences. In my own experience, it was the powerful attraction of steep rocks and high mountains which exercised an almost fatal attraction. It is hard to say why this was so, but it may be because we are groping towards the identification of a deep force which energises all self-education. I will not try to explore it further, but end with a quotation from a gifted contemporary anthropologist, Tim Ingold. For some years he has been exploring new ideas about how a person's or, indeed, how an animal's, learning energies operate in a Winnicott-style field where environment, tools, instruments and the exploratory learner are all involved in the emergence of pattern and form. Not surprisingly Ingold quotes Gregory Bateson as well as Suzanne Langer in introducing his ideas on the apparent *pull* of a frontier. It is as though it opens a door to the pressure of creativity and to the emergence of form. 'What we call mind', Ingold suggests, 'Is the cutting edge of the life process itself, the ever-moving front of what Alfred North Whitehead called "a creative advance into novelty"' (Ingold 1998: 169).

References

Boden, M. (1979) *Piaget*. London: Fontana.

Gardner, H. (1983) *Frames of Mind: the Theory of Multiple Intelligences*. New York: Basic Books.

Goodwin, B. (1995) *How the Leopard Changed its Spots*. London: Methuen.

Hodgkin, A. (1992) *Chance and Design*. Cambridge: Cambridge University Press, 22–3.

Hodgkin, G. K. H. (1963) *Towards an Earlier Diagnosis*. Edinburgh: Livingstone.

Hodgkin, R. A. (1983) *Playing and Exploring*. London: Methuen.

Holland, J. H. (1998) *Emergence from Chaos to Order*. Oxford: Oxford University Press.

Ingold, T. (1998) 'Culture, nature and environment: steps towards an ecology of mind', in E. Cartledge (ed.) *Mind, Brain, and the Environment*. Oxford: Oxford University Press, 169.

Ingold, T. (2000) *The Perception of the Environment: Essays in Livelihood, Dwelling and Skill*. London: Routledge.

Kauffman, S. (1995) *At Home in the Universe*. Oxford: Oxford University Press.

Langer, S. (1957) *Philosophy in a New Key*. Cambridge, Mass.: Harvard University Press.

MacIntyre, A. (1987) *After Virtue*. London: Duckworth.

Polanyi, M. (1958) *Personal Knowledge*. London: Routledge.

Winnicott, D. W. (1970) *Playing and Reality*. London: Tavistock.

Chapter 6

Learning to be a genetic counsellor

Patterns of life-world knowledge

Vivian Leyser da Rosa and Joan Solomon

Introduction

It is basic to most kinds of professional work that its practitioners should combine a high level of specific knowledge together with a capacity to empathise with their clients. This requires two very different types of understanding, and research indicates that they may, at times, be in conflict with each other. Genetic counsellors, like doctors, lawyers, and teachers, show other professional characteristics which include making decisions about new situations, autonomously, 'on the hoof'. How can genetic counsellors be prepared for this decision-making when, armed only with difficult and sometimes uncertain knowledge from the world of genetics, they stand alone amid the raw emotion of a family which may have had to face a terrible prognosis for their new baby, or the recent death of a child?

Genetic counselling is a field of increasing importance which used to be limited to the confirmation of diagnosis, mostly in the newborn, and the quantification of risks for the parents' and the other relatives' future family plans. With the increasing public acceptance of patients' right to know in a wider sense, counsellors have begun offering their clients a more theoretical gloss on the subject during their counselling sessions. During the last twenty years, the situation has been changed dramatically by the introduction of new prenatal diagnostic techniques which increased both the numbers of clients involved and also the nature of the advice being sought. Some of these tests have even become routine population screening programmes, such as those for the detection of carriers of thalassemia and other hemoglobinopathies, and more recently for conditions such as cystic fibrosis and Huntington's chorea. With the promise of possible new gene therapies based on genomics, counselling is likely to become even more in demand by those wanting to be reassured of their healthy genetic status, as well as that of their potential offspring.

All this new knowledge and new procedures mean, at the least, that more knowledge has to be conveyed to the public. Some of this is very taxing for a lay person, and the psychological reactions to it can be profoundly mixed. The expression 'New Human Genetics' has been coined to describe not just the latest advances in this field, but also the great number of interlinked social, cultural, moral and ethical issues that have been raised. Sally McIntyre (1995), commenting on the new situation, has written that it is no longer just a question of how much the public understands about genetics but also *what the geneticists understand about members of the public*.

The separate purposes of genetic counselling?

The general purposes of genetic counselling were described by one of its early practitioners (Fraser 1974).

> This process involves an attempt by one or more appropriately trained persons to help the individual or the family to
> i. comprehend the medical facts, including the diagnosis, the probable course of the disorder and the available management;
> ii. appreciate the way heredity contributes to the disorder and the risk of recurrence in specific relatives;
> iii. understand the options for dealing with the risk of recurrence;
> iv. choose the course of action which seems appropriate to them in view of their risk and their family goals and act in accordance with that decision; and
> v. make the best possible adjustment to the disorder in an affected family member and/or to the risk of recurrence of that disorder.

This formulation is still quite often quoted and, superficially, seems orderly and convincing. The first three points may call for traditional teaching from one who knows to those who don't, and are referred to as the provision of 'objective information . . . in a way that allows a decision to be made' by Revel (1995). On the face of it this seems quite the simplest part of the counselling process, as long as the clients have sufficient intelligence to understand what they are being told.

The last two of Fraser's points are more psychological, and more similar to the everyday meaning of counselling. Clients usually come to the genetic services from stressful personal situations which involve having to take life-long decisions. So an important aspect of counselling is to 'provide support in reaching decisions about options' as Revel wrote. But clients' affective reactions towards receiving and comprehending information are extremely variable; some optimistic clients receive bad news without much apparent distress, others who are more pessimistic need reassurance to believe in any test result, even when it is reassuringly negative. To deal with these effects several different counselling protocols have been designed and used. Sadly the results have all been disappointing. This suggests that the normal transmission model of learning may be inappropriate for the task.

Research evaluating the outcomes of counselling

We have two ways of evaluating the counselling procedures:

1   Was knowledge about genetics retained and understood?
2   Could it be applied in the clients' situations?

In the simplest type of evaluation, the clients and their families are tested after counselling for the knowledge they have acquired, in order to find out the efficiency of the teaching/learning process. Serra and her colleagues (1995) provide us with a typical example of this kind of evalua- tion. Genetic counselling was given to 200 Brazilian adults with the beta- thalassemia trait. After a period ranging from one to thirteen years later around 50 per cent of the patients interviewed could give correct answers about the name of the condition and meaning of the trait, and about two-thirds of them were able to refer to practical health and reproductive issues. Although the researchers used this data to show that the counsel- ling had been fairly effective in its own terms, their research also threw up two unexpected findings which were much less satisfactory.

First, the researchers noted that their clients found it much easier to understand practical advice than scientific knowledge. Perhaps that was not surprising. Second, and clearly coming as a surprise to these researchers, their results showed that even when the practical advice had been received and remembered many clients did not act upon it. For example clients understood the precautions to be taken because of their carrier status, such as bringing future spouses for testing, but they seemed *not* to be taking the required actions. Although there are under- standable reasons for this, such as not wanting to scare off a boy/girl friend, the clients' behaviour seemed to be in marked contrast to their understanding. This effect is well-known in social psychology where recorded knowledge and attitude are rarely reflected in actions. Similarly, in general education, motivation usually shows a surprisingly weak cor- relation with achievement.

Learning about one's inherited condition seems not, as Fraser's categor- isation had suggested, to be independent of the psychological processes. On the contrary, the clients' learning takes place within a framework of personal experience where emotional reactions become inextricably inter- woven with the learning of abstract genetic knowledge. This teaching/ learning part of the process, previously thought to be unproblematic, is now seen as deeply affected by the emotional condition of the clients.

This linking together of our cognition with our emotions is now well recognised in the field of memory studies. It is a common experience of daily life that we suddenly remember some incident from the past which may have been triggered by a visual image, or even by a familiar smell, and we retrieve the whole incident together with the emotions we experienced at the time. The present understanding of memory defines it in three quite different modes of operation (Tulving 1984) – procedural knowledge, which is about how to do something; semantic knowledge which is what teachers and counsellors try to pass on so that their students or clients can describe world-events in terms of overarching concepts; and episodic knowledge, remembering a whole incident which is triggered by a single probe that is intimately linked with the person's sense of identity. We have to be put into what Tulving calls retrieval mode by being in a certain place (such as going back upstairs to where we previously thought about it) in order to recall the episode. In the context of genetic counselling this theory explains why even a low-key discussion of what decision might be taken often triggers all the original symptoms of distress.

The clients' emotions may be aggravated by cultural insensitivity. As genetics services become more accessible clients may arrive from different ethnic and cultural backgrounds seeking help. The counsellors may hold to the Western ethic of a non-directive approach and patient autonomy, nevertheless this ignorance of the patients' preventive health practices, and their traditional beliefs, makes the counselling process even more fraught. Studies with Latino populations in the United States, and Pakistani and Indians in the UK have shown that cultural barriers increase the clients' lack of understanding.

Genetic counselling, especially in the early days, continued to treat psychological objectives separately from the knowledge objectives. Counsellors were told about the importance of listening to what clients want to know *before* proceeding to the actual conveying of information. But at this level of complexity (see Chapter 17) the process may not be as linear as that logic suggests. Clients' perceptions and needs, including expressing guilt, or mourning for a dead baby, should be foremost in the counsellor's mind throughout the whole counselling process. Listening may appear to be non-controversial, but in practice it can make the process very drawn out. In his excellent book on the practice of genetic counselling, Clarke (1994) expresses no doubts about the prime importance of carefully attending to the clients' wishes during the whole process because it would allow the clients to set both the pace of the discussion and its agenda. For those who have been referred for genetic counselling without their explicit consent, as is becoming more and more frequent, or for those from different cultural backgrounds, skilled and patient listening is of even greater importance, and their absence may amount to an unacceptable level of counsellor domination.

Problems with scientific knowledge and expertise

From a sociological perspective these results were not completely new and unexpected. In his book *The Consequences of Modernity* (1990) Anthony Giddens argued that the increasing sophistication and specialisation of modern science has inevitably led to a situation where very few can hope to assess the validity of its conclusions. When lay people are at serious risk (Beck 1986), the valid path to patient decision-making may be not so much an assessment of the knowledge on offer, as of finding an expert whose thinking they feel they can trust. This moves the clients' activity away from the struggle to understand the genetic knowledge and towards the development of empathy with the expert.

The sociology of knowledge suggests that life-world knowledge, which includes practical advice about actions of many kinds, is far more accessible to most people than specialised semantic knowledge. It is the paramount reality of everyday life. When a person has to confront the reality of a crisis which requires sharp decision-making, fuzzy life-world knowledge, with its tolerance of alternative points of view, may seem to be of little help. The client needs to make what Schutz and Luckmann (1973) call 'a leap into another province of reality' where the genetic semantic knowledge which explains aspects of their situation is situated. These two forms of knowing contrast sharply with semantic knowledge rarely called upon for action, while life-world knowing offers practical and proverb-driven advice.

If a client comes to a session not only stressed, but immersed in images of grossly handicapped children, of threats of early death, feelings of guilt, or fear of family rejection, then making the required leap into the abstract intellectual domain of scientific concepts may become very hard indeed (see Solomon 1983 for corroborative research with school children). Some recent research has shown that the attempt to teach ethics, which is clearly a decontextualised system of semantic knowledge, to senior medical students did not at first seem to improve either their applied competence or their clients' decision-making. Only when the course was changed to refocus upon actual clinical cases did it produce any real and lasting effect (Myser *et al.* 1995).

Teaching genetics to Brazilian medical students

In many Brazilian universities, human genetics is taught to medical students as a short first or early second year course. What makes this course different from those in elementary genetics in British schools is its placement in a vocational setting. Even though its genetic content runs from Mendelian laws to DNA and the molecular basis of inheritance, as it would do in the curriculum of most countries, it also includes some more practical teaching. The students find the whole area of genetics interesting and not particularly difficult.

We might expect the students to keep the two knowledge domains separate – the life-world domain of emotion and lay maxims, and the scientific domain of abstract knowledge – which they do. They are usually very keen to learn the biochemical details of genetic molecules and the way DNA commands biological processes. Indeed when subject to academic tests on these complex matters, the students usually do very well.

The next stage in the teaching schedule brings out quite different responses. When the students are asked about their own DNA – where it is, its parental origin and how it works inside their bodies – some actually seem surprised that genetic processes are happening within them. For these young doctors in training, formal scientific knowledge about body chemistry may be learned successfully but seems to be kept in a separate domain of thinking which is not easily accessed when it comes to explaining their heritage in terms of their father's blood group or their mother's blue eyes. The reverse also happens. When asked about relatives' physical resemblance, they revert to explaining it in lay terms such as 'blood mixtures' – even if they later claim that they only intended this as a figure of speech!

The students show consistent enthusiasm for scientific problem-solving when they are asked to build hypothetical family trees, using conventional symbols such as little squares, dots and marriage lines. But when it comes to representing their own families, all sort of doubts arise, such as 'Should an adopted child be represented in a family tree?' and 'How do I represent my older sister who was married once and now has a child with a boyfriend?' For the students this represents the first confrontation between life-world reality and scientific knowledge.

Finally, at the end of this genetics semester, the students are confronted with a situation where it is not possible to avoid the psychological dimensions of the problem. At the beginning they are told that genetic counselling relies heavily on the ethic of a trusting doctor-patient relationship which will be imbued with non-directive advice, moral neutrality, the client's *autonomy*, and complete confidentiality. For this exercise the students are given protocols of mythical patients who have come seeking information and advice. In every case they are asked to consider what scientific information should be provided and the possible outcomes of the counselling.

In the course of these exercises the students begin to appreciate that:

- The knowledge they can provide is not enough for the clients' needs,
- What they do provide may still leave the clients uncertain,

- There will be different outcomes depending on the clients' moral or cultural positions, and
- These positions often do not match their own.

At this point the students frequently display unease and frustration. So far they have experienced a simple simulation of the practical application of medical knowledge, in which they are studying to become experts, applied to a reality in which every client is already 'an expert in their own morality'. The problem which training will have to address is how to help them to recognise and understand the wide variety of the life-world moralities which surround them in the general population.

In Brazil training begins with the learning of up to date but sometimes ambiguous genetic information. This is followed by a number of actual case studies, with a significant part of the necessary competence being acquired on the job, sometimes alongside experienced counsellors who present different counselling styles for different situations. The ethical principle of non-directiveness (considered one of the hallmarks of good counselling) will also require a variety of approaches. The trainee counsellors have to be able to approach each patient or family knowing that the clients will be bound to assimilate scientific knowledge unevenly into their life-world frame of reference.

Decision-making and autodidactism

One other feature of the two sorts of knowledge is the very different ways in which they can be indexed and retrieved. Journals and textbooks have a bibliography or a search facility for the retrieval of knowledge, and even in these days of rapidly expanding genomics it does not need special dedication to keep up to date. It is quite simply a part of every counsellor's duty to do so (in much the same way as the scientist in Chapter 9 did) and search engines become easier to use every few months. The more difficult question is the general one of how complex empathic knowledge about people can be stored and accessed, if at all.

In this process we are dealing with episodic chunks of memory. The next and most important phase is to find out how the memory of these episodes can be used. This might be the categorising of an episode, for example the client 'is not listening', 'likely to break down in tears', 'seems ready to learn more', or 'does not understand' etc. It is these aspects that provide the 'sense' of the episode, as the new counsellor struggles to retain something useful from the experience. There could be a parallel here between this experience and the making sense of a puzzle picture which seems at first to be no more than blobs of black and white (see Figure 6.1).

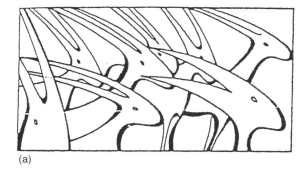

(a)

(b)

Figure 6.1 Recognising patterns.

Learning to 'see' these pictures is similar to the learning problem of the counsellors trying to 'see' the social situation, in different ways. It is notoriously difficult to guide someone else into seeing the picture as you do by the use of words. Sometimes the student counsellors are accompanied by a more experienced nurse but the non-verbal nature of the evidence makes even oral communication difficult. Seeing the man in the picture (Figure 6.1b) at last is immensely satisfying because it 'makes sense', and our aim is to see how signals from a potentially emotional situation in genetic counselling may do the same. N. R. Hanson (1958), who was the first to explore the pattern recognition through which we make discoveries, emphasised that the meaning of the whole pattern, in our case the whole counselling incident, is more than any list of the parts which we perceive. For genetic counsellors the clients' emotions are the social fabric of the incident, not an extra irritating addition to it. Hanson's view that what we look for has to make sense is not to be confused with a summary of the incidents which have taken place. It becomes first a recognisable pattern of prevalent emotions and then, by association, it may become a hypothesis about how best to deliver genetic counselling.

But how reliable are our interpretations of human expressions, out of which the patterns will be built? Despite all the laboratory research (e.g. Sternberg 1985) on social intelligence, as psychologists call the ability to read emotions into facial expressions, the assessment of this skill remains notoriously unreliable. We might recall that little children who are not much bigger than babies in arms, are already beginning to react to the feelings of others. At first it is the smile on their mother's face that makes them wriggle all over and then, at about ten months of age, the baby begins to copy facial expressions (Karmiloff-Smith 1997) and by 18 months they may begin pretend play in which they are someone else. It is at this stage, the psychologists say, that the child is beginning to acquire 'a theory of mind' which is firmly established by about the age of three years, so long as the child is not suffering from any form of autism (Baron-Cohen 1990). To have achieved this stage of social development means that the children are now able to impute feelings and motives to other people. They are on the way to becoming experts in recognising other's emotions.

Pattern recognition is typically an expert trait. Laboratory studies have shown that chess experts, as compared with chess novices, produce their amazing feats of memory concerning the positions of all the chess pieces after one brief look at the board by means of visual pattern recognition which is linked to their familiarity with the game (Larkin *et al.* 1970). The expert in genetic counselling also uses the recognition of pattern, albeit a much more humanistic one, by some self-taught method. That is what makes them autodidacts; there is no other way to learn. It is not difficult to see that no one can teach each stage. Genetic counsellors can only master the process by uncertain autonomous processes based on experiential learning about their clients' behaviour.

The next task is the linking of these observed patterns of behaviour with how their clients might react to genetic information. Committed practitioners may spend the rest of their professional lives informally evaluating their hypotheses about how clients will react to counselling. Feedback from this process not only provides a basis for practice, it also finds its way back into the original *recognition process*, incorporating highlighted patterns which need attention.

So far this has been a very fragmented account of the research evidence we have of processes and part processes which might explain how the trainee genetic counsellor teaches him/herself to recognise an appropriate moment for the delivery of genetic knowledge. Even if we think we can understand how patterns which, as Hanson remarked, are themselves rather like hypotheses, come into existence, how is it that the patterns from different episodes are brought together to make a tentative theory in action? (Schon 1983). All of us collect a repertoire of episodes from which we can make predictions about human reactions in everyday life. This kind of experiential learning, which we need to go through for effective pattern recognition, is learning without teaching. That makes it an autodidactic function, from which we learn to reflect on a private store of similar episodes which are non-verbally remembered.

What else do we know about pattern recognition? Artificial Intelligence experts have made some progress in creating programs which mimic it. Neurobiologists using PET-scanners are becoming ever more convinced that chunks of learning migrate about the brain, probably even more powerfully when we are asleep than when awake, making new connections as they do so. Does this process help in the ordering of knowledge through the recognition of recurring patterns? For such a personal non-verbal experiential kind of learning, an indexing of remembered counselling episodes may seem to be almost prohibitively difficult. Nevertheless we all know how very vividly we remember episodes which raised strong emotions, even though they cannot be couched in verbal terms. Perhaps then the main lesson of this chapter is that emotion may be a strong and essential part of much learning, and not just a component of motivation as has so frequently been assumed. This is especially important both for those who are experiencing so much unhappiness while they try to learn how genetics may be applied to their problems, and also for those who try to counsel them.

References

Baron-Cohen, S. (1990) 'Autism: a specific cognitive disorder of mind-blindness', *International Review of Psychiatry* 2: 81–90.

Beck, U. (1986) *The Risk Society*. London: Sage.

Clarke, A. (1994) 'What is genetic counselling?', in A. Clarke (ed.) *Genetic Counselling – Practice and Principles*. London: Routledge, 1–28.

Fraser, F. C. (1974) 'Genetic counselling', *American Journal of Human Genetics* 26: 636–659.

Giddens, A. (1990) *The Consequences of Modernity*. Cambridge: Polity Press.

Hanson, N. R. (1958) *Patterns of Discovery*, Cambridge: Cambridge University Press.

Karmiloff-Smith, A. (1997) *Beyond Modularity. A Developmental Perspective on Cognitive Science*. Cambridge, Mass.: MIT Press.

Larkin, J., McDermot, L., Simon, D. and Simon, L. (1970) 'Expert and novice performance in solving physics problems', *Science* 208(20): 1335–1342.

Lippman, A. (1991) 'Prenatal genetic testing and screening: constructing needs and reinforcing inequities', *American Journal of Law in Medicine* 17: 15–50.

McIntyre, S. (1995) 'The public understanding of science or the scientific understanding of the public? A review of the social context of the new genetics', *Public Understanding of Science* 4: 223–232.

Myser, C., Kerridge, I. and Mitchell, K. (1995) 'Ethical reasoning and decision-making in the clinical setting: assessing the process', *Medical Education* 29: 29–33.

Rapp, R. (1998) 'Refusing prenatal diagnosis: the meaning of bioscience in a multi-cultural world', *Science, Technology and Human Values* 23(1): 45–70.

Revel, M. (1995) 'Genetic Counseling', *Proceedings of the International Bioethics Committee.* UNESCO 1: 9–37. Paris, France.

Schon, D. (1983) *The Reflective Practitioner.* London: Routledge.

Schutz, A. and Luckmann, T. (1973) *Structures of the Life-World.* London: Heinemann.

Serra, H. G., Martins, C. S. B., Paiva e Silva, R. B. and Ramalho, A. S. (1995) 'Evaluation of genetic counselling offered to Brazilian carriers of the beta-thalassemia trait and to their relatives', *Brazilian Journal of Genetics* 18(3): 479–484.

Sternberg, R. (1985) *Beyond IQ. A Triadic Theory of Human Intelligence.* Cambridge: Cambridge University Press.

Solomon, J. (1983) 'Learning about energy. How children think in two domains', *European Journal of Science Education* 9: 49–59.

Tulving, E. (1984) 'How many memory systems are there?', *American Psychologist* 40(4): 385–398.

Chapter 7

Apprenticeship and lifelong learning

Autodidactism in the workplace

Richard Edwards

The contemporary workplace has increasingly been identified as a very important learning setting. Whether it is from the perspective of human capital theory or related to advances in technology and the associated importance of information and symbolic analysis (Castells 1999, Reich 1991), the workforce's capacity to increase its productivity by means of learning has become a central issue of policy and practice. These changes in the commercial evaluation of workers' learning have occurred at the same time as a shift in practice, in the UK at least, from traditional apprenticeship towards a less clear idea of lifelong learning. We may define apprenticeship as an initiation into an area of work in which the apprentice may hope to become an expert, often in a specified length of time. A capacity for lifelong learning, on the other hand, is a goal that required the workers to learn how they could continuously update their skills and knowledge. For this they needed a more generalised and autonomous expertise as a learner. With this shift comes also a move away from focusing on the formal provision of training by the employers, to the less formal learning practices in which people engage because of their own interests, and a recognition that people do not simply want to learn what is designated as training for the immediate job in hand. Increased importance is placed on informal methods of learning and the ways in which the workers teach themselves to participate in the workplace.

I identify the notion of self-teaching, or autodidactism, very much with the idea of informal learning, the learning that we engage in through our own actions and motivation rather than as receivers of learning specified and provided for us by others. In the workplace this is the learning of skills that we engage in as we practice our work, working with others, autonomously searching for information, and the like. It is not the learning associated with structured training programmes that might be offered by our employers, or that we seek out from formal providers of learning programmes, such as colleges and universities. There is increasing research evidence that informal learning of this kind is valued more highly by workers themselves, and that it plays a crucial role in organisational effectiveness (Ashton 1998, Eraut *et al.* 1998).

This chapter attempts to explore aspects of informal learning in the workplace and to suggest that the self-teaching it involves results in life-long learning which displaces apprenticeship seen as a specific set of insti-tutional structures. However, paradoxically, at the same time it positions workers as constantly in a new form of apprenticeship, where the latter is taken as a theory of learning (Ainley and Rainbird 1999, Lave and Wenger 1991). It is important to distinguish between the two kinds of apprenticeship. The institutional structures of apprenticeship can take many forms; often in the past it has taken place in horrendous conditions, which we might consider much less than educationally beneficial. On the whole it was, and still is in some developing countries, a process of the transmission of skills of the narrowest kind. Apprenticeship as a theory of learning is quite different, being more about the social and cultural processes through which one becomes inducted into a certain community of practice. It is apprenticeship of this latter sort which is of interest here. This is because there is a sense in which lifelong learning suggests that the movement from the periphery to the centre in notions of moving from becoming a novice to an expert who might be increasingly misplaced as the centre – unchanging expertise and mastery – ceases to hold. How-ever, before exploring this in more detail, I want to briefly outline some of the current trends in employment and the workplace, to provide a context for the later discussion.

Changing workplaces?

One of the key demands that have been made of contemporary work-places is that they and the people working within them need to become more flexible. The discussion of flexibility is often associated with debates about Fordism, neo-Fordism and post-Fordism and a shift from routine to increasingly non-routine work, in which problem-solving and being part of a team take on greater significance. Flexibility was first pro-mulgated as a response to the economic problems of lack of growth and inflation in many countries in the 1970s. It has been pursued since then by governments of many different political persuasions and supported by major regional and international economic organisations, such as the European Union (EU) and the Organisation of Economic Cooperation and Development (OECD).

For some, it is the changing nature of markets and the moves from mass to niche markets that is central to these processes, resulting in a shift from Fordist mass production to what some term post-Fordist flexible speciali-sation to service different sections of the consumer market. Webster (1995) identifies three flexibilities associated with post Fordism:

1   Flexibility of employees,
2   Flexibility of production, and
3   Flexibility of consumption.

For others it is the technological and institutional flexibility made possible by information and communications technologies (ICT) and resulting innovation and productivity gains that is central (Castells 1999) to the changes we experience. Harvey (1991: 147) identifies the defining qualities of the emerging regime as 'flexibility with respect to labour processes, labour markets, products and patterns of consumption'.

Flexibility was pursued through much of the 1980s and 1990s as central to transforming organisations and making them more competitive. If national economies are to be competitive in the increasingly integrated global market, it is argued that they have to be more flexible, and this requires both organisations and individuals to become more flexible as well. This was thought to require more than the generalised skills of the workplace, as mentioned above, obtained through informal learning. Now the goal of lifelong learning is being pursued through policies that place increasing emphasis on rather more formal learning. The latter is dominantly focused on vocational competence and learning for credit, during which the workplace itself becomes a central site for formal certificated learning. Greater emphasis therefore has been placed on the capabilities of workers and the practices through which these competences are assessed.

Politically this has been pursued through deregulation and the legislative transformation of labour relations. The multiskilled, flexible worker has been promoted as paradigmatic of the economically successful organisation, moving on from task to task, team working, problem-solving, and learning as they so do. It is the capacity to cope with the non-routine in work that characterises the flexible worker with generic rather than specialised skills. Alongside and as part of this flexibility have been:

• Shifts from manufacturing to services,
• The increased importance of information and knowledge,
• Downsizing and a casualisation of much employment,
• Changes in the age and gender structure of the labour force,
• The development of notions of the core and periphery workforce, and
• The growth of insecurity and inequality (Edwards 1997).

All these shifts and changes in working conditions are threatening to many of the older accepted conditions of work. This, for example, is how Ulrick Beck saw the downside of flexibility in the workplace.

> In the current and coming waves of automation this [industrial] *system of standardised full employment* is beginning to soften and fray at the margins into flexiblizations of its three supporting pillars: labour law, work site and working hours . . . Flexible, pluralized forms of under-employment are spreading.
>
> (Beck 1992: 142)

Organisations have pursued their own flexibility through a range of strategies – numerical flexibility, functional flexibility, distancing strategies, pay flexibility (Atkinson and Meager 1990). However human resource development, the learning of the workers, has been central to the implementation of all these strategies, although its precise impact is dependent on the organisational size and the sector of the economy within which the strategy is operating.

In the process, there has been the attempt to develop new workplace identities characterised by what some call 'an ethos of enterprise', similar perhaps to the professional identities which support autodidactism in teachers and scientists (Chapters 8 and 9). Workers themselves, as well as workplaces, are subject to the new practices of management, appraisal and development, which position them as enterprising and engaged in a curious 'enterprise of the self'. In this position:

> No matter what hand circumstances may have dealt a person, he or she remains always continuously engaged . . . in that one enterprise . . . In this sense the character of the entrepreneur can no longer be seen as just one among a plurality of ethical personalities *but must rather be seen as assuming an ontological priority.*
>
> (du Gay 1996: 181)

Exposure to the risks and costs of their activities is constructed as enabling workers to take responsibility for their actions, signifying a form of empowerment and success within the organisation. This requires members of the workforce to be developing not simply in the flexible use of skills and knowledge, but also to be engaging affectively with the well-being of the firm. Thus the workers even become empowered to participate in shaping the organisation's goals and practices. In her study of a large manufacturing multinational in the USA, Casey (1996: 320), for instance, argues that:

> The archetypical new Hephaestus employee is one who enthusiastically manifests the values of dedication, loyalty, self-sacrifice and passion for the product and customer, and who is willing to go the extra mile for his or her team.

This entails an active subjectivity aligned to organisational goals, producing what Casey rather coldly terms 'designer employees'. Here the alienation of industrialisation is supposed to be replaced by an enthusiasm for work. This has been particularly marked in those organisations involved in human resource practices such as employee development schemes, action learning sets, quality circles and the like. It should be added, however, that for many workers the downside of this is an intensification of the demands of the job.

Indeed, such trends towards designer employees can be overstated and over-generalised. Where employee development schemes provide workers with the potential to choose to learn what interests them, irrespective of the role they play in the workplace, there has been an unexpectedly broad take-up of opportunities in terms of subject matter and level. Indeed, some use these opportunities precisely to skill themselves to be ready for new employment and self-employment opportunities when they meet the almost inevitable moment of redundancy. Such people may have taken on board the message that standing still is not an option in the labour market, and that learning is a way of enhancing employability and self-employability. Alternately some may use this not to tie themselves ever more closely to the workplace in which they presently are, but to develop strategies that go beyond their immediate circumstances. Adopting a learning approach to life is a way of negotiating the insecurities of employment and developing some form of career or job resilience. Avoiding unemployment can be a major motivator to teaching oneself new skills and developing different capacities.

On certain readings, the rigidities and regularities of the Fordist production line have been displaced by the post-Fordist learning organisation. Learning organisations therefore seek to promote a culture of lifelong learning and people in the organisation are free to take it up for their own development. The notion of learning organisations is most often associated with private sector employers and commercial environments. However, it has come to have a wider applicability, partly as a result of changes in the public and voluntary sectors in many countries, wherein organisations have had to restructure to become more entrepreneurial. Burgoyne (1992: 327) identifies a number of characteristics of a learning organisation. These can be found to varying degrees within workplaces and may operate differentially within the gendered division of labour (Butler 1996). Learning organisations require at least some of the following:

- A learning approach to strategy
- Participative policy-making
- Open information systems
- Formative accounting and control

- Mutual adjustment between departments
- Reward flexibility
- Adaptable structures
- Boundary workers as environment scanners
- Interorganisational learning
- A learning culture and climate, and
- Self-development opportunities for all.

It is not simply the provision of learning opportunities that distinguishes learning organisations from other types of workplace, but also the form and content that such provision takes. Solving a problem, introducing a new product, scrapping an old one or reaching a different market have all been constructed as requiring participants to see the future in a new way. Success in this rapidly changing environment involves not only continuous learning but also different types of behaviour. Organisations change only if the people within them are prepared to change and do change. Increasingly, learning is focused around topics which are held to help the organisation to achieve its goals, processes organised through the practices of human resource development, and their emphasis on values and attitudes as well as skills. A goal as ambitious as changing values and attitudes may, as some argue, be more myth than reality (Avis 1996), with Taylorist approaches to management continuing, despite the opportunities for changes in the practices of production. These result in an organisational form often termed neo-Fordism. There is thus a continuation of routine work and of work discipline for many of the workforce, at the same time as opportunities existing for others to learn and perform more creative kinds of work.

Flexibility is not a single or simple phenomenon, but is differentiated according to nation, sector, organisation and management strategy. Early notions of the post-Fordist artisan with a more holistic approach to the job and more opportunities for innovation have given way to more cautious assessments. Indeed, the possibilities for innovation can be said to lie in the pedagogic assumptions and management approaches within the specific notions of flexibility adopted. The existence or otherwise of human resource development which encourages self learning as well as development, and the diverse forms it can take, is often argued to be a condition for these different forms of flexibility. In simple terms, Johnson and Lundvall (1991) argue that there are both reactive and active forms of flexibility. If flexibility is constructed as an adaptive process by which the worker finds a comfortable non-entrepreneurial niche within the firm, the notion of learning associated with this will be the old stimulus-response, and the possibilities for innovation are severely constrained. Flexibly valuable people and organisations react quite differently to externally imposed conditions. Their flexibility is constructed as an active process of learning, and by such an approach Johnson and Lundvall argue there is far greater potential for innovation.

This suggests two types of flexible organisation. First, there is the adaptive type, developing flexibility in response to changing markets wherein innovation is pursued through competition. This promotes considerable worker insecurity that is left unregulated or unmanaged. Management may be delayered but it will remain hierarchical and Taylorist in its approach, a situation of low trust. Human resource development may be marginal to such organisations or completely absent. Second, there is a more creative type of flexibility which seeks to develop and position itself within markets, and where innovation is pursued through cooperation. Here both flexibility and insecurity are regulated and managed as a single phenomenon. Different forms of human resource development may be associated with different forms of flexibility and with different types of learning. Each may be said to be a learning organisation, but they have quite different pedagogical underpinning. The first is based on stimulus-response; the second is fuelled by self-regulated learning which is developmental, with the degree of development circumscribed only by the extent of participation by the different stakeholders in the decision-making processes of the organisation.

From apprenticeship to lifelong learning and back again . . .

In the UK, the institutional arrangements for apprenticeship were very much tied to the provision of skilled workers for parts of the manufacturing sector. To have successfully completed an apprenticeship was a mark of honour and a demonstration of expertise in a specialised area. It tended to provide higher paid, and more secure employment. However, apprenticeship was only available for a small percentage of the whole workforce and those who received it were overwhelmingly male. In part, this might be said to rest in the skills to be acquired – only some workers could be good enough – but it was also due to the bargaining power of trade unions and professional bodies to restrict access as a way of obtaining higher pay and better work conditions. With the collapse of the manufacturing industry and the deregulation of labour markets from the 1980s, the institutional arrangements for apprenticeships were largely dismantled.

Central to that kind of apprenticeship was a combination of workplace and off-the-job learning through which the apprentice was inducted into the work and culture of the particular area of expertise they were developing. This was a process that took place in the transition from school to work and once completed, it was assumed that the expertise acquired would be enough for a whole working lifetime. It took a finite period of time to move from novice to expert. The conditions of one's apprenticeship and the forms of pedagogy and discipline to which one was subject were often far from pleasant, but this was a price worth paying should one succeed in becoming a qualified, skilled worker for life.

However, the changing nature of employment and work and the flexibility required from the workforce now means that the notion of apprenticeship as a transition from school to work is totally insufficient. Lifelong learning has therefore come to the fore in policy and practice as a characterisation of what is required of the workforce. Given the non-routine nature of much employment and work, the labour force needs to update their skills and knowledge on an ongoing basis. Skilled behaviour entails pattern recognition and chunking (Sloboda 1993 and da Rosa and Solomon, Chapter 6 above), with expertise quickly becoming dated. This is particularly marked in those areas in which the use of information and communications technology is prevalent. The notion that initial training, or any later training of a formal nature is sufficient to ensure a lifetime mastery in a particular area of work, has been replaced by the recognition of a constant need to learn autonomously from our own experiences, the attempt to engage in updating these for oneself, and to take a general learning approach to life.

There are many ways through which this facet of human resource development can be approached. Members of the workforce can be sent on courses run by public or private institutions, in their own workplace or elsewhere. Forms of open, distance and distributed learning can be provided. Mentoring schemes and action learning sets can make a contribution. There are also the more informal learning practices in which people engage for themselves, not explicitly organised for them, nor following the employers' agenda. It is such practices that can be said to be characteristic of autodidactism in the workplace, embodying personal forms of creativity, and learning through doing and self-invention.

Informal learning has been an important topic of debate and research for adult educators for many years. More recently, it has become a focus for research among those interested in workplace learning. Previously most attention had been given to the (lack of) provision of training in and for the workplace. Yet formal training, as we have seen, is only one aspect of the learning that takes place. In their characterisations of different workplaces, Marsick and Watkins (1999) draw a link between the nature of the work, organisational structure and types of learning. Each has an organisational metaphor associated with it (see Table 7.1).

This is useful in pointing to the ways in which the different forms of work imply their own approach to learning. It would also seem to point to a more developmental model of learning in the workplace – proactive flexibility – in those areas that are not governed by bureaucratic and

Table 7.1 Learning design

Metaphor	Nature of work	Organisation's structure	Learning design
Machine	Clearly defined, separate, coordinated	Bureaucratic and hierarchical	Instructional systems design: systematic training designed and conducted by experts
Open systems	Interactive with other work, interrelated	Networked	Learning is negotiated, self-directed and participatory
Brains	Work is self-regulated	More autonomy for individuals: increasing boundarylessness	Informal and incidental learning: continuous learning: that is single and double loop
Complexity	Work is self-initiated, subject to random shifts	High level of decentralisation: virtual and knowledge-based structures	Action-based learning; little clear guidance in weighing choices

Adapted from Marsick and Watkins 1999

hierarchical organisational structures. Inevitably, however, these are ideal types and therefore oversimplified. For one thing, most workplaces would probably contain a range of work and a mix of organisational structures. For the discussion here however, it is the location of informal learning in situations where work is self-regulated or self chosen that is of most interest. This seems a somewhat narrow reading of informal learning, as the latter might be said to also embrace the forms of action-based learning that Marsick and Watkins (1999) see as distinctive categories in their typology. There is an implied hierarchy in the structuring of learning within their typology that is not altogether convincing. Informal learning may be negotiated, continuous and action-based but it is the capacity to learn in a range of ways from the variety of situations that one finds in the workplace which might be said to characterise autonomous learning practice.

These practices are associated with different forms of cognition, which Eraut (2000) highlights in a very erudite exploration of what he terms 'non-formal learning' (Table 7.2). What is interesting here is that we can identify one of these modes – instant/reflex – as less associated with the creativity and self-teaching which we might want to associate with auto-didactism. In other words, not all informal learning in the workplace may be autodidactic. It appears that this is a feature only of proactive intuitive and autonomous individuals who have reflected and gained knowledge

Table 7.2 Mode of cognition

Thought/ action	Mode of cognition		
	Instant/reflex	*Rapid/intuitive*	*Deliberative/analytic*
Reading of the situation	Pattern recognition	Rapid interpretation	Review involving discussions and/or analysis
Decision making	Instant response	Intuitive	Deliberative with some analysis or discussion
Overt activity	Routinised action	Routines punctuated by rapid decisions	Planned actions with periodic progress reviews
Metacognitive processes	Situational awareness	Implicit monitoring Short, reactive reflections	Conscious monitoring of thought and activity Self-management Evaluation

Adapted from Eraut 2000

about how they best learn. This learning Eraut sees as being based on metacognitive processes.

Those who seek to learn from the processes in which they are engaged are those who are most likely to adopt a lifelong autonomous stance.

> These people adopt a variety of other methods in order to do their jobs and sometimes they transform those jobs in the process. The most active informal learners are in a process of constant transformation, both of themselves and of what they do.
>
> (Fevre *et al.* 2000: 64–65)

However, there may be little opportunity for this in workplaces where routine is still the norm and reflex responses required. It is also the case that not all such learning will be linked to the specific job that the worker does. In some circumstances it may be that the interest in teaching oneself becomes so great that one cannot or does not accept the teaching of others at all (as we have seen in other chapters), the consequence of which can be disaffection and eventual loss of employment.

The changing nature of employment and work, as we have seen, is requiring people to become lifelong learners. Central to such learning is the informal learning in the workplace. Certain practices associated with informal learning – rapid/intuitive and deliberative/analytic – are those that might also be said to characterise autodidactism. This might be said to position the lifelong learner in a constant condition of apprenticeship, as there is no end point to the expertise or mastery that can be attained

(Edwards and Usher 2000). Expertise is just being able to 'learning to learn' which has been given increased emphasis. Thus, even as the restricted institutional arrangements for apprenticeship have declined, apprenticeship, in the form of an autonomous learning approach to life, becomes ever more pervasive.

Conclusion

This chapter has offered a sketch of some possible links between auto-didactism and learning in the workplace. It provides a broad theoretical framework, within which more differentiation and colour can be developed. I have been suggesting that changes in the workplace are resulting in a shift towards notions of lifelong learning which involve a redefining of apprenticeship from an initial preparation for work, which was often behaviourist in its approach, to a constant condition of self learning and becoming. This shifting emphasis also entails increased emphasis on informal learning and some of the autonomous processes involved in this. The danger may be that in the process of providing qualification courses, we may be seeking to harness such learning too tightly, thereby undermining its informality and the powerful role it plays in people's lives (Davies 2000). Another problem might be that autodidactism, which is the natural way of learning for engaged adults who are well beyond the stage of compulsory education, might be schooled out of us by the need to be continually working for an accumulation of credits, backed up by a fear of dismissal and unemployment.

References

Ainley, P. and Rainbird, H. (eds) (1999) *Apprenticeship: Towards a New Paradigm for Learning.* London: Kogan Page.

Ashton, D. (1998) 'Skill formation: redirecting the research agenda', in F. Coffield (ed.) *Learning at Work.* Bristol: Policy Press.

Atkinson, J. and Meager, N. (1990) 'Changing working patterns: how companies achieve flexibility to meet new needs', in G. Esland (ed.) *Education, Training and Employment,* Volume 1, Wokingham: Addison-Wesley.

Avis, J. (1996) 'The myth of the post-fordist society', in J. Avis, M. Bloomer, G. Esland, D. Gleeson and P. Hodkinson (eds) *Knowledge and Nationhood.* London: Cassell.

Beck, U. (1992) *The Risk Society.* London: Sage.

Burgoyne, J. (1992) 'Creating a learning organisation', *RSA Journal* April: 321–330.

Butler, E. (1996) 'Equity and workplace learning: emerging discourses and conditions of possibility', unpublished paper delivered to the National Colloquium on Workplace Learning, University of Technology, Sydney, July.

Casey, C. (1996) *Work, Self, Society: After Industrialism.* London: Routledge.

Castells, M. (1999) *The Information Age: Economy, Society and Culture, Volume I: The Rise of the Network Society.* Oxford: Blackwell.

Davies, P. (2000) 'Formalising learning: the impact of accreditation', in F. Coffield (ed.) *The Necessity of Informal Learning*. Bristol: Policy Press.

Du Gay, P. (1996) *Consumption and Identity at Work*. London: Sage.

Edwards, R. (1997) *Changing Places? Flexibility, Lifelong Learning and a Learning Society*. London: Routledge.

Edwards, R. and Usher, R. (2000) 'Lifelong learning: the postmodern condition of education?', paper presented at the Adult Education Research Conference, Vancouver, June.

Eraut, M. (2000) 'Non-formal learning: implicit learning and tacit knowledge in professional work', in F. Coffield (ed.) *The Necessity of Informal Learning*. Bristol: Policy Press.

Eraut, M., Alderton, J., Cole, G. and Senker, P. (1998) 'Learning from other people at work', in F. Coffield (ed.) *Learning at Work*. Bristol: Policy Press.

Fevre, R., Gorard, S. and Rees, G. (2000) 'Necessary and unnecessary learning: the acquisition of knowledge and "skills" in and outside employment in South Wales in the 20th century', in F. Coffield (ed.) *The Necessity of Informal Learning*. Bristol: Policy Press.

Harvey, D. (1991) *The Condition of Postmodernity*. Oxford: Basil Blackwell.

Johnston, B. and Lundvall, B. (1991) 'Flexibility and institutional learning', in B. Jessop, H. Kastendiek, K. Nielsen and O. Pedersen (eds) *The Politics of Flexibility*. Aldershot: Edward Elgar.

Lave, J. and Wenger, E. (1991) *Situated Learning*. Cambridge: Cambridge University Press.

Marsick, V. and Watkins, K. (1999) 'Envisioning new organisations for learning', in D. Boud and J. Garrick (eds) *Understanding Learning at Work*. London: Routledge.

Reich, R. (1991) *The Work of Nations*. London: Simon and Schuster.

Sloboda, J. (1993) 'What is skill and how is it acquired?', in M. Thorpe, R. Edwards and A. Hanson (eds) *Culture and Processes of Adult Learning*. London: Routledge.

Webster, F. (1995) *Theories of the Information Society*. London: Routledge.

Chapter 8

Learning autonomously to be a primary teacher of science

Stephen Lunn

Introduction

The implementation of the National Curriculum in England and Wales from 1988 saw science move from being an option that was taught in primary schools at the teacher's discretion and according to the teacher's interests, to its current status as a core subject alongside English and maths, with a tightly specified curriculum. Many policy-makers and educationalists believed that 'generalist' primary teachers could not do justice to the science element of the curriculum, through lack of subject knowledge, preferring an approach based on specialist subject teachers (e.g. Alexander *et al.* 1992). They argued for the correction of deficiencies in teachers' knowledge through in-service training (e.g. Summers 1994). Such training as there was, however, was frequently directed at the science coordinator in each school, who was expected to cascade what they had learnt to their colleagues. This approach failed to recognise the central importance of the values brought to the teaching process (Harland and Kinder 1997), leaving the majority of teachers having to construct their own way of teaching science.

Early reports (e.g. Wragg *et al.* 1989) suggested a severe lack of confidence amongst primary teachers, who ranked science amongst the bottom three of the ten subjects that they were required to teach. Only two years later, science had moved up to third place in this ranking (Bennett *et al.* 1992) – a surprising result in the light of papers such as Kruger *et al.* (1990) and Mant and Summers (1993), which showed apparently severe continuing gaps in teachers' scientific content knowledge.

However teachers' confidence was not misplaced, as national, international, and local evidence shows. Attainment in science in national tests at the end of Key Stage 2 (Year 6, 11 years old) rose steadily once the assessment regime had settled down. Reports from the Department of Education and Employment, and Qualifications Curriculum and Assessment showed attainment rising more rapidly than in maths and English.

Our primary pupils were also found to be amongst the best in the world in international comparisons of attainment in science.

So teachers were becoming more confident, and their pupils' attainment was high and improving. All this was despite teachers' subject knowledge being consistently found to be poor, and the severely limited reach and effectiveness of in-service training. This suggested that through some act of self-help the teachers were somehow transcending the subject matter, and gaining confidence by another route. What could this be?

Research method

During the last decade there have been several claims of a close connection between self-constructed autobiography and personal identity (e.g. Harré 1983). In the case of Helms (1998), and Lunn and Solomon (2000) this was taken to be the teachers' professional identity and its associated values. So it seemed that if there were a mystery about how primary teachers had gained effective confidence in the teaching of science it would best be solved by an in-depth interview study. This was done recently in great detail for five primary teachers at different points in their teaching careers (Lunn 2000). Each case study explored a teacher's science and education-related 'learning biography' (Day 1993), their current lesson-planning and teaching practice, and their ideas about the nature of science. In the following five short sections there is only room to examine briefly the evidence from three areas which might show traces of their powers of self-learning: their own youth and schooling, their decision to teach and pre-service training, and their continued reflection and professional development.

Irene

Now in her early fifties, Irene had qualified as a teacher in 1994. She herself went to the old Victorian village school, which her children were also later to attend. She moved on to a secondary modern school in a local town where she became interested in biology. She thought about a career in nursing, but encouragement from the head teacher coincided with personal interest, and she decided to take all three sciences to GCE O level. When she passed biology but failed physics and chemistry, she left school to retake them at a college of further education. This time she passed, and at eighteen left college to take up her first job as a laboratory technician at a local girls' high school, taking a three-year day-release course for lab technicians at the local college. She gained a wide range of technical skills, in 'metal work, wood work, glass blowing, you name it', and she came to derive great enjoyment and satisfaction from using these skills to create good quality work. After working as a laboratory technician in several schools, and a career break while her children were young, divorce prompted her to find better-paid work as a pharmacology technician in a university.

Although she loved the job, she experienced a strong vocation to teach which she describes in this arresting way:

> I suddenly thought . . . my generation has ruined the world, we've consumed everything, polluted everything . . . I felt if I could teach the next generation to put it right, to know what to do and at least to make them care so they do something about it, then I'd have perhaps put back a little bit of what my generation has done wrong. So I just sold everything, upped sticks and went. I did a four year BEd course and specialised in environmental science and that's how I became a teacher.

Having taught for nearly five years, she enjoys and feels most confident in teaching science and technology, running a craft and technology after-school club, but her greatest satisfaction comes from her pastoral role. Irene is concerned about her own professional development, and teaches herself through journal articles and relevant Open University programmes on television, and is keen to learn more about her favourite areas such as ecological fieldwork. She recognises that some kinds of teaching knowledge can only develop through initial difficulties, citing an example of a role-play that got 'totally out of hand'. Reflecting on her professional development since she started teaching, Irene identifies the main change being in her approach to planning. She feels that she gains in confidence and competence each time she teaches a topic, gradually building up a stock of ideas and understanding, and becoming more relaxed and less uncertain, knowing what is coming and that she can cope with it. Her main concern when preparing to teach a science topic is being able to present the concepts at the children's level.

Outside school she has worked with AIDS patients. She follows everything to do with science in the press and on television; she used to take *New Scientist*, but found that it 'went over her head'. Irene valued taking part in the interview project, feeling that it held up a non-judgemental mirror to her teaching, and showed her new ways of looking at what she was doing. It had led her to recognise the centrality of 'making connections' to the moral dimensions of science, and suspects that this changes the implicit messages about values and identity that she unconsciously communicates to her pupils.

Howard

Now in his late forties, Howard has been teaching for nearly thirty years. He grew up in the outskirts of Manchester in the 1950s, attending a 'good, very formal' primary school where he was able to get out of lessons one afternoon a week by tidying the science stock cupboard. At secondary school he was attracted to science by the 'wonderful language', especially in biology, and chose to take botany, zoology and English, to A level. He went into teaching by default rather than vocation – his mother was a teacher, and he was 'too short to be a policeman' – and chose a Junior Secondary course at a college near Manchester, deferring the choice between primary or secondary teaching for as long as possible.

He has taught continuously in primary schools since qualifying, and has been at the same school for most of the last fifteen years. When the National Curriculum was introduced he became science coordinator, and went on a course where he was taught physics 'to degree level', he says. At the end of it he had forgotten everything it had covered, and remarks that since then he has never had occasion to refer to the copious course notes, having always been comfortable with what he was doing in the classroom. 'You don't have to be a scientist to teach science', he often said. The science in the Key Stage 2 programme of study was easy enough to 'mug up' before a lesson.

Howard sees himself as the lynch-pin of science teaching in the school, but also as the most nervous and stressed person on the staff, especially during inspections. He feels that he is 'too long in the tooth' to change his approach to teaching, and indeed takes pride in the fact that it has not changed since he came into teaching, though primary teaching is now 'totally different'. For him, professional development has effectively ceased. His main concerns in science teaching are covering the concepts required by the programme of study; translating the science into 'child-speak' and teaching it correctly; and making his teaching entertaining.

Taking part in the project made Howard more anxious about his personal performance, and suspicious of the goals of the research. In some areas he had not known what his opinions were until he articulated them: he admitted to being impressed with the 'great aplomb' with which he had done so! However he did not expect anything from our conversations to change the way he teaches.

Keith

At the time the project began Keith was twenty-six years old, and halfway through his third year of teaching. At the age of twelve or thirteen he realised he was beginning to do well in science and maths, and with the encouragement of a teacher he was soon amongst those with highest marks in physics and chemistry. He began to develop self-confidence and a reputation for asking questions.

Despite enjoying science, he had a growing feeling of being 'trapped', 'labelled the maths and science type', and at the beginning of A levels tried to escape, opting for humanities; but soon ended up back on track, studying maths, physics, chemistry and general studies to A level. Having been independent-minded in primary school, his habit of frequently and persistently questioning his teachers grew as he got older, until his A level maths teacher had to shut him up in order to get through the course. So, well before he started teaching, Keith was already experiencing the tension between external constraints, and his internal drive towards autonomy.

At university he read geomatics (roughly equivalent to land surveying). The course involved physics, astrophysics, computing, and some 'very, very hard maths'. He was considering a career in teaching, but his 'driving motivation' was towards the church. He spent a year working with a church organisation helping young people in south London, which he found enjoyable and challenging. During that year he applied for and was accepted on a PGCE course. He chose an upper primary course, partly because he was worried about his subject knowledge, believing it to be inadequate to teach to A level standard; and partly because he preferred the primary approach where he could develop a strong relationship with one class, and see the children through 'in every aspect of their education'. His first teaching practice was difficult: his second wonderful. His mentor gave him a great deal of freedom to try out his ideas, and he felt he succeeded in giving the children as authentic an experience of doing science as he could. His concern with the 'whole child' was reinforced by an experience in his first year after qualifying, when he managed to 'turn round' a child who had 'a very black history'.

Keith realises that, in his concerns for the whole child, and for their learning through authentic activity in an atmosphere of freedom and autonomy, he is bucking what he sees as an inevitable national move towards increasingly inflexible subject timetabling and specialist teaching in primary schools. This is driven by fact-oriented assessment, which runs counter to his professional values, and compromises his autonomy. He is also uncomfortable about teaching in a 'secular school', and would prefer the 'God-centred foundation' of a Christian school.

Keith sees himself as someone who learns best by watching and doing, with guidance, rather than by reading or being told. He feels that he is becoming increasingly responsible and autonomous as a teacher, and increasingly ready to challenge established practice and follow his own ideas. But he feels that his planning is being forced to be less creative, and more restricted to delivering content. He is finding teaching less stimulating, and is less hopeful that things will change for the better. At the end of the school year, Keith left the school, the area, and also the teaching profession. He now lives in the north, and works with 'problem youngsters', for a Christian organisation in the inner city.

Linda

At the start of the project Linda was in her mid-thirties, and in her fourth year of teaching. She had happy memories of attending a 'tiny little village school' in a pretty valley on the western edge of the Pennines. Being academically able, she was often left to get on with things alone, but outside school, from a very early age, all she wanted to do was to 'play teachers'. At secondary school she enjoyed biology and chemistry, and disliked physics, but took all three to GCSE on the basis of bad careers advice, becoming the first girl in the school's history to take physics, although intimidated and made to feel unwelcome by the physics teacher. She passed biology, just failed chemistry, and was defiantly proud of her 'U' (unclassified) in physics. Having earlier wanted to be a vet, her ambition shifted to graphic design, and she decided to take a foundation course at art school. In her second term she was offered a well-paid job as a ceramic artist with a local pottery, and was pushed into it by her father. She kept the job for eleven years, earning 'tons of money', on piecework, painting figurines.

Her husband worked in local government, and was always studying for exams, prompting Linda to start a one-year foundation evening class in catering – a very positive experience: for the first time in her life she felt like a 'leader'. Her self-esteem grew, and she went to see a 'brilliant careers advisor', who suggested she build a broad-based pyramid of qualifications – first more GCSEs, then A levels, then a degree. In the next year she took and passed maths and chemistry GCSEs, and her interest in science was rekindled by an inspirational chemistry teacher. During this period her desire to become a teacher had crystallised into a firm decision, and she applied to do a four-year BA with parallel Certificate in Education, specialising in English and visual arts, at a local college.

Linda preferred an approach where learning objectives were set and shared with the children, and debated such points vigorously with her education tutors – who have now, she thinks, come round to her view. She feels she has learnt more about teaching science 'on the hoof', by doing it, than she learnt in college, though she still has worries about it and is working hard on 'scientific enquiry'.

In her first school Linda says science meant 'pouring in facts' in order to get good SATs results. The school was 'so rigid' that she stopped doing things which she values highly, like investigations and team presentations, and was delighted to move to her current school. She is full of praise for her colleagues, admiring their teaching and 'always pinching ideas'. The school as a whole focuses on particular areas for development – in the first year of the project the push is on investigative science, generating lively debate amongst the staff. From the beginning of her training she took to heart the belief that 'education is not the filling of a pail, but the lighting of a fire': her mission as a teacher is to find and ignite the fire within every child. To this end she adopts a deliberate policy of trying to imagine what each child would most like to do, and finding something (not necessarily academic) that they are 'brilliant at'.

Linda is purposefully completing a portfolio of experience across the primary age range. Having taught Years 2 and 6 in the past, and reception/ Year 1 at the start of the project, she moved to Years 3 and 4 the following year, in a conscious effort to learn about child development at first hand and at all stages. There is a strong sense of her being 'in control', setting herself challenging but achievable targets. She is now confident enough to expose her lack of knowledge by 'driving the science coordinator crazy' with endless questions. One problem that preoccupies her is that of integrating process and content in her science teaching. She often uses the wrestling metaphor to describe her struggle to come to terms with scientific enquiry. Her most acute 'wrestling' arises when trying to fit a very simple statement from the curriculum into this framework.

Given carte blanche to improve her own science teaching, Linda says she would spend a month learning in a library. She would then spend another month or two working on both theoretical and practical aspects of these topics, with the help of a knowledgeable mentor. In this fantasy, she shows her need to be in control of her own learning, to have access to guidance when she needs it – an autodidactic model of learning which she consciously tries to recreate in the experiences of her pupils.

Taking part in the project had, Linda said, been interesting and illuminating, and had made her question things, adding 'the minute that you stop questioning how and what you teach, you become a bad teacher'.

Andrew

Andrew is in his late forties, grew up in rural Zimbabwe with a father who was a teacher, civil servant, farmer, insurance agent, keen gardener and natural historian. At primary school he remembers the excitement of rare nature walks, and of bringing back interesting finds to study. One teacher made a great impression: he would encourage children to bring in interesting things that they found, and would 'build the lesson round them'. At secondary school, still in Rhodesia, he took a general science option to GCE O level, and English and history at A level. He gained a teaching certificate in Britain, specialising in English and science.

Andrew entered teaching in the 1970s and has taught continually ever since apart from one break for travel and voluntary service, and one for study at a local college. From the outset he had always taught 'quite a lot of science', finding it interesting and enjoyable, and believing children 'got a lot out of it'. He has strong views on teaching science, and has managed to assert himself to the extent that he can do as he wishes, within the practical constraints of curriculum and timetable. He believes that children's responses to being trusted and given autonomy include enhanced self-esteem, interest and engagement, and these lead to better learning.

He has constructed a robust theory of teaching and learning, drawing on research and theoretical sources, but forged through practice into a very personal network of beliefs and values. He sets up the bulk of his science teaching so that children can choose who they want to work with, if anyone, pursue their own lines of enquiry and take as much time as they need to have a full concrete experience. He wants them to devise their own tests and reach their own conclusions.

Andrew said that, for children, a question creates a vacuum that must be filled: they will make up and accept *any* explanation rather than have none at all, and these pre-conceived ideas can be very resistant to change. The difficulty of helping children to consider alternatives seriously is 'all tied up with self concept, because the knowledge you have and the theories you have is part of you, and to admit that perhaps it's not quite the right one, is moving quite a way'. The teacher's job can be seen as one of persuasion alongside the preservation of children's self-esteem, by leading children to the point where they believe they have thought out for themselves whatever you wanted to teach them.

Andrew reported that he now makes 'far more allowances for individual differences' than he used to, trying to picture the children in the context of their whole lives, what they will be like as adults; varying pace, expectation and method to accommodate them. Few topics come up that he has not taught before but he varies his approaches to try out new ideas, and to adapt to the particular children he is teaching. Throughout our discussions, a large proportion of what he said was in the form of reported or imagined speech, thought or action. Andrew can run through a whole gamut of experiences, playing any or all of the roles, describing vivid images or 'mental video clips' of experiences that have been or are becoming important, or that exemplify and perhaps 'encode' something of value (Elbaz 1983).

Andrew works hard to develop his own professional knowledge, and feels that he has benefited from the opportunity to talk about his practice, although he described feeling 'totally wrung out' after an interview, from the effort of putting into words things that are usually tacit or implicit. He was aware of changes in his teaching suggesting that our discussions had left him 'rather less dogmatic, less sure about what science or any other area of human knowledge can ultimately achieve'. However he became more convinced than ever of long-standing 'basic thoughts about teaching science at this level'; and 'more interested in science education, and indeed in science'.

Discussion

It is not claimed that this group of five teachers were especially represen-
tative of the whole workforce, but the data from them collected over
many hours during 18 months of research is very rich and illuminating.
They are used here to see how far teachers need to be self-directed in
their daily work of teaching, in a curriculum climate where the load of
subject knowledge may increase from one year to the next. If it is true
that teachers can and do teach effectively subjects, like science, in which
they are not specialists, we would like to know:

- If they had strong qualities of autodidactism in their own youth.
- Did they develop these qualities before or after they became teachers?
- What connection, if any, was there between their own learning and
  how they wanted their pupils to learn?

Autodidactism when young?

Keith was the one who described himself as learning 'best by watching
and doing, with guidance, rather than by reading or being told'. He also
took a precociously autonomous learning stance when in school, asking
an uncomfortable number of questions. He acquired considerable self-
confidence from scholastic success but, during A levels, was more or less
told to stop thinking for himself and start absorbing what he was being
taught. This, coupled with his desire for autonomy, made him 'feel
trapped'. Later Keith found he could only enjoy his introduction to teaching when given freedom by his second mentor to try out his own ideas.

   At the time this study took place Keith was halfway through his third
year of teaching and troubled by his concerns for 'the whole child'. His
desire for his pupils to learn in an atmosphere of freedom and autonomy,
and also for his own freedom from the directional pressure of the National
Curriculum were troubling him. He felt that his planning was becoming
less creative, and his teaching less stimulating.

   We know that he was shortly to give up teaching altogether and,
although he himself saw the reason for this as a wish to work in a more
Christian environment, it is tempting to see his desire for autonomy and
freedom as forming a substantial part of this flight from teaching. At the
very least we can deduce that anyone as autodidactic as Keith is only too
likely to fit poorly into the pressure of school life today. A wish to learn
by oneself without reading or being taught must militate against the kind
of continuous professional development which has become necessary. As
was suggested in the description of young people in special schools
(Chapter 4) the characteristic of autodidactism can sometimes become a

serious barrier to learning if the orthodox method is too rich in instruction. This discussion is taken further in the epilogue.

How does autonomy develop?

For Irene, Linda, Andrew, and one suspects for many more, the wish for autonomy develops later in life, along with the vocation to teach. It may be an integral part of embracing a career. Some, perhaps most, have remembered a teacher from their own schooling as Andrew did. Irene went into teaching in order to prepare her pupils to protect the environment. This was a sudden inspiration, but it moved her into teaching and made at least some autonomy essential if her inspiration were to be realised.

Both Linda and Irene came into teaching rather late. Both had been encouraged by others to take a job on leaving school, which they did with some docility although neither of them were very satisfied. This has been a common story with women and it results in a change of career much later in life, sometimes, as in the case of Irene, after children have been raised and/or divorce has ended some earlier relationship. Older entrants like these may look for a great deal more from their new profession than they had expected from their first job taken straight from school (Solomon 1997). They want the sense of satisfaction which is born of autonomy and creativity, and terms like those are to be found in many of their transcripts. Linda, for example, reports that after eleven years in pottery she took a foundation course in catering and, perhaps as a result of following her own preference, for the first time in her life felt like a 'leader'. (Such questions about autonomy in learning related to age and to gender are discussed in Chapter 17.)

Andrew is so much the hero of this study it is hard to fit him and his self-directed ideas into a tight scheme. His words are full of the understanding of children and their needs in terms of autonomous experiences, and reaching their own conclusions. We have little or no idea of his own early progression except that he had always taught quite a lot of science, even before it was compulsory. Andrew had once spent 18 months travelling and teaching abroad, he had a sabbatical year in the days when long-serving and successful teachers still got them on full salary, and he had taken part in quite a few classroom research projects.

What is really surprising is that Andrew remained a classroom primary teacher, even turning down the offer of becoming the school's science coordinator. Most teachers who have had such an introduction to the world of educational theory and have enjoyed it as much as he did, soon leave the classroom for university or college. One can only suspect that the excitement of the professional life he found so absorbing, coupled with following a completely autonomous career path, was in itself satisfying enough for him. Certainly an introduction to research always does a great deal for the professional self-esteem that is the bedrock of auto-didacticsm in career development.

Teachers' autonomy and that of their pupils

The transcripts of these five teachers talking about their development and the learning of their pupils shows an almost perfect match. Those who have come to relish autonomy in their professional life also want it for their pupils. Andrew, Irene, Linda and Keith all mention this. Yet in a curious way it is Howard who rejects, by forgetting, the substance of his long in-service course, and also perceives no opportunity to use the research interviews for reflection or action, who makes this point most clearly. He wants no more professional development. When asked what changes in the National Curriculum he would like to see, he retorts firmly 'none at all' while the others all mention their favourite parts of science. Wanting no autonomy for himself, he allows none for the pupils.

Inside the classroom the learning community comprises both the teacher and the children. If the teachers claim autonomy for themselves, they also have to claim it for their pupils.

References

Alexander, R., Rose, J. and Woodhead, C. (1992) *Curriculum Organisation and Classroom Practice in Primary Schools: a Discussion Paper*. London: DES.

ATL (1996) *Doing our Level Best: an Evaluation of Statutory Assessment in 1995*. London: Association of Teachers and Lecturers.

Bennett, S. N., Wragg, E. C., Carre, C. G. and Carter, D. S. G. (1992) 'A longitudinal study of primary teachers' perceived competence in, and concerns about, National Curriculum implementation', *Research Papers in Education* 7(1): March.

Bromme, R. (1984) 'On the limitations of the theory metaphor for the study of teachers' expert knowledge', in R. Halkes and J. K. Olson (eds) *Teacher Thinking: a New Perspective on Persisting Problems in Education*. Lisse: Swets and Zeitlinger 43–57.

Close, G., Furlong, T. and Simon, S. (1997) *The Validity of the 1996 Key Stage 2 Tests in English, Mathematics and Science*. A report form King's College London, University of London, commissioned by the Association of Teachers and Lecturers.

Day, C. (1993) 'The importance of learning biography in supporting teacher development: an empirical study', in C. Day, J. Calderhead and P. Denicolo (eds) *Research on Teacher Thinking: Understanding Professional Development*. London: Falmer.

Elbaz, F. (1985) *Teacher Thinking. A Study of Political Knowledge*. London: Croom Helm.

Harré, R. (1983) *Personal Being*. Oxford: Basil Blackwell.

Harland, J. and Kinder, K. (1997) 'Teachers' continuing professional development: framing a model of outcomes', *British Journal of In-service Education* 23(1): 71–84.

Helms, J. V. (1998) 'Science – and me: subject matter and identity in secondary science teachers', *Journal of Research in Science Teaching* 35(7): 811–834.

Kruger, C., Palacio, D. and Summers, M. (1990) 'An investigation of some primary school teachers' understanding of the concepts of force and gravity', *British Educational Research Journal* 16(4): 383–397.

Lunn, S. (2000) 'Primary Teachers' understandings of the nature of science and the purposes of science education', unpublished PhD Thesis, The Open University.

Lunn, S. and Solomon, J. (2000) 'Primary teachers' thinking about the English National Curriculum for science: auto-biographies, warrants, and autonomy', *Journal of Research in Science Teaching* 37(10): 1045–1056.

Mant, J. and Summers, M. (1993) 'Some primary-school teachers' understanding of the Earth's place in the universe', *Research Papers in Education* 8(1): March 1993.

QCA (1998) *Standards at Key Stage 2, English, Mathematics and Science: Report on the 1998 Curriculum Assessments for 11-year-olds. A report for headteachers, class teachers and assessment co-ordinators.* London: Qualifications and Curriculum Authority.

QCA (1999) *Standards at Key Stage 2, English, Mathematics and Science: Report on the 1999 Curriculum Assessments for 11-year-olds. A report for headteachers, class teachers and assessment co-ordinators.* London: Qualifications and Curriculum Authority.

QCA (2000) *Standards at Key Stage 2, English, Mathematics and Science: Report on the 2000 Curriculum Assessments for 11-year-olds. A report for headteachers, class teachers and assessment co-ordinators.* London: Qualifications and Curriculum Authority.

Solomon, J. (1997) 'Girls' science education: choice, solidarity and culture', *International Journal of Science Education* 19(4): 407–417.

Summers, M. (1994) 'Science in the primary school: the problem of teachers' curricular expertise', *The Curriculum Journal* 5(2): 179–193.

Wragg, E. C., Bennett, S. N. and Carre, C. G. (1989) 'Primary teachers and the National Curriculum', *Research Papers in Education* 4(3): 17–45.

Chapter 9

The scientist as autodidact

John Ziman

Every scientist – indeed every professional scholar worthy of the name – has to be an autodidact. That is, he or she must become seriously knowledgeable about subjects on which they could never find a teacher. Research is always at the edge of the unknown, where previously unsuspected ideas or techniques are required to travel further. Very often, however, they already exist in some other corner of the vast techno-scientific world, and have to be learned by the researcher. Researchers will never get anywhere unless they are willing and able to become aware of this knowledge, locate it and take steps to learn it for themselves.

This autodidactic capability is enjoined by the scientific norm of originality, and summed up in the character trait of being 'self-winding'. Anyone familiar with the scientific life – in the human sciences as much as in the natural sciences – will be able to report numerous instances of it. My favourite example was a man I came across in an investigation of the personal aspects of change in scientific careers (Ziman 1987). In the course of an extended group interview, he revealed successive episodes of autodidactic effort. Initially he defined himself as a narrow specialist, who knew nothing about anything except the uptake of potassium by plants growing in clay soils. He had had a fairly conventional school and university education in biochemistry but he said that when he began research in soil science he had had ('of course') to bone up on the physical chemistry of ionic salts. Then, a few minutes later, he mentioned that a lot of new electronic techniques had been introduced into the subject, so 'I went down to the local technical college, and picked up enough about transistors and things to begin to build my own apparatus'. Later in the interview he remarked: 'In the '70s the Americans began to make computer models of the whole system, so there was nothing for it but to teach myself computing to show how wrong those guys were'. And as we were finishing, he explained that he had to go, because 'my research is not just laboratory work: every now and then I have to put on my Wellies and go down to the field, and talk to the farmer about how to plant the crops'.

But notice that this archetypical researcher did not apply for a year's paid leave in order to study full-time for a diploma in electronic engineering or computer science. He just went to 'an introductory course [in computing] at the Polytechnic . . . it was one evening a week for two months and after that it was just a matter of picking the rest up from a manual. But it was just the introduction, getting over the psychological barrier of actually talking to a computer'. Science advances too rapidly, the competition for discovery is too intense, for such learning to be a leisurely process of 'going to school' in the conventional sense. To pick up the intellectual or practical skills one thinks one needs, we have to get into the library or surf the Internet, find the appropriate books or consult appropriate experts, puzzle out difficulties, do some of the practical exercises, set up laboratory experiments, make some field observations, perhaps even start up a little research project – all for oneself, by oneself, under one's own personal control.

Very often, indeed, you find that those new ideas or techniques don't really exist in the form in which you plan to use them. After all, if you are doing serious research, then nobody would have previously thought of applying these particular methods to this particular problem. So the standard textbook techniques will have to be adapted to these novel circumstances. You will have to do a certain amount of tinkering, to make them fit your problem. Cautiously – for now you are getting out of your official area of expertise – you modify the default settings in the hope that the instrument will work better, or bolt on an accessory that ought to extend the scope of your observations. If this succeeds, you start to reconfigure the whole operating system, or devise a much more sensitive control mechanism. To do this, you draw on other skills or items of knowledge that you happen to have picked up. Before you realise it, your modest autodidactic exercise has become a creative research project – combinatorial in Boden's terms – from which others, in turn, will learn novel ideas and techniques.

In other words, to be a professional scientist one must be able to completely transcend one's basic professional education. It requires sufficient confidence to learn from personal experience with these skills, to speak them well enough to grasp their strengths and weaknesses, and thence to develop new vocabularies of thought and action. Within the scientific enterprise as a whole, there is no definable boundary between voluntarily accepted formal instruction and entirely idiosyncratic research. For a research scientist, all modes of learning are at heart autodidactic.

Now I suppose that some people are born like that. It comes along with curiosity as an inbuilt personal trait. But the evidence from detailed personality studies of professional scientists is that it often emerges only when they are forced into autodidactism by the sheer necessities of research. One of the questions that university teachers ask themselves is whether autonomy can be encouraged and developed at an earlier stage of formal education. That is why, for example, they usually strongly favour project work at school and university. In ideal circumstances (see Chapter 14) the student is put into an intellectual hole from which they can only escape with honour by letting go of the helping hand of a teacher and instructing themselves alone or in a group. If the educational frame is designed so that they usually (more or less) succeed, this is such a positive achievement that it enormously strengthens their intellectual self-confidence and self-esteem. They begin to see themselves as competent, independent actors on the scientific stage, motivating themselves and inventing their own lines rather than mouthing those of a long-dead author. In other words, they are being prepared, in advance, for the much more strenuous self-instruction ordeals of real research.

The celebratory literature of science – for example, the lectures of Nobel Prize winners – glows with pride in the virtues of autonomy. The mode of autonomy that is most admired is, of course, what Tom Jagtenberg (Jagtenberg 1983) called 'strategic autonomy' – that is, freedom to choose one's own research problem. Certainly, the recognition of an enigma capable of being unravelled is almost the supreme scientific gift (Ziman 1981). A few rare folk are able to perceive quite distant, almost unattainable research goals, and then they school themselves in the formal knowledge and tacit skills required to move towards them. It is well known, for example, that as a schoolboy Einstein had begun to imagine what a light wave would look like if one were travelling at the same speed, and then went off to the university to learn the theoretical physics needed to make mathematical sense of his conjectures.

Very often one new skill learned and practised leads on to another, with the goal posts being moved along in advance. Thus Einstein, having relativised mechanics and electromagnetism, perceived that gravity could perhaps be understood in a similar way, so he turned to mathematical colleagues and texts to teach himself the tensor calculus, a recondite branch of pure mathematics which he would never have encountered in his otherwise excellent education as a theoretical physicist. I don't think that he actually made any advances in this calculus as a mathematical formalism, but by applying it to physical events in the space-time continuum he completely changed its scientific significance. Sometimes, as Tim Hunkin's story illustrates (Chapter 11), an autodidact keeps on reinventing himself or herself over a much wider range of their personality – their motives, goals, self-image etc. – than simply what they might now know. Interestingly, however, by the time Einstein was fifty he had evidently lost his autodidactic bent, for he made no effort to acquire the attitude of mind required to grasp the new quantum mechanics that was conquering theoretical physics.

In practice, of course, most scientists are very far indeed from being like Einstein. They are not amazed by enigmas (like Aeron in Chapter 3), nor even highly motivated to try to answer challenging grand questions. As Thomas Kuhn put it (Kuhn 1962), they occupy themselves with applying normal science to the innumerable puzzles that seem soluble by reasonable mental and practical exertion under the sheltering paradigm of their discipline. But we must not take too seriously Kuhn's notion that this is entirely different from 'revolutionary science', which is supposedly devoted to the resolution of manifest anomalies. In practice, a good research scientist does normal science on Mondays, Wednesdays and Fridays, and revolutionary science on Tuesdays, Thursdays and Saturdays: Sundays are often fully occupied with catching up with the literature – that is, learning what other scientists have been discovering. Research is not, after all, a matter of setting off into the unknown with no idea of what one might expect to find. It is precisely through continued reflection on their own experience and the reported experiences of their contemporaries that top class professional researchers are distinguishable from apprentices. They are able to anticipate, to some extent, the results of quite ambitious projects, and to devise reliable methods for undertaking them (Reuter and Tripier 1980).

The notion of pure epistemic liberty should not be romanticised. To put it another way: the sheer tactics of scientific research are immensely demanding and immensely rewarding as games of skill. Most researchers, including the great majority of academic scientists, are really happy enough to settle for what Jagtenberg called technical autonomy – meaning freedom to choose the methodology, conceptual frame, experimental technique, etc. with which to attack the problems assigned to them by circumstance or managerial fiat. That still leaves plenty of space for the exercise of personal autonomy in what needs to be learnt. The distinction between the scientist (engineer, scholar, etc.) and the technician (research assistant, etc.) is precisely this freedom to acquire new knowledge without having to be taught it.

What can be disconcerting is that this freedom is seldom exercised beyond very narrow bounds. Notoriously, research scientists are extreme specialists. They work within the parish boundaries of a tiny area of the scientific world, typically in a field that is just a part of one of the dozen or so subdisciplines into which each of the scores of academic disciplines are conventionally divided (Ziman 1987, 2000). The trouble is that just to get anywhere near the frontier region in their field requires many years of systematic learning – learning that has had to be assembled, compressed and packaged into elaborate courses of instruction. As I have remarked, even Einstein, despite myths to the contrary, had been through this mill. Like any other good, creative scientist, he had had to learn to speak the basic language of his subject, for which a research university was the only reliable source.

This did not apply, of course, until the early nineteenth century. Until then, higher education did not officially include much science, and was not closely associated with scientific research. Just occasionally, even now, one still finds a scientist or scholar who has had to pick up all that basic routine grammar, five-finger exercises, parts of verbs, algebraic manipulations, etc. in less organised ways. But such extreme auto-didactism is not to be recommended, especially in a sophisticated science such as molecular biology where the discourse is as obscure as Chinese to the uninstructed. It is not uncommon to find senior scientists who entered the research world as technicians and rose from the ranks, rather than following a glittering student career through high school, college, graduate school into post-doctoral employment. On closer inspection, however, it usually emerges that they are not completely self-taught, in that at one time or another they have taken, or been given, time off to study for a conventional degree in the field of their research.

Nevertheless, the question arises of just how far such preliminary formal instruction should go before the autodidactic regime of research takes over. About fifty years ago, when I came into the world of physics research, the British tradition was to give very thorough, quite advanced formal instruction up to the Bachelor's degree level, and then to encourage a few of the best students to throw themselves, without lifebelts, into the deep water of research and just swim. In a major university a few enthusiastic dons might advertise courses of lectures on their specialties, less for systematic instruction than as a medium for arguing with their colleagues and attracting acolytes. Even a Ph.D. supervisor could not be relied on to provide guidance into the literature. Those who survived had to be self-winding, self-sustaining swimmers, although whether they were really well-informed even over their field or subdiscipline was some-times questionable.

In the United States, by contrast, these same students – and perhaps a more extensive cadre of their cohort – would have to undergo several more years of graduate school before they were deemed to be ready to do research on their own. That is, regular courses of instruction and exam-ination in all the supposedly relevant subjects were obligatory for the student, and a major mode of employment for the professoriate. We in Britain said that this was spoon feeding, and that it tended to entrench fashionable doctrines, that it did not encourage independence of mind, etc. – in other words, it was contrary to the autodidactic ideology of our whole postgraduate system. The Americans said that our students were narrow, ignorant, and intellectually idiosyncratic. Read David Lodge in *Changing Places* (Lodge 1975) for a satire on this dispute. In the event, the American style has become more and more prevalent in British universities, and in most others throughout the world. This was probably inevitable but it would be interesting to look at other great modern scholarly cultures, such as those of France and Germany, to see how this tension is resolved in practice. For example, does the requirement to submit a doctoral dissertation at several later stages in a career foster an autonomous approach?

Mostly scientists pedal along not too strenuously through their careers, learning enough as they go along to maintain the momentum of their original education and the strong autodidactic impulse of their doctoral and postdoctoral years. But their autonomous capabilities are sometimes tested to near breaking point by having to make an abrupt change in their field of research in mid career. This can happen for a number of reasons, under various personal and social circumstances, such as loss of employment, war, disaffection with ones career path, etc., which I have discussed in detail elsewhere (Ziman 1987). What then becomes very urgently necessary is a decent background of knowledge about a new field – very often, a field that is highly specialised in quite a different language from the one that has been left.

It would be too large a task here to discuss the various factors and considerations that influence success or failure in such an event. For example, personal morale and motivation plays a very large part, and can undoubtedly be facilitated by sympathetic, supportive attitudes and actions by more senior colleagues. Generally speaking, the transition usually turns out to be easier than feared when it first looms over the horizon. Perhaps this is because a scientist or scholar with twenty years of active research experience has acquired a metascientific skill in the art of research as such. This applies to the autonomous experiential aspects of learning, such as knowing how to pick and skim-read relevant texts, when and how to approach acknowledged authorities, at what stage to begin experimental or work in the new field in order to back up or make vivid – sometimes even to controvert – bookish theoretical discourse, and so on.

One point that did become clear, however, was that scientists who had concentrated throughout their previous careers on a very narrow range of problems had great difficulty in making large changes. In particular, it was usually asking too much of them to jump from one scientific language area to another. Here I mean a somewhat larger domain of knowledge than a conventional discipline. For example, most physicists can teach themselves to do mechanical or electrical engineering, since these use much the same conceptual schemes. Again, there is a large area of research in biochemistry, molecular biology and cellular-level physiology where there are no major difficulties of interpretation – that is, where someone highly specialised in one field can soon get the hang of what is going on in another. But the scope of ordinary scientific (and scholarly) didactics does not extend normally to include the trained physicist who needs quickly to become a palaeontologist, or the economist who wants to contribute urgently to cognitive psychology.

Indeed, in spite of a strong personal bias against erecting barriers between scholarly disciplines, I am coming round to the belief that these are not just social conventions. Sciences differ in the way that they observe, analyse, represent and reconstruct various aspects of the world, and these different perspectives take years to learn and unlearn. For example, when physicists began to build large instruments such as radio telescopes and particle accelerators, they tended to treat them as enlarged pieces of laboratory apparatus. It took some years before it was realised that the design principles and practical skills laboriously learnt by professional engineers are also required to build structure on this scale. Again, the physicists and chemists who flooded into biology as it inflated have tended to ignore the vast differences between an inanimate mechanism and a living organism, and thus to seriously underrate the scientific understanding of field biologists.

Yet even such limits can sometimes be transcended. In practice, many scientists enlarge the range of their knowledge outside of their formal disciplines, not just out of intellectual curiosity but because that is what is required by their research. If we are to take the generalised demand for interdisciplinarity seriously, then such requirements are becoming more and more insistent (Ziman 1997). The problems to be tackled nowadays in most domains of technoscience do not present themselves precisely in the terms of a conventional academic discipline, and cannot be solved by multidisciplinary teams of specialists each quite ignorant of each other's specialties. So quite a large proportion of active professional scientists have acquired, slowly over the years, a perfectly adequate understanding of the thought processes and paradigms of other disciplines. This is brought out very well in Peter Galison's brilliant study of high energy particle physics (Galison 1997) where there were people who could think well enough as both experimenters and theorists, or as both experimental physicists and engineers, to bridge the gap. But let it be clear that this was experientially acquired knowledge, picked up by active participation in common enterprises over a period of years. It was not something that could be learnt in a crash course of study, whether self- or other-instructed.

Nevertheless, the transdisciplinary autodidact should not just brush aside the conventional wisdom of the discipline into which he or she has parachuted down. It is all too easy to imagine that a fresh look from an unbiased but well-trained mind will immediately reveal truths that were hidden amongst the nitty gritty of orthodox research. Thus, a distinguished theoretical physicist may claim that all that sociology needs is a mathematical theory based on statistical mechanics, or an evolutionary biologist insists that cultural systems are just assemblies of self-preserving memes, entirely anologous to biological genes. Sometimes, as in the heroic tragedy of the meteorologist, Alfred Wegener, breaking the veil of silence of the geologists about the shapes of the continents, a crude alien thrust is indeed required to penetrate a complacent paradigm. Much more usually, the amateur outsider is quickly stalled by genuine difficulties that are very familiar to the local professionals.

Creative scientific autodidactism is not just a matter of thinking things out for oneself. As an academic theoretical physicist I often used to receive hopeful texts from obsessive DIY authors claiming to put Einstein right on the nature of space and time: invariably these were simply inconsistent with incontrovertible facts and mathematical theorems known to every physics graduate. Indeed, one of these cranks was himself a physics professor, who asserted that the famous 'twins paradox' of special relativity had never been seriously analysed, regardless of the fact that it had been discussed in detail in regular textbooks and review articles right back to the 1920s. The danger of feeling that one has to do it all oneself is exemplified in a Nobel prize-winning paper by a well-known theoretical physicist who laboured for scores of pages, rather unconvincingly, to derive a result which he could have found proven as a basic theorem in a standard treatise on the mathematics of probability.

Let me return, finally, to my soil scientist, who had defined himself as a very narrow specialist, but who had unselfconsciously revealed that he was, in fact, an Admirable Crichton, with a wonderful range of practical skills. Each of these had been acquired autodidactically, and represents a channel of potentiality for further self-instruction. If driven to it, he could surely have become a perfectly competent electronic engineer, or computer programmer or farmer, primarily by the exercise of his own self-winding, self-confident personal powers. I am reminded of the man laying beach-pebble cobbles, outside King's College Cambridge. A bystander asked whether he had perhaps learnt this craft from his father. 'Nope!' he said, 'Never tried it before. Just picked it up as I went along!'

Remember also the protean scientist's reference to the local technical college where he had gone at first to get the technical knowledge that he knew that he wanted. It might have been, for all we know, a rather average educational institution, with poor facilities and mediocre teachers. But it did provide the site and the source for the knowledge gleaning that was needed by this particular citizen, and, one must presume, for many others. Nowadays, I suppose, a lot of that knowledge would be available in reasonably bite-sized packages on the Internet. But we must not overlook the social and political importance of the various institutions – including especially the Open University – which make it possible for individuals to exercise their democratic right to pull themselves up by their own bootstraps to the highest levels of learning and technical expertise.

References

Galison, P. (1997) *Image and Logic: A Material Culture of Microphysics*. Chicago, IL: University of Chicago Press.

Jagtenberg, T. (1983) *The Social Construction of Science*. Dordrecht: Reidel.

Kuhn, T. S. (1962) *The Structure of Scientific Revolutions*. Chicago, IL: University of Chicago Press.

Lodge, D. (1975) *Changing Places*. London: Penguin.

Reuter, H. and Tripier, P. (1980) 'Travail et créativité dans un marché interne', *Sociologie du Travail* 3: 241–256.

Ziman, J. M. (1981) *Puzzles, Problems and Enigmas: Occasional Pieces on the Human Aspects of Science*. Cambridge: Cambridge University Press.

Ziman, J. M. (1987) *Knowing Everything About Nothing: Specialization and Change in Scientific Careers*. Cambridge: Cambridge University Press.

Ziman, J. M. (1997) 'Disciplinarity and interdisciplinarity in research', in R. Cunningham (ed.) *Interdisciplinarity and the Organisation of Knowledge in Europe*. Conference Proceedings. Cambridge: Academia Europaea.

Ziman, J. M. (2000) *Real Science: What it is and What it Means*. Cambridge: Cambridge University Press.

Chapter 10

The autodidactic museum in France and other countries

Paul Caro

Autodidactism is a very natural way of learning in a museum. Anyone deeply interested in a topic will try to access the relevant knowledge, either through talking to people, reading books in libraries, visits to museums, or searches on the Internet. The subjects studied by the auto-didactic visitor to museums may not be taught in schools: they may be 'hobbies' sometimes supported by weekly or monthly periodicals which are another communal source of learning, giving advice for example on medicinal plants, cooking recipes, hunting for mushrooms, stamp collections, games such as chess, mechanics, or do-it-yourself jobs. Interest in truly academic matters may be less common, but subjects which have a romantic flavour, allow for day dreaming and have a poetic or emotional background – such as astronomy, dinosaurs, botany, alchemy, history etc. – attract a great number of people with genuine interests. Because many of these visitors write to the museum curators with questions, comments or alternative personal theories, we see something of the nature and passions of this curious cohort.

For a long time, one might say that almost all science was the product of autodidacts. Many of the great scientists of the past centuries created all their own knowledge. The reason was that there were no schools, most of the Universities in Europe basically teaching theology, law and medicine. In France science was only taught in the 'Grandes Écoles' from the beginning of the nineteenth century, and the 'science' presented was mostly mathematics. Some of the great French scientists of the end of the century, 100 years ago, had no academic background at all and were truly self-taught 'amateurs'.

Science popularisation started very early. For instance one of the first chemistry popularisation books, *La Chymie charitable et facile en faveur des Dames* (Meurdrac 1999 [1666]) was written by a self-taught woman, Marie Meurdrac, in 1666. It was a series of recipes for beauty and health which drew on the knowledge of plants, and had a good overview of the experimental equipment available at the time. What may be more surprising is the foreword, written by the lady herself, which turned out to be one of the first historical pleas in favour of the education of women, asserting their intellectual equality with men. The plants were to be seen in the botanical gardens, a kind of outside museum, created by the State (at Montpellier in 1593 and in Paris in 1635). Medicinal gardens were already in use in the Middle Ages, such as the famous physik gardens at Hampton Court, London. The Jardin du Roi in Paris was later to be developed into a museum of natural history. Besides the displays, lectures were delivered there to the general public by the scientists. Experimental physics (electro-statics and magnetism) was the subject of public performances demon-strated for instance by the famous Abbé Nollet in Paris in the eighteenth century. These new areas of learning that the scientists of the times were opening up, were sustained by the publication of books such as the *Great Encyclopaedia* of Diderot and d'Alembert (published from 1751 to 1772).

Today interested members of the public make use of all the available facilities to learn about their particular interest. The Collège de France in Paris, the Sorbonne's main rival, is where well-known scientists from all disciplinary fields have delivered annual courses of lectures to a lay public since the sixteenth century. The place is usually overcrowded, just as it was when public lectures were given at the Conservatoire des Arts et Métiers during the year 2000 as part of 'The University of all Branches of Knowledge' (Université de tous les savoirs' a series of one-day confer-ences over 360 days covering all branches of knowledge). Through those traditional means autodidacts were encouraged to come and learn what they chose from the subjects on offer.

As we have seen in the previous chapter, scientists are also autodidacts: there are new things they need to learn from colleagues, from literature, from visits to laboratories or manufacturers. And what they learn they are likely to have to teach later to others some day. Every teacher knows that teaching is of itself an autodidactic process because we learn by the act of teaching. Some teachers, as we saw in Chapter 8, learn autono-mously once they are motivated by the discipline. In consequence the museums and other kinds of institution which we describe here, where they are free to come and help themselves as they might do at a knowl-edge cafeteria, are useful to teachers, as well as other autodidacts.

Teaching yourself is a process which should, ideally, be entirely free from the constraints of time and place. It should depend entirely on the taste of the individual and the amount of time he wants to invest. This freedom of 'customer choice' implies competition between resource centres to attract as many visitors as possible.

Three types of museums

There are, roughly, about 3000 museums in France (Sallois 1995), rather more than in England, of which some 880 are under technical control of the State as either national museums, local museums or museums of associations. They are very different from each other, with the enormous Louvre at the top, and at the bottom a score of small hide-outs catering to local specialities. From the figures it is clear that museums are a huge national asset both in terms of potential learning and as tourist centres, and they present a wide-ranging cultural offering which is designed to cater for all tastes. Museums however have different policies and styles. The classification we present below is somewhat arbitrary (Caro 1998) because the same institution can house, side by side, as many as three separate museums, as does the Science Museum in London.

The first type: the Collection museum

Curiosity is the main motor for both autodidacts and the museums which feed them. Most began in the seventeenth century from the polymathic 'Cabinets des Curiosities' for amateurs who were usually rich and already entrapped by curiosity (Stafford 1994). The private display of a mixture of strange natural samples along with unusual work of arts within a museum which was itself built, often in flamboyant antique style, in an urban setting commonly provide an exotic spectacle against a utilitarian background. Most museums evolved as places specialising in systematic exhibitions, rather than just intriguing but unsystematic collections showing a mixture of curiosities. In science the objective was to have collections as complete as possible either in natural history or technology. Collections were often built up by professional scientists as a system which could provide references for fellow scientists. They were a wonderful tool for science. But museums were also public facilities and had to function as a showcase for society. As a consequence, their displays were expected to be available to the public to satisfy lay curiosity, rather than to teach any branch of science in a systematic way. This approach necessitated the opening up of museums which had previously been collections for the use of academic scientists, and was very unpopular with those who expected them to serve science.[1] As late as 1992 the famous French anthropologist Claude Lévi-Strauss was complaining loudly about the need to have curators open 'their' museums to the public. . . .[2]

The close connection between museums and education was clear almost from the beginning. In the middle of the eighteenth century some of the 'Cabinets des Curiosités' were designed to complement teaching by lectures (Stafford 1994). The first official science museum in Paris (1781), was created as a teaching institution to 'unite theory and practice'. It had as founder and director a young chemist who was himself a remarkable experimentalist, Jean-François Pilâtre de Rozier, later to become the first man to fly, on 21 November 1783. He was also the first fatality in an air accident during an early attempt to cross the Channel in a balloon (Dollfus 1993).

Museums were one of the few areas in which the public could come in direct contact with real science through the viewing of authentic objects. Science museums which had been essentially private collections had, in common with the art galleries, little or no detailed information for their visitors: they gave the name of the specimen and nothing more, as a gallery provides the title and author of a work or picture. For the curious it was a chance to see real things, collections of minerals, plants in a botanical garden, paleontological skeletons and so on, and form their own opinion about them, as any autodidact would want to do. Children would have little experience of animals were it not for the zoos, which are another kind of museum specialising in living animals, the only alternative to a circus. Museums came into being as a resource to complement books. They provided a feeling of reality, and occasionally offered the experience of a kind of practical work.

The visitors can draw their own conclusion about a scientific sample or be their own critic of a work of art. This first type of museum caters for those who want to draw their own conclusions, and the result of those visits can be read in the largely enthusiastic comments written on personal websites on the Internet. However recently there has been a tendency to produce a new kind of presentation which is more like an elaborate show of actors, lights and sounds. That move towards sensationalism may even have damaged some of the classic autodidactic effect (for instance in 'la Grande Galerie du Museum d'Histoire Naturelle' in Paris (Van Präet 1996)).

The educational contribution of museums for those who want to teach themselves is well known. We have evidence that many youngsters have taken up science studies after spending long hours contemplating samples in a museum. The solemn atmosphere, together with the fascination of the unknown, has always given a distinctive flavour to the act of learning in a museum. In some ways it can seem like a journey around the world as samples from many different countries are presented one after the other. The setting of the stage – the *mise en scène* – is a serious didactic component of the presentation of the educational material to which considerable attention is paid in French museums. To do it well means being able to rely on an expert team of architectural and scenographic staff who ensure that the whole exhibition, items and setting together, give the knowledge a higher prestige and help the museum to become a landmark in a major city. The museums of today, it seems, have some part of the function of the old Romano-Greek temples of long ago. These were not only dedicated to gods in the cities, they also provided a kind of social unity so that people could gather there and marvel at what they saw. The temples, like our present day museums, housed those components of knowledge in which people of good repute were expected to be interested. To be present was to be a truly educated citizen sharing ideas with others from the same cultural background. This is another facet of the auto-didactic function of museums.

This sociocultural function may explain why troops of young children, still too young to really understand the contents on display, are made to visit so many museums. It is true that the school and their parents may encourage such visits, but the children themselves react emotionally to these halls of learning. They are impressed by the grandeur of the place, may well have treasured memories of it, and at the very least will know that it exists. This is a kind of 'experiential' education completely outside normal teaching.

The second type: interactive or 'hands-on' museums

This second type of museum was created by scientists for special educational purposes. The Exploratorium in San Francisco and the Ontario Science Centre in Toronto both developed about 1970 became known as 'hands-on exhibits'. The public, mostly children, manipulate the display and are supposed to learn by themselves some basic science in the process, usually the elements of physics (Duensing 1996). Classical hands-on experiments are now exhibited in a large number of museums across the world. The Cité des Sciences et de l'Industrie in Paris, as well as the Science Museum in London, have a large hands-on section, which includes new designs developed by the staff, clustered round such topics as mechanics, life, the human body, communication, electricity and light.

The idea of presenting experiments rather than just objects is an old one. Physics experiments were attractions at fairs from the eighteenth until the middle of the twentieth century. By 1900 there was a place in Brussels where people could come to do electrical experiments for themselves. The Palais de la Découverte in Paris was created in 1937 by scientists in order to make demonstrations based on those done in the university. Understanding the concepts of science depends very much on experiments, and allowing people to do some of them makes them more memorable and may help the audience to penetrate a little way into the mysteries of science. Many young students start their future careers in science by conducting all sorts of experiments in the kitchen or the garden. This is often a very different kind of practical work from that described in Chapter 3, where the goal is for the children to make their own discoveries. Here there are labels to read and a particular piece of science to be learnt in association with specified action. There is even a market for small scientific instruments (microscopes, telescopes) in many of these museums.

The third type: describing outcomes

The third type of museum is mostly the creation of politicians. Their intention is to show the importance of new technologies or industrial achievements on behalf of either a whole nation or a local area.[3] The displays present technology at work, rather than the fundamental principles of science. They focus on results, materials, products, apparatus, economics, and explain how they contribute to daily life or open new ways towards the future. That type of museum directly inherits the tradition of the Great Exhibitions (starting with the Crystal Palace in London in 1851). The intention is not to create familiarity with the concepts but to awe the visitors and promote the achievements of industry. The Cité des Sciences et de l'Industrie in Paris has many examples of this sort of presentation. Here there may be some confusion with entertainment theme-parks which also have scientific displays with heavy commercial support (for example Disneyland in Paris has a Space exhibit). Another Disney theme-park, EPCOT in Orlando (Florida), also has presentations of this type. The visitor does not walk around as real autodidacts might do, but is transported slowly across the exhibit in a train system. Personal control of the time factor, which is such an important component of the visit of autodidacts to classical museums, is totally removed, since the visitor cannot stop the train at will. The main problem for all visitors to these huge museums is simple fatigue!

In recent years another component, also of political origin, was added to the displays of this kind. This is the presentation of problems and hazards created by industrial and scientific progress, such as pollution, the greenhouse effect and climate change, new methods in agriculture, and even education (e.g. the exhibit 'Désir d'apprendre' presented in the year 2000 at the Cité).[4] The exhibits are clearly a resource for autodidacts who are interested in citizenship issues and there has been a growing demand for them in many museums. In recent months still another component has been introduced which greatly improves the understanding of topics in the news. This is the presence of scientists, mostly young, alongside the displays.[5] They can then answer questions from the public and present some of their own work.

Museums and learning

The second edition of a governmental report, first published in January 1997, called *A Common Wealth: Museums in the Learning Age* was published in the UK in July 1999. It was addressed to the Department of Culture Media and Sport and written by David Anderson. In the foreword the then Minister of the Arts, Alan Howarth, wrote: 'Education surely should be central to the work of museums and galleries. . . . The government wants to encourage and develop this so that there is a more consistent spread of expertise and benefit throughout the country.'

This is different from the usual remit of museums. As a learning resource the museum can have exhibits, programmes and facilities for self-directed learning. This may include staff trained in education problems and a service in charge of research and evaluation of public learning, both informal and formal. Now, it seems, there are to be stronger connections with teachers and educational institutions in order to increase the impact on our children's education.

Science museums offer help to groups through guided tours adapted to their special interests. This educational practice encourages neither autonomy nor the escape from imposed teaching that autodidacts want. Watching groups of children visiting some organised hands-on centres may suggest that they cannot learn very much because of the excitement and noise as they run from display to display. The group visit just acts as an introduction for the children who may wish to come back later with their parents or by themselves. The couple, child and parent (or grandparent) is interesting to observe because much more attention is given to the displays. Either the child explains it to the parents, or the reverse. There is a possible interaction between them in what might be considered as a 'family autodidactic' process in which the usual authoritative kind of teaching is absent. At the Cité it is estimated that roughly 20 per cent of the visitors can be called 'attentive' and spend a reasonable length of time watching presentations, asking the questions, or taking part in demonstrations.

Museums also offer another type of educational facility – workshops to help those who might want to study specific subjects. Internet 'classes' are typical of this. Some museums have libraries of educational resources such as CD-Rom, teaching materials or language laboratories, as well as collections of books. The Cité has a 'Cité des Métiers' as a guide to careers, where youngsters can browse the information and get counselling from specialised staff. Many museums have now become almost a component of the educational system, active partners working in close collaboration with the schools. The use of the museum as a resource for learning now begins early in the life of a child and we must hope that its programmed nature does not preclude the child's autonomy.

There is one other autodidactic process in the operation of museums. It concerns the staff themselves when planning new exhibits. They may use experts but also work in groups characterised by what is called a 'symmetry of ignorance' (Fisher 1999). This is very conducive to social creativity. Members of the groups have very different types of knowledge (artists, designers, and scientists for instance). They have to explain what kind of contribution they would like to make to the project: they have to interact with each other and take decisions. They learn by creating shared understanding as different mini-cultures meet. It can also be part of project-oriented pedagogy, with the role of the teacher being that of an observer (see Chapter 14). This is almost the negative pedagogy recommended by Jean-Jacques Rousseau (1969) in which the teacher creates situations in which the pupils have to learn by themselves from the facts which they can observe (Chapter 3).

So we see that there are many different ways of learning in a museum. The first is passive learning, by the student from the teacher in the old familiar one-way, top-down process. Here museums can help the teacher to reinforce his or her message, introduce examples, and suggest homework. Students are not autonomous and have no control over this kind of study. A second type is self-directed learning now quite developed in Europe (see Chapters 14 and 15). Students and teacher make the choice of a topic on which the class will work to produce a report, a movie, a show, anything. The work is shared and knowledge is constructed through use of resources, dialogues, discussions, creation of products. The teacher is then a facilitator, but still always present. Some of these projects may be very close to real scientific research, for example a local archaeological excavation, but if in the course of study there is a breakdown due to lack of knowledge expert help will be needed.

Museums face competition from the Web

Many museums offer information about their displays on the Web, taking care to avoid giving so much away that a visit is no longer necessary! Meanwhile wholly virtual museums are also in operation on the Web. A typical example is the Paleontology Museum created at Berkeley at the University of California, an outstanding resource fulfilling elementary as well as sophisticated needs. Any autodidact interested in the topics and wishing to avoid being taught in a conventional way can draw a large amount of information from the presentations on offer. The search engines save the visitor both time and money when compared with a trip to the conventional museum. The number of these websites is large, especially in science, with additional contributions from research laboratories or agencies. Their expertise is much larger than that of any single member of the museum staff, and they are quickly learning pedagogical principles. The only remaining advantage of the regular museums is that they offer a real human contact and allow the visitors to meet experts face to face. Bringing in more professional people to talk to the public in the museums – scientists or artists or engineers – may prove to be a valuable way forward in this fight between the virtual and the human. Museums have to continue to be culturally appropriate as they always have been, but the educational actors in public space should see to it that they appear far more than mere repositories of knowledge.

Notes

1 On the British Museum in 1761 see the remark by Jean-Claude Guédon in *La science en scène*, Presses de l'Ecole Normale Supérieure et Palais de la Découverte, Paris, 1996, p. 76 and p. 85.
2 In a series of articles published in *Le Monde* in September 1992.
3 A series of papers describing industrial museums and their stories in different countries is to be found in Brigitte Schroeder-Gudehus (editor) *La société industrielle et ses musées*, demande sociale et choix politiques 1890–1990, Gordon and Breach, Montreux, 1992.
4 *Désir d'apprendre*, expo-Découverte, le livre, Cité des Sciences et de l'Industrie, Paris, 1999.
5 A series of 10 exhibits entitled 'Oser le savoir', each dealing with a different topic was organised as a joint-venture by the Cité des Sciences et de l'Industrie and the CNRS during the year 2000.

References

Anderson, D. (1997) *A Common Wealth: Museums in the Learning Age*. London: Department of Culture, Media and Sport.

Caro, P. (1998) 'Informal education through science museums', *Alberta Museums Review* 24(1): 31–35.

Dollfus, A. (1993) *Pilâtre de Rozier, premier navigateur aérien première victime de l'air*. Paris: Association Française pour l'Avancement des Sciences, pp. 10–22.

Duensing, S. (1996) 'Exhibit development as a way of thinking and communicating. Exploratorium, a case study', in *La science en scène*. Paris: Presses de l'Ecole Normale Supérieure et Palais de la Découverte, pp. 265–273.

Fisher, G. (1999) 'Symmetry of ignorance, social creativity, and meta-design', *Knowledge-Based Systems*. Special Issue on Creativity and Cognition C&C '99.

Meurdrac, M. (1999 [1666]) *La Chymie charitable et facile en faveur des Dames*, nouvelle édition présentée et annotée par Jean Jacques. Paris: CNRS Editions.

Rousseau, J. J. (1969) 'Lettre à Christophe de Beaumont', in *Oeuvres Complètes Tome IV*. Bibliothèque de la Pléiade. Paris: Gallimard, p. 945.

Sallois, J. (1995) *Les musées de France*, 'Que sais-je?'. Paris: Presses Universitaires de France, p. 3.

Stafford. B. M. (1994) *Artful Science, Enlightenment Entertainment and the Eclipse of Visual Education*. Cambridge, Mass.: MIT Press.

Van Praët, M. (1996) 'Le Muséum d'Histoire Naturelle', in *La science en scène*. Paris: Presses de l'Ecole Normale Supérieure et Palais de la Découverte, pp. 217–230.

Chapter 11

The useful arts

Tim Hunkin

Between arts and science

This chapter is about art and science and some of the links between them. It is named after the section in a library sandwiched between the pure sciences (the 500s) and the fine arts (the 700s). It is partly autobiographical, partly historical and partly about Mr Dewey, who devised the absurdly ambitious classification system for all human knowledge that libraries round the world have used ever since. My favourite part of any public library has always been this large amorphous section usually simply labelled 'The Useful Arts'. It contains everything from rocketry to crochet, engineering, hobbies, cookery, etc. Mr Dewey has become a hero of mine. There are many connections between the arts and sciences, but his one seems particularly strong.

As a child I constantly made things at home, mechanical things like a burglar catching machine (a female figure that beckoned the burglar and hit him on the head with a hammer). I never thought that making them was doing art, although I lavished attention on their appearance, or doing science although I was constantly experimenting with electricity, materials and mechanisms to get them to work.

At school subjects became rapidly polarised. Arts subjects seemed to consist mainly of writing essays, science subjects of doing sums. Not particularly interested in any school subject, I chose sciences because I found sums much quicker to do than essays. Things have improved since the 1960s when I was at school, but teaching still has to centre round activities that can be done in the classroom, sitting at desks, and which can be examined.

Drawings and cartoons

I was good at sums and eventually got to Cambridge with a scholarship to read engineering science. This was an intensely theoretical course and, although some of the mathematics was quite elegant, I found it frustrating

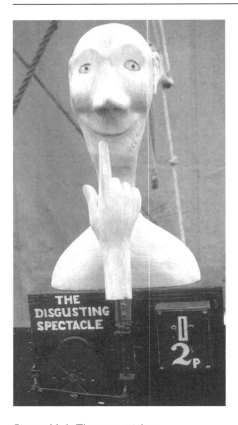

Figure 11.1 The nose-picker.

being without any tools or workshop. Instead I started to draw cartoons, eventually contributing a regular strip, called *The Rudiments of Wisdom*, for a student newspaper. Throughout my time there, despite regular engineering drawing, my 'arty' external activities seemed to have no connection with my engineering. Since leaving twenty-four years ago I have gradually realised how wrong I was. Cartoons and engineering design have much in common, united as elements of Mr Dewey's useful arts.

An early commission I took on was drawing a cross-section of a brewery, showing how the beer was made. Showing the pipes going from one process I needed far fewer words than a wholly written explanation; the drawing was not only decorative, it was also conveying information. The use of drawings to convey information is widespread – consider diagrams, graphs and maps – imagine trying to express all the information in a map in words. Edward Tufty's book *Envisioning Information* is stuffed full of extraordinary examples of visual information of this sort.

I have continued to find new applications, only recently discovering that I could decimate the number of words on labels in the Science Museum by adding cartoon drawings to show how the objects were used.

Engineering drawings serve the same purpose – to convey information. The idea of drafting engineering drawings is surprisingly recent; James Watt was one of the first people to use them. His early beautifully hand-coloured steam engine drawings from about 1800 were executed after the engines had been finished, mainly to demonstrate the workings. The idea of using drawings to proscribe how every part should be made caught on rather later, as engineering feats became more ambitious and increasingly depended on coordinating the efforts of large teams of workers.

What I have realised is that formal engineering drawings are almost exclusively intended for conveying information, to ensure all the parts fit together, and not for designing the parts in the first place. Despite what school Design Technology (DT) teachers instruct their students to do, parts are frequently only 'drawn up' once a prototype has been perfected; doing the initial design is a separate process.

Prototypes can be made without any drawing. I don't remember drawing my machines much as a child, and when I started making things again after leaving Cambridge, I still did very little drawing, just working out the detail by trial and error. There were so many factors, particularly with moving parts, that drawings did not help with – Will a lever be rigid enough? Will a spring counteract a weight? Will a grub screw be enough to hold a pulley on a shaft? Will a motor be powerful enough? Will it stop quickly enough? The quickest way to find out things like this was to try them.

Engineers originally used to work with 'dirty hands', but things had started to change by the mid-nineteenth century when James Nasmyth wrote:

> The eyes and the fingers, the bare fingers, are the two principle trust-worthy inlets to trustworthy knowledge in all the materials and operations which the engineer has to deal with . . . Hence I have no faith in young engineers who are addicted to wearing gloves. Gloves, especially kid-gloves, are the perfect non-conductors of technical knowledge.

There is something intuitively obvious in the idea of making use of as many of the senses as possible – smells and sounds can also be very useful in identifying a problem – but in practice trying everything out becomes very slow. With experience it becomes possible to solve many design problems indirectly, on paper. I now sketch most of the parts I make. Sketching and back of the envelope plans are very different from

Figure 11.2 The refuse android.

precise engineering drawings – I can change my mind all the time, scrubbing over the lines again and again. Drawing becomes a tool for thinking, for exploring different solutions, rejecting bad ones and developing good ones. Design engineers in large companies like Black and Decker, despite their sophisticated CAD suites, still do most of their design work sketching with pen and paper. Only when they have perfected a component do they draw it on the computer.

This process is not very different from doing drawings as a cartoonist – scrubbing over lines, trying to make the image clear and concise, thinking of endless variations or embellishments. It is obviously an intellectual skill, not verbal or mathematical, but something shared by most of those involved in engineering and applied arts and often unrecognised. An academic art historian once asked me if it was really possible to think by drawing. That's how deeply she equated thinking with verbal reasoning!

The world of fine art

Mr Dewey was not only right in recognising the useful arts as the link between fine art and pure science, he was also right in seeing it as something distinct. About fifteen years ago I had a brief period of respectability in the fine art world as a sculptor, with an exhibition at the ICA, followed by nearly twenty years in regional city art centres. At first I was flattered and enjoyed seeing my coin operated machines, which I had previously been taking to local fairs and fetes, immaculately displayed and I was impressed by the art magazines and their intense theoretical discussions about contemporary art.

However, disillusionment soon set in and I felt the fine art world was increasingly alien. I found the hushed, respectful atmosphere of art galleries arid, compared to the boisterous, cheeky atmosphere of the fairs. I became suspicious of the art world's difficulty with humour and popular commercial art forms. I found their writing elitist and I began to suspect it was meaningless empty hype. I felt that the whole point of exhibiting was to communicate something, yet here there seemed to be an ethos that obscurity was a virtue! I started to think that the art world views today's artists in the romantic tradition of William Blake, close to the tradition of mad art. I had tried briefly working as the romantic artist in a garret, drawing entirely on my imagination, but it didn't suit me. I liked being out in the world, being inquisitive, doing something useful which was more akin to the renaissance artists. This did mean making compromises in what I produced, but I found I didn't really mind. In fact I rather enjoyed all the discussions and arguments. I haven't had any contact with the fine art world for ten years now, and have never regretted my departure.

One of my first designs was a coin operated device called *The Birth of Venus* that I made for a friend; an arrangement of pumps, buckets and weights etc. which pulled a poster of Raquel Welch out of a bath of murky water.

I have always found it very satisfying creating things that make people laugh. It is true that, unlike great art, humour does not last. Nineteenth century cartoons, for instance, now seem completely unfunny. However I suspect that the art world's main problem with humour is that it undermines the idea of fine art as a serious and important subject. This baffling front that fine art presents to the world partly explains its minority interest. I suspect it stems from a terror of the art being dismissed as slight and superficial, which is odd because other art forms are assumed to work on many different levels. Films for example can have a rigid plot, fulfil Hollywood's need for sex, violence and sentimentality, but still raise interesting issues and ideas. My own films about domestic machines have a story, demystify the machine's workings, but also have undercurrents, poking fun at consumerism etc.

It is the fine art world of the curators and the dealers and the critics that is alien. Fine artists themselves have many of the same practical skills and interests as those involved in the useful arts. Few fine artists that I have met have much respect for the art world, but feel themselves trapped within it.

Machines and models

I have spent a considerable amount of time demystifying everyday machines, making films and designing museum galleries. I have become increasingly aware that understanding the principles behind even sophisticated machines like photocopiers and video recorders, is distinctly separate from understanding contemporary pure science. It is separate because the theories and models of the universe that today's scientists find useful in their work – quantum physics, DNA genetics, chaos theory, etc. – are generally not the same as the models most useful for everybody else who is curious to understand more about the world around them. Newtonian physics is far more relevant to the machines I've filmed than relativity. Victorian electricity is more useful than quantum theory. Even surprising devices like transistors have their Victorian origins in the point-contact devices in the first radio receivers. When sophisticated modern models are relevant, real understanding depends on an awareness of the basic science from which they were developed.

In many cases the machines are developed first, with scientific principles applied after the event. Science and mathematics can help in perfecting the machine, but the heart of the design process is still an art – knowing what will work, knowing what size and shape to make the parts. Even the humble washing machine is a considerable achievement, each of the hundreds of parts has undergone intensive development, often involving years of work. It is because of this thoroughness that we have come to expect our machines to be so reliable that we don't need to know anything about what's inside them. Once again Mr Dewey was right, this sort of achievement of the useful arts is separate from pure science.

Status of the useful arts

Despite the importance of the useful arts in creating the modern world, the subject and the skills are often ignored. Engineers, designers and skilled workers are not usually good at talking about their work, not surprisingly because, as we have seen, it is essentially non-verbal. There are no great works of literature in the shelves of the useful arts. Interest in the abstract and the theoretical has always been seen as intellectually superior to interest in the tangible and the practical. Academic study requires the use of words or mathematics, ignoring areas to which they cannot be applied. Schools also favour academic subjects, with the added incentive that they don't require expensive materials and equipment, and don't pose awkward health and safety problems. Journalists, critics and politicians principally work with words, and are not in a good position to grasp the nature of the useful arts either.

I now see my Cambridge Engineering Science course as a result of the engineers feeling inferior to all the other subjects in the university. The course was set up to prove that engineering could be made into a theoretical mathematical discipline.

As far as this book is concerned I feel a fraud as an autodidact. I had a good education, even if I didn't enjoy it. I picked up the ability to write and do sums; O level physics is still very useful to me. I didn't find my university course useful, but it did shape my engineering attitude to the world and this has stayed with me ever since. The elitism of Cambridge, which I now feel rather embarrassed about, also gave me an absurd confidence to do whatever I wanted and teach myself whatever I wanted to know. Almost every scientist or artist needs to teach themselves new skills or disciplines at times. I am just an extreme case.

However, even though I don't consider myself to be a true autodidact because I was taught by others, the territory of The Useful Arts is inhabited by many of them. Practical skills involved are not well taught at school, particularly since the widespread removal of metal and woodworking equipment in recent years. The practical skills were best taught by the apprenticeship system, but this has also virtually disappeared. Several people I've worked with have little formal education but a brilliant grasp of intuitive engineering, much better than mine, and an unquenchable thirst to teach themselves more. The sad and unjust reality is that their huge talent remains largely unrecognised and little respected by society. It seems unfair that my privileged education has left me with the confidence that they lack.

Chapter 12

Indian market women and their mathematics

Anita Rampal

Introduction

Draupadi earns her living as a domestic worker, sweeping floors, washing clothes and utensils, running from house to house throughout the day, and is very keen to educate her daughter Sunita so that she will not have a similar life. On talking to Sunita, however, we find she is unable to do her sums at school and says she has problems making sense of 'division'. 'But you know how to do division, don't you? If your mother wants to divide Rs. 180 equally between her three children how much would she give you?' we ask her reassuringly, expecting a pat reply. Sunita seems confused and stares blankly at us, but her mother, unschooled and barely literate, laughs and provides the right answer instantly.

It becomes clear that Sunita is muddled by the algorithms she has been taught at school, and is unable to use her lived experience to operate with numbers the way her mother can, so effortlessly. When confronted with the problem Sunita first tries desperately to translate it into some mathematical operation between the numbers 180 and 3, but cannot decide whether to multiply, add, or something else. Even when asked to divide 180 by 3, she can only visualise the school method, of writing numbers in some meaningless pattern of long division, and soon gives up.

Draupadi, on the contrary, is confident and uses many different ways of handling the numbers depending on the problem posed. In a flash she has broken the problem into manageable parts, has first distributed 50 to each of the three children, and then from the remaining 30 she has doled out 10 each, so that finally each child has been given Rs. 60. Had we asked her to divide 190 she would continue the same process iteratively, with an extra 10 to distribute among the three (Rampal *et al.* 1998, 2000).

Next we ask Draupadi how much she would need if, she had to give Rs. 180 to each child. Again promptly, almost without batting an eyelid she says 'Rs. 180 for three of them? . . . that's Rs. 540' without knowing any tables or being able to write these figures down. How did she do it? Like other autodidacts in this book, she is superbly self-confident and has her own private methods. First she pictures three 180s in her mind. Of the last 180 she mentally gives 20 to each of the first two, 'completing' 200 each time, and then adds 200 + 200 + 140. She hardly ever gets it wrong, and has ways of checking the answer if in doubt. She challenges her husband, a skilled and literate mason, that she could perform mental computations faster than he could, using written methods. Draupadi does not try to teach her own way of performing mathematical operations to her daughter, assuming that these are available to anyone who can write. Unfortunately it is not so for young Sunita and her generation. At school they are taught in a different way and learn very little. Children who drop out early or who have been to school grow up to be part of the large numbers of adult non-literates. If there had been better teaching strategies in elementary school in the fifty years since our country became independent, we would not have had to face the stupendous task of teaching millions through Mass Literacy Campaigns.

Lessons from the Mass Literacy Campaigns

The voluntary spirit of this programme and serious efforts towards community mobilisation ensured that large numbers of adults initially came to the classes. Major problems arose later when trying to sustain the motivation of learners and teachers. The programme had called for the preparation of local primers at the district level, a historic decision in Indian education, though this did not happen in all places. The State Resource Centres printed primers in the vernacular, and district authorities either adapted or adopted these for their programmes.

For teaching reading and writing there seemed to be an understanding that teaching methods must attempt to codify speech and verbal thought, through whole words and phrases, and not start from the alphabet. However, there has not been any such attempt to understand the verbal meaning of numbers, and to locate that in the domain of adults' lived experience. Neither were the autodidactic ways that adults so often discover for themselves ever included. Oral numeracy is actually more natural among unschooled adults than is literacy, which means that they are more familiar with numbers or measurements than with letters. However, the strategies they use in oral arithmetic are often distinct from the routine methods of written arithmetic (Nunes *et al.* 1993).

Just as we do not start by teaching adults how to speak before teaching them to read and write, we do not have to teach them to count simple numbers or to add before teaching them written numeracy. Moreover, adults are aware of the limitations of using only their memory for keeping numbers in their mind, especially when they have to keep track of sub-totals during complex calculations. They would find it a great help to be able to write down numbers, but they do not want to be taught only how to write 1 or 8 or 22. They want to learn *quickly* to write larger numbers, and our numeracy programme must reach this level of teaching useful skills at an early stage. We must also reinforce their mental arithmetic skills (instead of trying to replace or ignore them), and help them with different types of record keeping that are of practical use in their daily lives. Unfortunately, our adult literacy primers do not do this.

The primers labour through the numbers in an absurdly linear fashion, with numbers 1–10 in Chapter 1, numbers 11–20 in Chapter 2, etc. Normally the first primer contains numbers 1–50, and simple addition and subtraction. The second primer deals with numbers 1–100, with some idea of place value, further exercises in addition and subtraction and an introduction to clock time. The third primer includes the operations of multiplication and division, measurement, basic concepts in decimals, fractions and money transactions.

Adults are not only treated like children, but are also taught in a painfully linear manner, far removed from the natural way in which the autodidactic women, like Draupadi, operate. Illustrations in the primers are taken from children's books, where they are asked to count eight ducks or five apples. When the poor mathematical performance of adult learners is brought to the attention of the curriculum committee, its knee-jerk reaction is to remove even more of the challenging concepts, such as decimals or fractions, in a misguided attempt at further simplification.

However, we now know that the process of learning in an adult is far from linear; it is contextually related to mathematical knowledge acquired through everyday life experience. Adults also want to move on quickly to more sophisticated and challenging tasks in mathematics, which can help them deal with market transactions more confidently. A number such as 87 may seem large to a child, but not to an adult, and does not justify being relegated to the second primer. Further, the operations of addition and multiplication make sense to adults as contextual problems, which can be stated in words. Just as Draupadi had solved the problems of division and multiplication of 180 by 3 effortlessly, using her own strategies; most of the adults are capable of doing word problems long before they learn to read and write. In fact, stating arithmetical problems in familiar *words* keeps the context alive and provides a real-world link. Calculations involving money, particularly those related to profit and loss, simple interest on loans, or even the probability of winning or losing a lottery, are important to the learners but are absent from the curriculum.

The adults who came to literacy classes were already using not only their own oral arithmetical strategies, but also a host of other mathematical transactions, such as sorting, measurement and estimation, as a part of their activities relating to life and labour. In this respect too the teaching practice was divorced from their knowledge and dismissive of the nonstandard methods they had developed for themselves. Metric units of measurement were cursorily defined as constituting the standard system, without any attempt to link them to the common systems in use. It is well known that new ideas and skills have to be interpreted by assigning meaning to them, codifying them according to the categories for which they have evolved and, more importantly, testing them out in real-life settings. The teaching practices used in adult literacy classes never attempt to encourage this, and fail to engage learners in reflection of any kind.

Thus there was a wide mismatch between the teaching methods and the learning strategies of these adults. Those who design primers and teaching methods for them seem totally unaware of the learning strategies they already use, and fall back instead upon outdated school methods for teaching children. So literacy classes impose on adults routines that make no sense to them and only cause boredom, frustration and failure, quite similar to the 'school maths syndrome' suffered by millions of children worldwide. Adults who have come to these literacy classes with tremendous effort soon get disheartened and drop out, often disappointing the campaign leaders.

Innumeracy – an international problem

Some of the concerns expressed in the UNESCO report, *Arithmetic in Daily Life and Literacy* were strikingly similar to the problems we continue to face a decade later in our own campaign. It pointed out that:

> An arithmetic programme must be able to transform the principal needs felt by adults into specific educational methods and content, by going directly to the most essential and useful matters. And quickly, for adults have only a limited time for learning. With them it is not possible, as it is at the school level, to put off the acquisition of more satisfying skills to a later time. . . . As we know, non-literates are almost always the poorest people, the most exploited and the most oppressed. They cannot be expected to agree to learn to read and write out of blind loyalty to moral or civic considerations, or out of devotion to some noble cause for their benefit. In order not to waste their time literacy must offer them a real opportunity to help change their situation.
>
> (Dalbera 1990)

The 1980s and 1990s have witnessed much soul searching in both the UK and the USA about large numbers of innumerate citizens who suffer from deep maths anxiety and are incapable of solving simple arithmetical problems. Despite having achieved universal schooling these industrialised countries are expressing concern about the level of mathematical performance of their adults, and are also questioning the efficacy of teaching mathematics in schools. The *Mathematics Report Card* (Dossey 1988) which sampled 80 per cent of 17-year-olds at school caused a furore in America. The study had shown that only 40 per cent of the nation's students could solve moderately sophisticated problems such as finding '87 per cent of 10', while only 6 per cent could find the square root of 17 to the nearest integer.

In his popular book *Innumeracy: Mathematical Illiteracy and its Consequences*, Paulos (1990) has criticised the education system and shown that widespread innumeracy resulted in even educated adults misinterpreting statistics or taking incorrect decisions about risk probability. For instance, quoting a study done by two researchers at the Washington University, he showed that most doctors' assessments of the risks involved in various operations and medications were off the mark by whole orders of magnitude. This theme has been analysed through studies of people's beliefs, their understanding of probabilistic events and hence the rational basis for decision-making, by psychologists Kahneman, Slovic and Tversky (1982). Much debate followed about people's decisions in relation to their survival in dangerous environments, which was more problematic than textbook definitions of logic or probability (Gardner 1985).

The Cockroft Commission (1982) had also generated concerned debate in England some years earlier, after large-scale tests and interviews with adults had shown very low levels of numeracy. The most striking feature of the British study was the extent of anxiety, helplessness, fear and guilt felt by common people in the face of simple problems. The report documented a widespread inability to handle percentages, such as those used in the context of tips and sales reductions. (Many adults thought that a fall in the rate of inflation reported in newspapers should cause a fall in prices.) The study also found that those needing to use job-related mathematics did so by methods and tricks passed on by fellow workers which had little connection with the methods taught at school.

In the last few years US–Japanese studies have attempted to see why children perform better in mathematics through the open methods used for teaching in Japan (Becker and Shimada 1997). The thrust of most of these and other similar studies in different parts of the world has been to review teaching and look at possible strategies that might instil more confidence (emotion) in learners and relate instruction better to their experience.

Autodidactism and sociocultural theories of learning

There has been worldwide concern over the need to improve the school mathematics curricula and to make teaching more contextually related to the learners' activities. Nevertheless there has been very little effort to understand how people learn and *do* mathematics in their own social and cultural settings. Autodidactism, as the term signifies, is the process of self-teaching, so it is not surprising that it is well tuned to the needs of daily life. However autodidactism need not necessarily imply a lone struggle by an individual who is working in isolation. Indeed, in unschooled working situations, learning takes place much more as the situated activity of a community.

Unlike traditional cognitive theories which distance the learning mind from the learner's experience, situated learning does the opposite. This not only makes it richer than the usually abstract school learning, but also bolsters self-confidence. Knowledge is always being constructed, retuned and transformed by autodidacts, as and when they need it for other processes (see Chapter 9). Learning cannot be pinned down to operations inside the head of an individual, or to the tasks undertaken, or to the tools in use, or the environment, but lies instead in the *active relations* between all of them.

The use of activity as the unit of analysis permits a reformulation of the relationship between individuals and the sociocultural environment. This interdependence between the individual, the task, and the environment needs to be understood without losing the holistic background, in much the same way as we focus on either a single person learning or the functioning of the whole community, without assuming that they are separate elements (Lave 1996).

The philosopher John Dewey also used a sociocultural approach. For him the idea of participation in the social environment, included learning as a process of mutual appropriation. This approach is probably the most suitable for a study of unschooled autodidactism, since people without formal instruction appropriate cultural knowledge in many ways. As early as 1916 Dewey had written, in his classic book *Democracy and Education*:

> For the living, experiencing being is an intimate participant in the activities of the world to which it belongs, then knowledge is a mode of participation, valuable in the degree to which it is effective. . . . By doing his share in the associated activity, the individual appropriates the purpose . . . becomes familiar with its methods and subject matter, acquires needed skill, and is saturated with its emotional spirit.
>
> (Dewey 1916)

To understand self-learning in practice, it is therefore crucial to examine the details of how people are involved in activities, within specific settings, and how their participation changes from being peripheral, as in observing and carrying out secondary roles, to being responsible for managing such activities. Moreover, it is also important to look at how people construe the purpose of their activity and seek meanings in those situations (Rogoff 1995).

It is within this perspective that we will proceed to look at the cultural repertoire of our adults, most of them unschooled and yet very efficient in doing mathematics as part of their daily activities. We shall attempt to give some idea of the rich traditions of folk mathematics still alive among the predominantly oral societies of our country and the cultural mechanisms used to preserve and appropriate such knowledge. We shall also briefly present some strategies of street mathematics used for arithmetical computations (as done by Draupadi) to see how these help the process of learning.

Folk and street mathematics

To understand learning in practice it is essential to know something about people's purposes, affective as well as cognitive, and what kinds of meaning they find in the different situations in which they have grown up.

> One big tree
> It has twelve branches
> On each branch there are thirty leaves
> Of which fifteen are black
> And fifteen white – what are they?

> It is impossible to count father's money
> And impossible to fold mother's sari
> What are these?

Such timeless riddles about time, the stars, or the sky, reveal the nature of observations made by a society that is sensitive and observant about its surroundings. More significantly, they also show how an oral society has managed to codify its knowledge to transmit to its learners. A poetic riddle, based on a rhythmic play of words and sounds, meant to tease and challenge the minds of learners, is a potent tool used by many traditional oral societies to develop creative thinking and imagination. Even today numerous such riddles, with wonderful philosophical, lyrical or mathematical content, are still used by the older members of rural societies. Unfortunately most of our school children no longer know these riddles, and are also losing most of the rest of their folk knowledge.

Indian societies have invested tremendous effort and ingenuity into devising mnemonics for transmitting their rich bodies of knowledge to future generations. *Shlokas, mantras* and *sutras* composed in elaborate rhythmic patterns were all used as means to ensure that the knowledge of such societies was made memorable. Verse and rhyme, which help in memorising long pieces of complicated information, have been woven creatively into the observations and philosophy of oral civilisations. Voluminous bodies of early scientific texts, including the Vedas, existed for centuries in purely oral form, composed and recited through complex techniques.

> [These] included not only grammatical and phonetic analyses but various methods of marking each uttered phrase with physical gestures and bodily movements, so that the texts were almost inscribed into the body's motor memory.
>
> (Daniels-Ramanujan and Harrison 2001)

Numbers of such poems, narratives, riddles, games and songs exist not in the repertoire of classical oral literature, meant for limited consumption by the learned elite, but in the folklore of ordinary people. Even today the older generations living in villages enjoy this rich repertoire of folklore. One might wonder what is the connection between these kinds of riddles, which are mathematical, a source of fun and games, rhymes and song, and the nature of autodidactism?

The innumerable poetic puzzles and stories about numbers existing in the folklore of different regions of India are often not easy to solve, even with written algorithms. However, people enjoy reciting them and trying to give answers using intuitive and empirical strategies. The first of the number riddles given below is simple, and yet more than a mere enumeration of the fingers of one's hand, it reflects on an important characteristic of *Homo sapiens*. This ability, which allows us to touch each finger separately to the opposing thumb, is known to be responsible for most human creation through the use and manufacture of tools. Thus the riddle is meant not just to help us think of numbers but also to appreciate the special construction of the human hand. Here again rhythm is used as an aid to the non-literate autodidact's memory in a way that is familiar in many other societies.

> Brothers there are five
> Without the help of the eldest
> The younger ones can barely survive.
> What are these?

The next number riddle is narrated as an oral story with dramatic nuances to hold the listener's attention. The puzzle is posed in verse and, interestingly, there are many other examples where the answers too are given as a repartee, in the same format as a poetic riddle. Indeed, the poetic pattern of *sawaal jawaab* or question and answer in verse, is still popular in some parts of the country, but is fast getting marginalised by more modern forms of literate and visual communication. In classical music and dance techniques, such creative duels or repartees in rhythmic patterns of beats or movements are still formally taught and carefully nurtured. It is as though room is deliberately being left for the defiant autodidacts (see Chapter 2) who want to display a different approach and through it to assert their autonomy, without breaching the rules of courtesy.

The story of the egg vendor

An egg vendor was moving along a road selling his wares. An idler who didn't have much work to do tried to engage the vendor in a duel of words. This grew into a fight and he pulled the basket of eggs and dashed it on the floor. The eggs broke. The vendor requested the village *panchayat* (the local committee of the five wise elders) to intervene and settle the dispute. The *panchayat* called a public meeting and asked the vendor to state how many of his eggs had been broken. This is what he said:

> If counted in pairs, one will remain,
> If counted in threes, two will remain,
> If counted in fours, three will remain,
> If counted in fives, four will remain,
> If counted in sevens, nothing remains.
> (One hundred and nineteen eggs).

Here verse is being used not just to aid memory, but also to challenge others, even the village elders. Challenge, humour, wit and autonomy all figure in one or the other tales of autodidacts.

Measurements for all

People participating in specific production processes use numerous methods of counting and sorting, through which they also acquire the ability to make very accurate estimations. Estimations form the basis of all measurements, and there is normally a consensus as to which type of unit is to be used for measuring what and when. Even though people use a variety of units for different situations, they may not know how to convert from one type to another. This is also true of the more educated ones like us, who may not easily estimate heights of persons in the metric system, though for cloth or distances we have been using standard metric units for some time.

An ancient poem in Tamil (the major language of the southern Indian state of Tamilnadu) illustrates how an amazingly wide range of length measures, from the atomic to an astronomical scale, had been visualised through the use of rich life-world imagery. Though the English translation cannot possibly match the sense of rhyme and sounds of the original, it is still worth giving an extract here.

8 atoms	= 1 speck in the sun's ray
8 specks in the sun's ray	= 1 speck of cotton dust
8 cotton specks	= 1 hair point tip
8 hair tips	= 1 small sand particle
8 sand particles	= 1 small mustard seed
8 small mustard seeds	= 1 sesame seed
8 sesame seeds	= 1 paddy seed
8 paddy seeds	= 1 finger width
12 finger widths	= 1 span
2 spans	= 1 cubit
12 cubits	= 1 stick (*kol*)
500 *kols*	= 1 *koopidu dooram* (calling distance)
4 *koopidu doorams*	= 1 *kaadam* (about 1.2 kms)

The measure *koopidu dooram* or calling distance is known to have been used in many early metrological systems. This suggests that there existed folk and empirical knowledge about finite distances travelled by sound, and an idea about how different frequencies attenuate at different distances. In fact, in the elaborate system of distance measurements developed by the Saharan nomads the carrying distance of the human voice was distinguished from that of various other animals, so as to generate different units.

As the economic historian Kula (1986) noted, the earlier measures were truly representational; they signified something real, and had a social meaning, through people's concrete activities of life and labour. Historically, the earliest stage in the development of units of measurement is anthropomorphic, corresponding to parts of the human body. Thus throughout the world there have been measures such as the foot (to mark distances when planting potatoes), the pace, or the elbow or ell (to measure cloth, etc.). Moreover, as has been pointed out in the context of old Slavonic measures, the peasant fisherman would refer to his net as being '30 fathoms long and 20 ells wide', thus choosing different convenient measures for the length and width respectively.

We need to acknowledge and build upon such measures, which are still in use today in most of our own rural societies. As part of our research we had studied various systems of estimation and measurement used by adults for measuring time, area, lengths, capacity, weights, volume etc. We found elaborate vocabularies and measurement systems created by people themselves, related to parts of the human body and also to standard objects of everyday use. Some of the ideas for using these are discussed in our book *Numeracy Counts!* (Rampal *et al.* 1998) and the enlarged Hindi version *Zindagi Ka Hisaab* (literally meaning 'Life's Accounts') (Rampal *et al.* 2000).

Effecting a metric and a cognitive shift

Historically it has been seen that traditional measures were not only more functional but also more technically sound for comparative purposes. In the case of differing quality of goods or resources, having only one unit was not considered the most convenient tool for measurement. For instance, for land measurement the hectare does not provide a directly addable measure, owing to the unequal quality of soils. The owner of two hectares is not twice as rich as the owner of one hectare, since the value of land depends upon many other factors. Thus mechanically adding hectares is not technically correct, since not every hectare is equal to another. The earlier measures, based on qualitative factors, such as the labour-time needed to till the land, or the amount of seed required for sowing a given crop, presented a more realistic value for a given piece of land.

People were used to thinking in terms of different measures for the different *quality* of an item, such as a 'better/larger' measure for poorer grain. This produced another hurdle in the metrification of measurement, which was not simply connected with the decimal base. Thinking in categories of invariable measures and variable prices (to adjust for the quality, purity, dampness, etc. of grain) amounted to a complete mental revolution. It was not enough simply to master the measures, or even to master the decimal way of counting.

The older 'quality' forms of measurement are still prevalent in India today, and coexist with the new standard systems. Ironically, most educators fail to appreciate the ingenuity of such measures, used effortlessly by autodidacts, and dismiss them as crude, inaccurate or even primitive. In this way they also thwart the possibility of a discussion with adults about the autonomous systems they use. This failure to acknowledge people's lived knowledge can violently disrupt the process of learning and the smooth appropriation of new knowledge.

The metric system demands a huge cognitive shift from the synthetic-qualitative way of thinking to a more abstract-quantitative process, which links in quite a different way with the lived knowledge of the marketplace. In the metric system, we tend to abstract just one of the many qualities of diverse objects, say the length, and view them all from a single perspective. So the pace of a woman, the length of her sari, the height of a tree, the thickness of a sheet of paper, or even the length of the earth's meridian are all contracted so as to use the same unit of measurement.

This, at least in large part, is what still causes resistance to the use of metric units.

There is yet another fundamental objection to the use of base ten which could be made on behalf of the self-taught women such as Draupadi. As they perform their calculations, approaching ever closer to the required answer, the repeated divisibility by two is of crucial significance in their counting systems. Thus in the duodecimal system the basic number twelve is twice divided by two – 'half and half again' – and in the sex-decimal system the basic number sixteen is divisible by two four times over. In this way people manage to cope with quarter quantities without resorting to fractions. Our own research in India has shown that even today people use continuous division and groupings effortlessly, in pre-dominantly oral processes of measurement and computation.

Historians have claimed that it is more feasible to change the values of measures than alter the ways of dividing and multiplying used for genera-tions in the mental arithmetic practised and self-learnt by common people. In fact, China had done just that to usher in metric reform. The Chinese reform, which began as early as 1912, also faced many difficulties owing to the new terminology, which even used sounds that did not exist in the Chinese language. In 1959 the government tried again, this time attempting a different route, which involved retaining many of the former names, standardising their dimensions and integrating them with the metric system. Thus 'cheng' was made equal to the litre, the 'tsin' to half a kilogram and the 'chi' to one-third the metre. Within five months the new measures were adopted all over China. In Britain where many market tradespeople try only rather half-heartedly to conform to European regulations about metric weights, the older pound (lb.) has often simply become half a kilo, in ordinary people's minds, in a similar way to that in China.

In many states of South India intricate fractions still exist in the every-day vocabulary. In Tamil and Malayalam (the languages of the states of Tamilnadu and Kerala, respectively), people still speak of 'half of one-fourth' as 'araikaal' or 'three-fourths of one-eighth' as 'mukaal arakaal'. This too is similar to the mental halving process used by autodidacts. Interestingly, these intricate fractions also seem to be related to the mark-edly more intricate rhythms used for the percussion instruments in the classical Carnatik music of South India. This suggests that for autodidacts too, rhythm may be just another powerful tool for memorising what is so intimately related to mathematical creation.

References

Becker, J. P. and Shimada, S. (eds) (1997) *The Open-Ended Approach – A New Proposal for Teaching Mathematics.* Reston, VA: NCTM.

Carpenter, T. P., Lindquist, M. M., Mathews, W. and Silver, E. A. (1983) 'Results of the Third NAEP Mathematics Assessment: Secondary School', *Mathematics Teacher* 76: 652–659.

Cockcroft, W. H. (1982) *Mathematic's Counts.* London: HMSO.

Dalbera, C. (1990) *Arithmetic in Daily Life and Literacy.* Paris: UNESCO, International Bureau of Education.

Daniels-Ramanujan, M. and Harrison, K. (eds) (2001) *A.K. Ramanujan: Uncollected Poems and Prose.* New Delhi: Oxford University Press.

Dewey, J. (1916) *Democracy and Education: an Introduction to the Philosophy of Education.* New York: Macmillan.

Dossey, J. (1988) *Mathematics Report Card.* Washington, DC: National Assessment for Educational Progress.

Gardner, H. (1985) *The Mind's New Science.* Basic Books: New York.

Kahneman, D., Slovic, P. and Tversky, A. (eds) (1982) *Judgement under Uncertainty: Heuristics and Biases.* New York: Cambridge University Press.

Kula, W. (1986) *Measures and Men.* Princeon, NJ: Princeton University Press.

Lave, J. (1996) 'The practice of learning', in S. Chaiklin and J. Lave (ed.), *Understanding Practice: Perspectives on Activity and Context.* Cambridge: Cambridge University Press.

Lave, J. and Wener, E. (1991) *Situated Knowledge.* Cambridge: Cambridge University Press.

Nunes, T., Schliemann, A. D. and Carraher, D. W. (1993) *Street Mathematics and School Mathematics.* Cambridge: Cambridge University Press.

Paulos, J. A. (1990) *Innumeracy: Mathematical Illiteracy and its Consequences.* New York: Vintage Books.

Rampal, A., Ramanujam, R. and Saraswati, L. S. (1998) *Numeracy Counts!* Mussoorie (India): National Literacy Resource Centre, LBSNAA.

Rampal, A., Ramanujam, R. and Saraswati, L. S. (2000) *Zindagi Ka Hisaab.* Mussoorie (India): National Literacy Resource Centre, LBSNAA.

Reed, H. J. and Lave, J. (1981) 'Arithmetic as a tool for investigating relations between culture and cognition', in R. W. Casson (ed.) *Language, Culture and Cognition.* London: Macmillan.

Rogoff, B. (1995) 'Sociocultural activity in three planes', in J. V. Wertsch, Pablo Del Rio and A. Alvarez (eds) *Sociocultural Studies of Mind.* Cambridge: Cambridge University Press.

Chapter 13

How does resource-based learning help the self-directed learner?

Eileen Scanlon

This chapter considers the way in which a resource-based approach to teaching has increased the opportunities for people to learn. The range of resources that the Open University has developed includes television and multimedia, and the consequences of the convergence of computer and communications technology. Resource-based learning developed in distance education in response to a growing interest in the capacity of different media for helping science learners.

The Open University context

The Open University (OU) was founded in 1969. Its charter specified that it should teach to wide objectives, and 'by a diversity of means such as broadcasting and technological devices appropriate to higher education *and* promote the educational well being of the community generally'.

The first Open University courses were produced in 1971. Students over 21 years old studying part time by distance learning began their study of a range of subjects including mathematics, social sciences and science. Walter Perry, the OU's first Vice Chancellor, traced the influences leading to its foundation as follows:

> The concept . . . evolved from the convergence of three major postwar educational trends. The first of these concerns developments in the provision for adult education, the second the growth of educational broadcasting and the third the political objective of promoting the spread of egalitarianism in education.
>
> (Perry 1976: 1)

The students study part time using the specially designed, multimedia packages of materials sent from the OU centre at Milton Keynes to their homes, throughout the UK and beyond. Two significant features of the original provision were a commitment to open access and to the use of a range of media, described in the 1970s as a multimedia approach but nowadays as multiple media courses. The commitment to open access meant that students were registered on courses in the order in which they applied, and there was no requirement for any entry qualifications. Students required only basic literacy and numeracy and some general knowledge. However students do need a great deal of motivation and persistence and at least twelve hours a week to set aside for study. The consequence of this open access policy is very apparent in the construction of the degree programme. Based on a model of the time spent by full-time undergraduates in four year honours degree courses in Scotland, the first year for all students was to be spent in Foundation level study (now called level 1) in one of the main areas. These foundation courses had to serve a dual function, to bring those with little knowledge to a level where they could proceed, and yet be sufficiently challenging for those who already had some prior knowledge.

The original decision to allow students to choose the components of their degrees has some implications for the more autonomous learners. Students are provided with advice, but the choice of courses is essentially their own. In 1989 a study of science graduates established that although most had elected to concentrate on one discipline, the freedom to mix and match courses was much valued.

> This diversity of degree profiles is hardly surprising in view of the range of previous experience and aspirations that UKOU students bring to their studies in science: some are updating or upgrading earlier science qualifications, others embarking on science courses for the first time, but with intentions of pursuing the field in either teaching or research, still others are doing the courses for their own interest.
>
> (Ross and Scanlon 1995: 24)

By 2000, the Open University was producing 9 per cent of all UK graduates (around 7000 per year), adding to the national total of almost 200,000 graduates, and 150,000 students who had studied one or more courses in science. Thirty per cent of these had entered with few or no qualifications.

The Open University public

From the beginning it was clear that people used the materials in different ways. The wider Open University audience includes students, associate lecturers who tutor groups of students locally, eavesdroppers who watch Open University TV broadcasts, families of students, and employers of students who in some cases had provided financial assistance.

Clark *et al.* (1998) made an attempt to characterise the impact of the Open University's television provision on the public understanding of

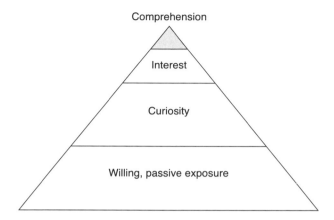

Figure 13.1 The impact of television reception on the public.

science using the public response to one programme. They worked to a four level model of impact describing an individual's involvement with media science. The levels identified were *awareness* (those who watched the TV programmes, *curiosity* (those who asked for further information), *interest* (those who entered a course of study) and *comprehension* (those who concluded a course with success). The salient point identified was that the number of people watching the programmes was some ninety times the number that actually enrolled on the course and passed it. This suggests a huge, if hidden, contribution to the general understanding of science.

Previous research on the audience for TV programmes (Taylor 1997) suggested that it consisted of a core of dedicated viewers, actively seeking out OU programmes, a 'horizon' audience which was less dedicated but still interested enough to follow up on programmes of particular interest and a 'grazing' audience. The latter approximated to the 'eavesdroppers'. The core audience was larger than the population of students and consisted of what BBC Education calls 'committed learners at home'. Research showed that:

> Their key interest in watching is cited as being 'particularly interested in the subject matter' this is buttressed by the fact that when asked why they like academic presentations they choose because 'they get deeply involved in the subject matter'.
>
> (Taylor 1997: 16)

Since the beginning of the Open University its Institute of Educational Technology has tracked the performance of students on OU courses, their opinions about course materials, their experiences on graduating and their motivation during the first year.

> We confined ourselves to asking students what had made them choose to study through the Open University. Looking at the reasons students gave we found that those stressing ends predominated over those stressing means. Thus the reasons most frequently mentioned were: to widen their knowledge (37%), to gain higher educational quali-fications (33%) and to help with present job (15%) or job change (15%). . . . Mention of educational qualifications and job was related to age with the younger students more likely to mention these in contrast to the proportion mentioning 'to widen knowledge' which increased with age.
>
> (McIntosh *et al.* 1974: 245)

A survey of graduates who had recently completed a course (Woodley 1996) found that 72 per cent of graduates continue to use course materials, while 50 per cent use TV to stay in touch. Almost all (99 per cent) of the students found their degrees enjoyable and 56 per cent had changed their job, of which 82 per cent found that their qualification was useful for this (Ross and Scanlon 1991). Others had moved into employment for the first time. One student wrote 'I started as a full-time housewife; my OU degree was my entrance ticket to the IBM' (Ross and Scanlon 1991: 7). In recent years shorter courses lasting only a few weeks have been designed for those who have specific interest in topical issues such as the human genome, global warming, or astronomy. This sort of teaching, which spreads science knowledge to members of the public who may not take a full degree, is a serious part of our academic remit.

When first developed in the early 1970s the programme was intended to be an interdisciplinary course *in* science, not a course *about* science. It had both to be suitable for students beginning their training in science, and also to be a single course for those who wished to have just a taste of science study. It was hoped that both groups would be enabled to read science magazines such as *New Scientist* with understanding. The first Dean of the science faculty, who was also the educational technologist involved in the course design, wrote of these course aims and objectives as follows:

> whether the student is an intending professional scientist, a teacher or simply a citizen interested in the understanding of science, he (sic) must be taught the external relevance as well as the internal content of science . . . An understanding of modern science and an ability to think and act scientifically are attributes required not only of profes-sional scientists . . . We believe the long term future of Britain requires

a massive increase and improvement in science education at all levels . . .
there is an objective for more and better educated scientists and more
and better science education in the community.

(Kaye and Pentz 1974: 52)

Media mix and student autonomy

The multiple media approach has particular benefits for self-directed
learning. Clear writing on science includes the construction of a logical
argument, but it is a challenge for the authors to combine this linear
structure of text-based instruction with encouraging free debate around
the social issues presented. This logical structure of the texts, and the
inclusion of compulsory activities within them, are sometimes condemned
for exerting too much control over the students' learning. Such control is
not easy to reconcile with the development of adult students as lifelong
autonomous learners. Lockwood (1992) reviewed the attitudes of students
and compared them with those who wrote the materials. Among the
reasons given for using activities within the text the writers mentioned
'fostering learner independence' as an instructional goal and 'creating
enthusiasm and interest' as another. Neither of these suggest a controlling
attitude.

There is a wide and increasing range of media, including television (and
videocassettes), radio (and audiocassettes), home experimental kits, residential schools and continuous assessment tutorials and examinations.
(As we shall see in the final chapter, not all of these attract autonomous
students.) Computers are used for multimedia CD-ROMs and to access
resources on the Internet. So, for example, students can take part in
vicarious experiments, go on virtual field trips, or access a mini-library
of research papers. Computers are also used for electronic conferencing
and to increase the opportunities for communication between isolated
students. By the 1980s, it was decided that a significant proportion of
courses would need access to a computer (mostly for computing and technology courses). By the late 1990s, with the addition of a modem to the
specification, many courses were making extensive use of multimedia
CD-ROMs and conferencing.

The use of such alternative media can replace some parts of the experience of a science student in a conventional higher education institution,
such as practical work. There are good arguments for a media mix being
a powerful aid to learning; a recent Vice Chancellor wrote: 'If the OU has
learned one thing in 30 years it is that there is no magic all-purpose
media – for University study at least' (Daniel 2000: 17). An early insight
was that one of the key design decisions involved a necessary element of
media redundancy:

It has been suggested that a valuable function of the different media in a multi-media system is to provide a degree of redundancy (by presenting the same materials through different media) on the assumption that some students learn most effectively from television or film and other more effectively from printed materials.

(Briggs 1967 quoted in Kaye and Pentz 1974: 26)

Science from TV

From its inception as 'the University of the Air' the role of television was seen as vital. Indeed students were advised not to register for science courses unless they were able to receive broadcasts, as these formed a key part of the strategy of providing practical work. The OU has always attracted a large general audience for its TV programmes. This became apparent from the fact that its programmes sometimes appeared in the BBC's Broadcasting Audience Research Board (BARB) ratings, for which the minimum audience for inclusion in the statistics is 500,000 viewers. Radcliffe (1990) estimates that audiences regularly reach 200,000. As we have seen, in some courses the eavesdroppers significantly outnumber the registered students. Surprisingly around half of these drop-in viewers were found by Taylor (1992) to engage in some follow up activity on their own – true autodidacts!

The difficulty of providing an experience of practical work is an important issue. There are several advantages of television for illustrating experiments especially if expensive, difficult or risky. A studio setting can make it possible to show students how cameras can be combined with other instruments like microscopes. Sometimes a film crew may penetrate into an industrial or laboratory setting or on a biology or geology field trip. Techniques such as slow motion, 3D effects or animations can be used to help explain difficult concepts (e.g. in stereo-chemistry). Television has also been used for providing information about the contexts in which science is carried out and applied, using scientists to talk about their work (see Ross and Scanlon 1995).

In recent years some attempts have been made to follow the opening objective of the OU – 'to promote the educational well being of the community generally' by making the most of the eavesdropper audience. So in 1997 the University was given the opportunity to build and sustain its audience for programmes on Saturday and Sunday mornings, spreading it to a much larger audience. Existing programmes were embedded in a 'themed' morning and an associated website with more information. A number of science themes were chosen (e.g. *The Body, Islands of Life, Is science finished?*) and the most popular of these, *Life on Mars*, attracted over 500,000 viewers. Viewers wrote of these types of programmes:

It gives you an insight into some of the things going on in the world you would normally never think about.

I just got bored with watching the same rubbish on the television and of talking about the same thing all the time.

A later series of four programmes, *Rough Science,* followed the exploits of five scientists marooned on a Mediterranean island, with challenges to improvise a radio and cook a banquet. It was broadcast on Friday evenings and supported by a website which contains follow up activities and some information on the science behind the programmes, providing a link to the OU courses and booklet. Its audience peaked at over 2 million. A sample of viewers was polled and 40 per cent gave as their reason for watching the series an existing interest in science. Comments from viewers published on the website gave a variety of views.

I'm 11 years old and I find your program amazing, it's astonishing. I know lots of people at my age or older would have to be paid quite a lot to watch your program (no afence) (sic) but I love the way you tackle the tasks you are given . . . from a great fan, viewer and not a nerd.

and from others a further indication that the OU was fulfilling its remit to provide education to the community,

We have been watching this as a family and have thoroughly enjoyed the series. For me it has been the best piece of Friday evening viewing for years, even though the competition is poor.

Computer-based resources for learning science

One result of the convergence of communications and computer technology has been an explosion in the possibilities for independent learners. The Web-based resources associated with OU BBC television programmes are part of this increased access.

Once you are connected to the Internet you have instant access to an almost indescribable wealth of information . . . through electronic mail and bulletin boards. . . . You can use a different kind of resource: a worldwide supply of knowledgeable people, some of whom are sure to share your interest, no matter how obscure.

(Krol 1994: xix)

The second part of the quote above refers to the potential for collaboration, which has been extensively used. This can be considered by looking at one of the MSc science courses.

Communicating Science is a post graduate Masters course for developing skills in communicating scientific ideas to a variety of audiences. A mini-library of extra resource materials is provided on CD-ROM. Tutorial support is mainly carried out electronically via the FirstClass conferencing system. Students also use the Internet to access electronic databases, and other examples of teaching available over the Web, a multimedia evaluation site, a number of museum-based sites and electronic debate surrounding controversial current and historical topics. Telematic conferences provide students with opportunities for communication and a Course Forum encourages students to raise and discuss issues which emerge from the course. A 'Café' is there for informal chat between students, and a tutor discussion forum for planning, and assessment. These interactions have been structured to involve groups of twenty students in discussion and group work, and for both students and tutors to assess whether the conferences have led them to revise their own opinion of the topic under discussion.

The provision of only limited opportunities for collaboration has been one of the major criticisms of distance learning. However these new electronic conferences have been highly rated by the students who participated. Some have commented on the way that this type of discussion forum has led to a change in the power relationships between students and lecturers, which also encourages student autonomy. The scale of the use of electronic communication in the University is certainly huge. John Daniel, our last Vice Chancellor, estimated that 150,000 student-to-student messages were sent each day during 6000 computer conferences!

Programmes for later versions of the Foundation Course include a multimedia visit to the Galapagos Islands, and to an oak wood, as well as an exploration of the periodic table with clips of relevant, but far too dangerous, experiments. Packages that include simulation or modelling features are particularly valuable as they allow students to ask 'what if' questions. Yarnell and Kafai (1996) report some interesting work with children learning science who were asked to produce a science-based computer game. They worked for several months conducting research programming screens and interactions creating stories and dialogues. Eventually these 11-year-olds had designed an educational game that teaches about the ocean environment. Such work highlights the sense of ownership in relation to the creation of a computer-based world, which was first encouraged by the work of Seymour Papert. In 1980 he described how programming in LOGO could be used to develop an understanding of Newton's Laws. This potential of independent learning through active programming has probably been best developed for young science learners by di Sessa (2000). No doubt such independent activity also has much to offer adult learners.

Review

In this chapter I have attempted to illustrate how the Open University has approached the development of open learning which could support students' learning without taking away their autonomy.

We have many quotations from students who were happy and productive in the structured experience provided, and descriptions of ways in which the University's provision can support different purposes for learning. One student's reason for registering with the OU was a deep interest in tropical fish. He intended to pursue a science degree culminating in a course on oceanography, and seemed typical of a specialised public who migrate from a hobby interest to active research.

> There is still considerable scope for amateurs as researchers armed with cheap instruments and for certain subjects, access to the Internet. Lewenstein identified 10 environmental organizations with US memberships in excess of 100,000; in all, some 15 million Americans belong to such groups. Drawing on these resources, for example, every Christmas thousands of amateur ornithologists are mobilized by the Audubon Society to chart the voyages of migrating birds; these 'twitchers' play a key part, too, in protecting rare species. In astronomy, thousands of amateurs organized into local associations play an irreplaceable role in looking for comets and studying variable stars.
>
> (Miller and Gregory 1998: 230)

The structure of scientific knowledge and the need for guidance from experienced teachers presents particular challenges for distance education in terms of the students' autonomy. Self regulation is the goal for education courses, in any university. The potential conflict is with the auto-didactic students' wish to follow their own interests without teaching, assignments or examinations. But is this possible?

> The science that is needed by an advanced industrial society cannot be learned by *Watching with Mother*, *'Sitting by Nelly'*, *Tomorrow's World* or *Horizon* on TV, reading the newspapers, poring over 'teach yourself' books in the evening or even by apprenticeships to a practical craft. Our technological civilisation . . . would slowly collapse if tens or hundreds of thousands of people were not spending some of the formative years of their lives learning science systematically from professional teachers.
>
> (Ziman 1986: 132)

However, there is another constituency of the public with a particular need for education in science of immediate relevance to problems in their lives. Rose describes these.

> As a sociologist, I would wish to argue that lay people, not least because we live in a scientific culture, and outside our narrow expertise we are all lay people, pick up some particular areas of science . . . those which are important or have some special interest for them, and that they make sense of this knowledge within the expertise in their own context. Often people do this without claiming that their knowledge is science but instead speak modestly of hard facts or reliable knowledge. Thus in my own PUS research on people with a cholesterol genetic disorder (autosomal, so handy for a researcher interested in gender) both women and men knew more about saturated and unsaturated fats than was revealed in a parallel quantitative study ascertaining public levels of scientific knowledge.
>
> (Rose 1997: 61)

In the study Rose describes the adults showed no interest in the basic science of metabolism. Groups of learners with a particular need for information have sometimes found the resources they need on the Internet. An interesting development of this (Preece 1999) is the part that 'empathic communities' on the Web may have to play.

OU voices?

Decisions made by the course teams at the OU have resulted in the production of some resources where autonomous learners are allowed a voice. This chapter has discussed planning assumptions, systems development, the opinions of science education experts and the findings of surveys. However none of this conveys well enough the passion with which many students describe what Entwistle and Entwistle (1992) refer to as the 'feeling tone' that we experience when beginning to understand a new topic.

One OU voice that captures some of this is that of a female student successful in gaining a science degree:

> I've always been interested in 'how come?' I was the elephant's child for questions never satisfactorily answered. And I believed that if I could just once get there, I would be able to find out how to find out the answers to any questions that I wanted to ask. I may choose not to ask it, but at least I am totally certain that I can go and explore anything.
>
> (Lunneborg 1994: 45)

The following extract is from a letter sent by a male 'drop-in viewer' representing the perspective of a non-student with just occasional contact with OU broadcasts.

> I was hopeless at school, always last in the class. I always seemed to be asking questions that no one else seemed to ask, and the teachers gave up on me I guess. May I say how much I enjoy the OU programmes. They really are terrific, and I often cry inside because they were not about when I was at school, for I now know education is far more than just learning and knowing.
>
> (Taylor 1997: 1)

References

BBC Audience Research (2000) *Rough Science: Analysis of the series based on the QUEST survey.*

Briggs, L. J. (1967) *Instructional Media: A Procedure for the Design of Multi-media Instruction.* Pittsburgh, Pennsylvania: Pittsburgh American Institutes for Research.

Daniel, J. (2000) *e-ducation@open.ac.uk* In o.zone magazine, Autumn/Winter BBC publications.

di Sessar, A. (2000) *Changing Minds: Computers, Learning and Literacy.* Cambridge, Mass.: MIT Press.

Donovan, C., Hodgson, B., Scanlon, E. and Whitelegg, E. (2000) *Associate Lecturers in Science at the Open University, http://. . .* , Report for the Athena Project.

Clark, P., Lambourne, R., Farmelo, G., Scanlon, E. and Ashby, A. (1998) *A Vision of Accessibility.* S804 CD Rom, Open University.

Entwistle, A. and Entwistle, N. (1992) 'Experiences of understanding when revising for degree examinations', *Learning and Instruction* 2(1): 1–22.

Gregory, J. and Miller, S. (1998) *Science in Public.* New York and London: Plenum Press.

Hartman, J. (1997) 'The popularisation of science through citizen volunteers', *Public Understanding of Science* 6: 69–86.

Irwin, A. and Wynne, B. (ed.) (1996) *Misunderstanding Science.* Cambridge: Cambridge University Press

Kaye, A. and Pentz, M. (1974) 'Integrating multi-media systems for science education which achieve a wide territorial coverage', in *New Trends in the Utilisation of Educational Technology for Science Education.* Paris: UNESCO Press.

Koslow, S. H. and Huerta, M. (2000) *Electronic Collaboration in Science.* Hillsdale, NJ: Lawrence Erlbaum Associates.

Krol, E. (1994) *The Whole Internet: Users Guide and Catalogue.* Sebastopol, CA: O'Reilly and Associated.

Levinson, R. and Thomas, J. (1997) *Science Today: Problem or Crisis?* London: Routledge.

Lockwood, F. (1992) *Activities in Self Instructional Texts.* London: Kogan Page.

Lunneborg, P. (1994) *OU Women: Undoing Educational Obstacles.* London: Cassells.

McIntosh, N., Calder, A. and Swift, B. (1974) *A Degree of Difference: a Study of the First Years' Intake of Students to the Open University of the United Kingdom*. London: Society for Research into Higher Education.

Moss, G. D. and Brewer, A. (1981) 'The contribution of the Open University to innovation in higher education', *Higher Education* 10: 141–151.

Papert, S. (1980) *Mindstorms: Children, Computers and Powerful Ideas*. New York: Basic Books.

Pentz, M. (1988) *It can't be done! a personal view and critical appraisal of science teaching at the Open University*, The second Ritchie Calder Lecture. London: The Royal Institution (unpublished).

Perry, W. (1976) *Open University: a Personal Account by the First Vice Chancellor*. Milton Keynes: Open University Press.

Preece, J. (1999) 'Empathic communities: balancing emotional and factual communication', *Interacting with Computers* 12: 63–77.

Radcliffe, J. (1990) 'Television and distance education in Europe: current roles and future trends', in A. W. Bates (ed.) *Media and Technology in European Distance Education*. Milton Keynes: EADTU, Open University.

Rose, H. (1997) *Science Wars*, in R. Levinson and J. Thomas (eds) *Science Today: Problem or Crisis?* London: Routledge.

Ross, S. and Scanlon, E. (1991) 'Physicists all: Are Open University graduates different?', *Open Learning* 6(2): 3–11.

Ross, S. and Scanlon, E. (1995) *Open Science: the Distance Teaching and Open Learning of Science Subjects*. London: Paul Chapman Publishing.

Rzepa, H. (1996) 'Science and the Internet: the world wide web', *Science Progress* 79(2): 97–118.

Scanlon, E. (1997) 'Learning science on-line', *Studies in Science Education* 30: 57–92.

Taylor, J. (1992) 'DIVA 93 Final report on the drop-in viewing audience survey', *Programme on Learner Use of Media report no 40*, Open University internal document, Milton Keynes.

Taylor, J. (1997) Open.saturday: Audience Research, *Programme on Learner Use of Media no. 84*. Milton Keynes: Open University.

Wolf, W. (1996) 'Science and the Internet', *Science and the Future, Britannica Year Book*, 34–39.

Woodley, A. (1996) Access to what? a study of mature graduate outcomes. Student Research Centre Report, Institute of Educational Technology, Open University.

Woodley, A. (1997) 'Early results form the 1996 Graduate survey'. Student Research Centre Report No 118, Open University internal report.

Yarnell, L. and Kafai, Y. (1996) *Issues in project based science activities: children's constructions of ocean software games*. Paper presented at American Educational Research Association Annual Meeting, New York.

Ziman, J. (1986) Science education for whom? in J. E. Brown, A. Cooper, T. Horton, F. Toates and D. Zeldin (eds) *Science in Schools*. Buckingham: Open University Press.

Chapter 14

Learning through project work at the University of Roskilde

Albert Paulsen

Introduction

This chapter describes the development of new learning procedures designed to encourage autonomy in learning. This scheme arose during a time of political unrest and has been surrounded by public controversy ever since. Autodidactism has often been thought of as a private and individualistic activity, but here it flourishes in the context of group project work, and within a semi-residential setting.

The University of Roskilde was founded in 1970 and studies began there in 1972. The 1960s had been a time of acute student unrest which was felt across Europe and provoked violent street demonstrations in several countries, particularly France and Germany. New universities had been built in the immediate post-war period but the demand for places from increasing numbers of would-be students was difficult to satisfy. This situation was further complicated by government promises to provide university education for all returning soldiers who wanted it. At first this produced a struggle for places which, in the UK, just fuelled a high level of competition for entry. But the real challenge was to provide what would be relevant to the much broader interests of the students now entering them. There was also an argument that study, and its outcomes, should better match what industry demanded – more flexibility of approach (see Chapter 7) – as well as problem-solving. In most countries the students who did gain entry to higher education found themselves in overcrowded or overspill classes where they were faced by exactly the same courses as had been held there for decades before the war. The student riots of 1968 had followed directly from this situation, a revolt against the kind of university education only suited to an old elite.

In Denmark there were strong educational traditions and aspirations dating from the first decades of the nineteenth century, concerning the purpose and structure of a 'folk high-school'. This is to be found in the voluminous writings of Nikolay Grundtvig, but how far his influence was directly invoked by those who planned the new curriculum for Roskilde

University is not clear (Illeris 1999). Grundtvig wrote about autonomy for the students which was to be exercised through a Student Council in an alternative kind of university – an academy – specially designed for the rural peasant youth. He wrote that knowledge should be relevant to the students instead of the dead classical languages, a 'living interaction' with knowledge, and of 'mutual education' as a free communication of ideas between students and teachers, with a stress on fellowship and a residential community. In his lifetime he never achieved his academy, however the more modest 'folk high-schools' in the spirit of Gundtvig's teaching did materialise, although not always approved by him in detail.

So when it seemed that a new kind of curriculum was required for a new University at Roskilde, to take the over-spill from Copenhagen, the outline of plans for student project work in groups lay ready to hand. In much the same way the Workers' Education Association and Higher National Diplomas (HND) in England had influenced planning for the UK Open University, in the sense that it was to be part-time and open access. The OU, as described in the previous chapter, was quite different from Roskilde in many ways but it too reflected the national educational traditions, being modestly radical at first, more concerned with winning confidence by establishing high academic standards. The OU began its first courses only one year earlier than Roskilde.

The idea of student directed project work was in place at the University of Roskilde from the first. Indeed the first proposal was that absolutely *all* studies should take the form of such projects, but the Ministry of Education was soon made aware of the concerns of the academic establishment about such a programme and a committee was set up to reform the proposed course structure so that only 50 per cent of the student studies were committed to project work. This kind of critical hostility from some quarters still dogs the University but, in spite of dramatic political turbulence in the seventies, the basic principles have been maintained. This has been questioned by politicians, the media, and with most hostility by groups in favour of traditional academic conventions and 'rigorous standards' – a phrase that is not unfamiliar in Britain! In 1976 the Danish parliament rejected a motion to close down Roskilde University by a majority of only one vote, while thousands of students were demonstrating noisily on the streets outside in its defence! However now, some twenty-five years later, there is such pressure from students wanting to enrol that it has become necessary to introduce rules for restricted admission (Legge 1997).

Those original ideas about autonomy and group work are still in place. Nevertheless it was not enough to stipulate that students should spend half their time on self-chosen projects, and to carry them out in auto-didactic groups. All sorts of difficulties were bound to arise, and they did.

It became the tutors' task to guide students through the several phases of the work. These guiding ideas can be summed up under seven headings:

- Formation of groups around topics (about 5–7 students to a group)
- The formulation of the problem
- Planning and writing up a report
- Collaboration and how to deal with conflicts within the group
- Student autonomy and the role of the tutor
- Evaluation and examination, and
- Competencies, academic recognition, and promotion of the type of study.

The study structure

The university offers two years of basic studies in the natural sciences, humanities, or social sciences. During these four semesters of study the students have to pass in four projects and eight courses. In the natural sciences there is a great variety of courses from which to choose, amounting to about thirty in science and related areas. However the choice of discipline restricts student choice during the basic study period in the first year. A further one year of study of one or two academic disciplines will qualify for a bachelor degree and two years of further study will then qualify for a Masters degree in either one or two disciplines.

The study environment

Project work was quite literally built into the university in recognition of the importance of the study environment. Besides normal resources like access to books and journals in libraries, and access to laboratories and computer-facilities, the students study and live in the houses. Each one is for about 100 students and consists of a number of group-rooms, offices for tutors, a secretary and facilities for photocopying. A politician and strong opponent of the project method once said in parliament: 'We will never get rid of project work at Roskilde University. They have built it in concrete'. The bachelor and master degree courses have houses of their own.

The project

The content of a project is confined to an obligatory framework within which the students have to commit themselves to a problem they want to investigate. (An example of a framework for degree studies in physics might be epistemology and history of physics.)

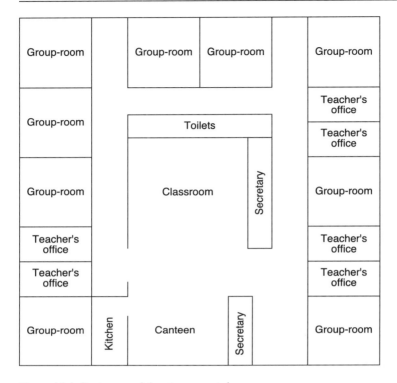

Figure 14.1 Project work 'set in concrete'.

Problem orientation serves as a guideline for the investigation, and sets the criteria for what is relevant and important for the project. This formulation of the problem is the most important part of the process because it provides a focus for the work.

Participant direction means that the students themselves are responsible for all the important decisions in the qualification process – assessment and interim discussion.

Interdisciplinary work is a complex issue but we are sure that that it is impossible to work on projects about authentic and controversial problems without a pluralist approach.

The study has to be exemplary for academic qualifications and for disciplinary content. Exemplary content is vital for avoiding complete subjectivism in project assessment.

It has to be borne in mind that these are not genuine research projects, but projects in an educational setting. Aspects of the learning are bound to be 'personal and hence a source of motivation' (Illeris 1999) but without some foundation in objectivity the educational content of the project will be lost. In more recent discussions about this the tutors are using terms like 'authenticity and apprenticeship' to show that they are encouraging the students to prepare for real life problems which will have more complexity and reality. These terms, which were not in the educational vocabulary in the 1960s and the beginning of the 1970s, are now in much wider use thanks to the work of general educators like Rogoff and Lave (1984).

Working in groups requires complex skills with wide psychological implications. The tutors believe that learning is a largely social enterprise, and that group work is closely connected with commitment, responsibility, and hence with quality. The exchange of ideas, the encouragement to express ideas in words and writing, and hence the urge to understand and reflect in depth may be some of the most important features of working in groups. A great deal depends on how the students deal with group-work, and how it is guided by the tutor.

What makes a good project?

Project work may be considered as an enculturation process where students progressively develop more independence and autonomy. Although students have autonomy and responsibility from the first semester at the university, they still have many other group skills to develop. When they come to the Bachelor and Masters studies the university with all its facilities, including the tutors and researchers, simply act as resources for the students' independent study. By this stage it is essential that all the project working skills are firmly in place.

A tutor who was recently questioned as to what makes a good project replied: 'good routines and good tutors' (Illeris 1999: 31). The routines or phases of project work can be explained in terms of student autonomy, the role of the tutor and the procedures for evaluation. A moment's reflection shows that there are ample opportunities for any one of these factors to militate against the others, so a discussion of all aspects of project work, as a kind of enculturation process, is essential. Although the tutors work very closely together and agree about the overall objectives, there are still some differences between them in the conception of project work. What follows are the author's own interpretations and experiences.

Project routine phase I: Problem formulation

Each project has a topical or thematic framework fixed to the semester. For example, in the Basic Studies for the Natural Sciences these themes are:

- Science in Society
- Theory and Modelling

Table 14.1 A short overview of the routines and roles of students and tutors in phase 1.

Routines phase 1	Student	Tutor
Introduction to the obligatory theme	Acceptance of the thematic framework	Offering explanations of the objectives and the thematic framework.
Topic for projects Formation of groups	Self-chosen by the group within the thematic framework	Offering advice and acceptance of the topic. Asking for the diary/logbook and an agenda for every meeting.
Formulation of the problem	Formulated independently by the group within the topic	Tutoring for focus and for formulation (and reformulation) of the problem. Final acceptance of the formulation.

- Communication of Science
- Theme of own choice

Programmes for the Masters degree have rather more discipline-related themes.

There are three types of activity for preparing the students for their important project choice. First, at the beginning of a semester the teachers, who are mostly academic staff with research and teaching responsibilities, give an introductory lecture on the theme. Second, the older students will give examples of relevant projects that they have done in their first year. Third, the students go on visits to relevant institutions and industries.

During this first phase, which lasts 2–3 weeks, topics and problems are announced by the students and the tutors and usually pinned up on a notice-board which is called 'The Marketplace'. This is an important moment. The students can sign up and join groups of fellow students with the same interests. They hold provisional group meetings and consultations with the tutors, and literature – journals, experts and other sources of information – are consulted. All this happens before the group is finally established and has reached an agreement about the project topic.

Plenary meetings finally settle the groups for their work, which includes an agreement about how many groups there should be, the projects to be addressed and the allocation of the teachers. This is not an easy process. It is important that the students' interests and teachers' expertise coincide. The final decisions and responsibility rest unequivocally with the students. In this way student autonomy is exercised in the context of original decision-making.

Table 14.2 A short overview of the routines and the roles in phase 2.

Routine phase 2	Student	Tutor
Planning	Independent group work	Offering advice for structure, provisional content and timetable for the work.
Internal evaluation (halfway evaluation)	Independently planned by the group in collaboration with an opponent group. Read and evaluate the work of an opponent group	Read and evaluate the work of an opponent group.
Evaluation of group work and of the group	Participate, collaborate and contribute individually	Participate on equal level in group evaluation but also offer advice and suggestions for solutions to conflicts.

A logbook is set up where every meeting and every activity is recorded. The first task of the group is to formulate the problem and focus on it. The formulation is often only provisional at the beginning and has to be refined as the students go deeper into the topic. A final formulation is important for the focus of the project, and during this phase the exemplarity – the suitability of the proposed topic for academic qualification and for disciplinary content – is an important issue. Despite the norm of student autonomy the teacher always carries a measure of responsibility for the complete programme; thus although the students' personal interests are important the central idea is that they should coincide with the overall educational objectives and exemplary content (Christiansen 1999).

Project routine phase 2: planning, evaluation and conflict!

The group present their project and receive critical feedback and advice for future work from the other group of peers and their teacher. The idea is that students should evaluate students and so learn from each other.

Another kind of evaluation – the group evaluation – is held whenever necessary, especially in the case of conflicts. The group meet with their tutor so that every student can express an opinion about their own efforts and those of the other members of the group. This is a very important part of the process. Without it there is a risk of unresolved conflict with consequent hidden agendas and defensive group processes. All of this could spoil the students' commitment.

Table 14.3 A short overview of the routines in phases 3 and 4

Routine	Student	Tutor
Phase 3: Theoretical and/or empirical work and investigations	Independently decided	Tutoring about the literature: investigative methods, research methodology and expertise from inside and outside the university. Reading drafts and giving advice about the structure of the report. Appreciating and evaluating the quality of work.
Phase 4: Writing up the report	Independently decided	Appreciating and evaluating quality. Last minute rescue actions.

Project routine phase 3: elaboration and compilation

The main part of this phase is the elaboration and clarification of the theoretical foundation and empirical work and investigations. This is where the tutor brings his or her expertise as a researcher into the project, offering methodological and theoretical advice. The interdisciplinary approaches of many projects will often demand expertise well beyond the expertise of the teacher, and in that case the student will need to

Table 14.4 The fifth phase of the project

Routine phase 5	Student	Tutor
Internal evaluation	Independently planned in collaboration with an opponent group. Read and evaluate the work of an opponent group	Read and evaluate the work of an opponent group
And/or group examination by an external examiner and the tutor (45 minutes per student in the group)	10–15 minutes presentation followed by a discussion of a topic given by the tutor 72 working hours before the examination. (Degree programmes: 10–15 minutes presentation of a self-chosen topic from the project followed by a discussion.	Scrutinising and discussing the project and give individual grades in agreement with the external examiner.
Final group evaluation of the tutor, the result and the process	To participate, collaborate and contribute	To participate, collaborate and contribute. Final approval of the project work of the individual students!

make arrangements with experts or laboratories in public or industrial institutions. Students following two subject programmes will need help for each subject.

Project routine phase 4: writing up the project report

Writing drafts of the project report is normally done concurrently by the group members, the final report will be edited to ensure a coherent approach. Last minute investigations and changes often make the final week rather hectic. Students may stay overnight at the campus to save travelling hours and work around the clock to finish before the deadline, which is appled mercilessly!

Project routine phase 5: internal and external evaluation and examination

At the end of the semester an internal evaluation is held, an 'opponent group' will be appointed for each group submitting. There will also be a final group evaluation, where each student will give an evaluation and express an opinion about the process, the result and their teacher. The teacher has to approve or reject the finished project for each individual student. This is a requirement if the individual student is to be allowed to participate in a final external examination. Then the teacher and the external examiner agree on the grade for each student.

Successes, fallacies, and problems

Since the 1980s Roskilde University has, somewhat reluctantly, been recognised as a bona fide university. The main reason for this is the success of its students in the labour market. The different competencies which employers wanted, and that the majority of Roskilde students exhibited, were:

- Cooperation and flexibility in teamwork
- Capacity to acquire new areas of knowledge
- Ability to work autonomously and study in depth
- Ability to express themselves orally and to write a report to time.

Students are also assessed according to traditional academic standards which are comparable with those who have studied at traditional universities (Niss 2000). They lack the breadth of knowledge within a discipline and the academic staff at Roskilde are continually discussing what constitutes an academic discipline, and what content would be considered satisfactory (Ulriksen 1999).

Reflections on autodidactism and group project work

The University of Roskilde stands apart as an institute of higher education committed to encouraging its students to be autonomous within a learning group. We would like to know much more about the motivations of those who have chosen to study at Roskilde University and to match them against those of other autodidacts. We have had examples of people who displayed a kind of creativity, or at least originality, in the search for new and effective ways of knowing.

The educationalists of Roskilde University are always aware of the novelty of their methods, possibly because they are made to suffer for it! Denmark is a country which allows for radical ideas but maintains the right to keep arguing about them. It is part of the culture of a small, but once large, nation which is prone to great social and democratic ideas. It is, for example, a country which spends more than any other in Europe per child on their schooling. What return do they get for 'the taxpayers' money' as British politicians and the tabloid papers tend to call it? They do not come first in the European section of the International Mathematics and Science tests (TIMSS) but they are often near the top in their adults' understanding of topical science.

The teachers of Roskilde feel that they are constantly being challenged, and much of what they write reflects the impact of this continual criticism. They are also aware that there is no single orthodox opinion about project work which is held by all the teachers. However they are clear, it seems, on two points – that their students were 'more political' in the 1970s and that at this time there were a greater number of political topics chosen for the projects. This is when Theodore Roszak famously wrote about politics and transcendence which was designed to encourage the young to resist all domination in what he saw as a post-industrial society (Roszak 1972). The Roskilde teachers feel that in those early days the university absorbed a greater number of mature autodidactic students who felt that they might not easily be able to accept the top-down lecturing and assessment regime that was common in the traditional universities.

In 1999 a book written on project studies at Roskilde was subtitled with Anthony Giddens' phrase 'late modernity' (Giddens 1990). He was referring to an accelerating increase of knowledge which he held responsible for a breakdown of rapport between the experts and the members of the public who had to take their knowledge on trust. In place of trust Giddens saw the development of a kind of protective identity which might help the public face down the power of the expert through the membership of a self-selected group, and the feeling of group identity that this provided. He wrote that 'tendencies towards dispersal (into groups) vie with those promoting integration' (Giddens 1991: 189). Now, a decade later, the staff at Roskilde see the same tendency in a new generation of students who are having difficulty in choosing projects with sufficient objectivity to satisfy the university's 'exemplification' objectives (Illeris 1999). The 'life politics' of single issue groups – animal rights, ecofeminism, protection of the environment, etc. – are often chosen by Roskilde's students, and developed along autodidactic lines.

At the same time industry calls for the skills of team-working, and students from Roskilde are certainly doing well in the employment stakes when compared with those from more conventional and individualistic courses. Meanwhile, for the teachers, the struggle to keep the objective aspects of project work as sharply defined as ever for these late modern students, may prove every bit as taxing as holding out against the forces of traditional academia in Denmark – a community for whom Roskilde's continuing experiment with project work forms an occasionally worrying but inspiring part.

References

Christiansen, F. V. (1999) 'Exemplarity and educational planning', in H. Oleson and J. Jensen (eds) *Project Studies – a Late Modern University Reform*. Roskilde: Roskilde University Press, 57–66.

Giddens, A. (1990) *The Consequences of Modernity*. Cambridge: Polity Press.

Giddens, A. (1991) *Modernity and Self-Identity*. Oxford: Polity Press.

Illeris, K. (1999) Project work in university studies, in H. Oleson and J. Jensen (eds) *Project Studies – a Late Modern University Reform*. Roskilde: Roskilde University Press, 25–32.

Legge, K. (1997) *Problem-orientated group project work at Roskilde*. Tekst 336. IMFUFA. University. Roskilde Universiteitscenter.

Niss, Mogens (2000) *University Mathematics based on problem oriented projects: 25 years of experience with the Roskilde Model*. In: *Tekst nr 389. IMFUFA*, Roskilde University.

Rogoff, B. and Lave, J. (eds) (1984) *Everyday Cognition: Its Development in Social Context*. Cambridge, Mass.: Harvard University Press.

Roszak, T. (1972) *Where the Wasteland Ends*. London: Faber & Faber.

Ulriksen, L. (1999) 'In the crossfire of tradition and modernisation', in H. Oleson and J. Jensen (eds) *Project Studies – a Late Modern University Reform*. Roskilde: Roskilde University Press, 136–150.

Chapter 15

A long life of learning

Jack Diamond

Uncued reflections during an interview with Lord Jack Diamond, Chief Secretary to the Treasury from 1964 to 1970, and after that a life peer and Leader of the SDP in the House of Lords. He was 94 years of age at the time of writing.

I was seven when the First World War broke out. A single Zeppelin came over Leeds where we lived and dropped some bombs somewhere or other, so everyone rushed around, and my mother sent me to a Jewish boarding school in Liverpool, because that was too far for a Zeppelin to reach, in theory! I was there for over a year; and it was a dreadful waste of time. When I went to the Grammar School back in Leeds they didn't even want to examine me because my elder brother had been such a brilliant scholar; they even put me into a form that was one year too high for me. But I had just come from this school where, for a year, I had learnt nothing at all and had forgotten most of what I already knew. After half a term they put me down into my own age group, and after that I did reasonably well.

I have no recollection of *not* enjoying my time at the Grammar School. I was beaten up the first day, of course, because I was a Jewish boy – that was inevitable in those days. There were the usual bullies in the class and three of them were waiting for me in the cloakroom. I bear no malice for that. If you were a Jewish boy you expected to get belted. That has changed ever since the influx of Asians and Caribbeans, who have taken the place of the Jews. And when, much later, I went to give out the prizes at my old school annual prize-giving, I found, instead of an endless line of Jewish boys coming up for the prizes, it was the Muslim boys now.

I had an extremely varied life at school. What I liked particularly was break in the middle of the morning when I would quickly take off my jacket and rush into the gym for a ten minutes work-out. But when I was about 15 years old I caught typhoid and was lucky to survive. Two of us in Leeds got typhoid and I was in hospital for three months. There was nothing the doctors could do except keep me flat on my back, and give me nothing to eat. Sadly the other boy died. It made a big break in my life in terms of thinking. I had lots of time to turn over in my mind what I had been learning.

I hadn't even been conscious of the pleasure of learning until I was well into the sixth form classics course. We were divided up when we went into the sixth form. Pupils went into Classics if they were thought suitable and lots went into either modern languages or science. I remember that ancient history was a subject I really liked, this was not so much for the wars and battles, as for the beginnings of ideas about philosophy and democracy.

I was always extremely busy in school being captain or vice-captain for a variety of sports. I also belonged to the debating society and the choral society and was the secretary of the Classics society for which I had to write up the minutes in Latin, which was probably very good for me. It had been assumed that I would go to university, and then become a solicitor so that I could feed briefs to my older brother who was a barrister. I did not object to this plan, even if I wasn't enthralled about it either. The one thing I had been looking forward to was seeing if I could beat the first-year Cambridge undergraduates in the 50 yards swimming races.

Then there came into my life one Joe Berger. He came over to talk to me, and I can still remember how thrilled I was to see him walk up the garden path. This was one of the occasions when the future seemed to open out. That has happened on two or three occasions in my life. I don't understand it, but each time I have known quite clearly that there was going to be a new turn in my life. We talked and it was soon decided that I would train to be a chartered accountant and be his articled clerk in London. This was a totally new idea. To go from being a classicist, with no interest whatsoever in mathematics, to becoming a chartered accountant was something I had never even considered. We talked and I was delighted – something told me 'This is your future!'

I didn't even finish my last term at school; I just went to London and began work. I had already passed 'the Matric' which was necessary to start, and then I had to work for the intermediate examination and then the final. We had to pass all the examinations and complete the necessary work experience with our employers. It was widely regarded as the toughest of all the professional qualifications; far more difficult, for example, than getting into the Bar. There was an enormous amount to learn, so the full five years of articles was necessary. I have always thought of it as the best possible introduction to the world of business, because we saw so many small and large firms from the inside, as we went round doing audits.

I was never critical about whether a course was good or bad. I just took the view that I had to learn it in order to pass the exams – it was going through a drill. I was a well disciplined person and knew that the exams had to be passed. At the same time I did realise that the accountancy part of it wasn't up my street. I had never much liked mathematics. I would certainly have been happier reading Sophocles, and it would also have been much easier for me.

The very day that my articles expired I said goodbye to the firm in the morning and started practice that very afternoon. I got a desk in the office of one of my brother's friends, and just had to wait for work to come in. Most of the first year was spent selling life insurance, but gradually clients came along, one introduced another, and soon it all built up. By the end of the first year I was earning enough to get married.

I learnt a lot during the five years of articles, but that was as nothing – *as nothing* – compared with what I learnt in just one year of practice. The questions I faced were quite different; now I was advising clients about important matters *on my own responsibility*. I already had a fair understanding of people which came, in part, from looking after the boys in my house at school. I had dealt with clients in a small way when I was an articled clerk, but now this was on quite a different level. They wanted my advice about what to do in their business, as well as working out their tax liability. That first year was very important, and the essential difference was the taking on of responsibility for what I was advising. It was an intensive learning experience, and from then onwards I just went on deepening my knowledge of business.

I am also quite sure that the vast amount of time I spent at the Boys' Club in the East End of London was an important part of my education. I had been helping those boys in important ways: taking them away from the corner lamp-post, and encouraging them to do sports and amateur dramatics. We joined with the local girls' club for drama, which was very popular, and we took the boys to camp once a year. I learnt an enormous amount from that, not consciously or deliberately but by expanding my understanding of boys from very different backgrounds – and, once more, through taking on new responsibilities.

About this time I took part in starting a local reading group. Victor Gollancz had the idea of setting up a number of groups all over the country where like-minded people could meet and discuss the social problems which were described in the books he had published. This was to become The Left Book Club. So I was reading these books about the practical problems of life and what was happening in the world. The group members did not necessarily belong to any political party; it was just an occasion for social learning, a group activity which encouraged us to learn from reading some of these rather tough books. Discussing in groups and exchanging views was new to me and I found it a very enjoyable way of learning.

By this time I had begun to realise that what I had been doing in the Boys' Club was dealing with effects, not causes, and that we must now move on and deal with causes. I was also influenced by a friend in the Labour Party who suddenly said to me one day while we were talking together, 'With your views, I don't know why you don't join the Labour Party!' I had always felt strongly about poverty and inequality in the distribution of the good things of life. So I joined the Labour Party – just like that – in 1933.

Throughout my life I have been given responsibilities because I was the only one prepared to do the work. So, in almost no time at all, I was made secretary of the local Labour Party and took part in its organisation. I never went to Spain during the Civil War, but I was keen enough to subject myself to the derision of passers-by by holding up a banner in the high street in Ruislip denouncing the evils of the Fascists!

Then, in the next local election, I stood for one of the wards. That was a learning experience – very much so – learning by experience, not learning out of a book. Practical politics begins with learning by doing, by getting up at street corners and talking to anyone who is prepared to listen. During the war I also learnt more about being a business man and a financial director, which is allied to, but not the same as, being a practising chartered accountant. Now I was taking really big decisions and running a large show that involved packing and transporting fighter aircraft for use in North Africa. During the war there was no time at all for reading, I was on Home Guard duties at least two nights a week. I don't remember taking part in any political activity during the war years.

At that time I was not yet thinking of going into Parliament. But then the chairman of a company I was asked to take over invited me to lunch at the House of Commons of which he was a member. We talked a lot, and at the end of the lunch I said to myself 'Well, if a bloody fool like that can be an MP, so can I!' It was a prompt to start learning about how politics works and how local authorities work, but for me it was emphatically *not* a prompt to enrol in any kind of academic learning.

As soon as the war came to an end I decided to stand for parliament. I had already begun preparing for the work of an MP by getting experience in local activities. I took on jobs like being on the Board of Governors of a boys' grammar school in the East End. There I found boys who were academically very good but had to leave school at the age of thirteen or fourteen because they needed to contribute to the family income. This was always on my mind, one of the motivating factors which drove me, and fed into my social thinking. Another way to learn how politics worked was to be on the Board of Governors of a large hospital, so I did that too. Most Labour MPs had come from being local councillors and I am not aware of anyone else having taken the same route as I did. But then I had left it very late for starting as an MP: I was already about 38, and so I had to learn fast, and the way I chose proved very valuable.

Most of the jobs I did in government were themselves learning experiences. I didn't know anywhere near enough economics for my work in the Treasury and I was aware of this all the time. I had learnt a little economics for my accountancy examinations, but I did *not* try to learn more from books: that would have been too theoretical for my taste. Somehow I have always wanted to get involved in the practical side of things. I knew very little about the Treasury, not too many people in the Labour Party did. In those days they tended to know a lot about the Trade Unions, and a lot knew about teaching, and some had been journalists. For a short time there was one other Chartered Accountant in the parliamentary Labour party, but he was very weak and didn't last long. Once you were in the House you fell into groups which studied this, or studied that. One such group was interested in finance: I became a member of that group and made some very good friends there, including Hugh Gaitskell. I was also doing a lot of committee work. In the early days of being an MP I still had to look after my practice and to see clients in the House of Commons because there wasn't enough time to get away for meetings. The pressure in government was fantastic. You had to limit your sleeping to five-and-a-half hours a night and your sit-down meals to two, because there simply was not enough time for three meals, so a sandwich had to do.

After I had lost my seat and had gone into the House of Lords I was given more jobs to do, like leading on one of the major bills for our side in the House of Lords – that was the Trades Union bill. And then I was Chairman of the Royal Commission, which took a lot of time. Even the Thatcher governments were very keen on me being Chairman of Committees. Of course, I learnt from all these jobs, and I had masses of papers to read, so I had to become a very quick reader. There was no difficulty in acquainting myself with what the papers were saying and in recollecting the important parts, which I would need in order to chair the committee effectively.

After the demise of the SDP which I had been leading in the House of Lords, when I was well into my seventies, I found I had a little more time, and I started in on a brand new kind of learning project. The thing which concerns politicians most, and also interested me enormously was 'What was it that moved people most . . . moved opinions most, and indeed moved feelings most, and from them went on to actions?' You need to understand that the main work of a politician is persuasion, altering people's opinions, and moving them towards what you believe they ought to think. And it's one hell of a job. People have their own thoughts, they have been brought up on those, and so to move a large body of public opinion one way or another is a gigantic task.

There was no doubt in my mind about the answer to those questions: what most moved the thinking, feelings and actions of people was the major religions. That meant that I should have to embark on reading the Old Testament and the New Testament (the Koran came much later). By this time I had already gone back to an interest in reading the classics: I was reading some Latin and some Greek, and enjoying it enormously. I liked the challenge and was learning in a different way from how one reads classics in school, when the master told us what to do and what to think. Now I formed my own thoughts, I was very much an autodidactic learner; nobody was guiding me at all.

I first read the *Odyssey* which seemed very good, and then I read the *Iliad*. To this day I can never understand why people put the two together. One is a marvellous story and the other is very second rate. The way the *Odyssey* is told and the way the two themes of the story, the travel adventures and the home circumstances, were brought together in wonderful climax at the end, that was beautiful storytelling – beautiful! And all this business in the *Iliad* about Hector being bad tempered and sulking in his tent, did not entertain me at all.

So I decided to begin by reading the books which had motivated people far more effectively than any political speeches: that was the texts of their respective faiths. I had never given up my personal faith in Judaism, and the older I got the more conscious I became of being a Jew. I regarded myself as being fortunate to have inherited the genes of this ancient race.

To do that learning properly I thought I should read these books in the original language; that was the kind of challenge I enjoyed. But Hebrew was nothing like as easy for me to read as Greek. I could manage that reasonably well. There was no problem with the alphabet; Greek is an Indo-European language related to English so there is always something familiar about it. Hebrew isn't the same at all. It was like being thrown into an entirely different world. I worked regularly at it – a little every day – and very gradually this began to show me how the persuasion of the Old Testament worked. Then I stupidly let some people know what I was doing. By this time I had read the whole of the New Testament and the five books of Moses. I finished up with an enormous respect for Jewish learning and Jewish writing. The people who knew what I was doing all said 'Well the next thing you have got to do is to read the *Koran*'. So that came next. Understanding ancient Arabic and reading the *Koran* proved next to impossible, but my motive was always the same – to find out how religious texts persuade people.

All my life I have been working with people, from being a prefect at school, to running the Boys' Club in the East End of London, and being a chartered accountant and advising clients about problems. I was always working with people and trying to find out what motivated them. Usually I did that directly while being with them, but this time I was doing it indirectly through books. Nevertheless it was, for me, a very successful exploit. It taught me more about where people stand, even about Muslim attitudes, than I could possibly have realised – their history and their writing. Even my own heritage in Judaism I understood better. Reading the Old Testament in Hebrew was slow going, but it gave me time to realise what was going on and to think it over. It filled in great blanks in my knowledge and I finished with an enormous respect for the Old Testament. I also understood Christianity better for having read the New Testament, and I found something inherently Jewish in that too. I came to regard the Christians as a Jewish group who had the good fortune to have someone who wrote about it all, a chap called Paul. Otherwise I don't think Christianity would have developed very far. Paul formed groups in various places to promote the good work. Perhaps what Paul's epistles did for the early Christians, was similar to what the group discussions in the Left Book Club had once done for me.

No, I haven't finished reading the *Koran* yet, but I am making progress.

Chapter 16

Common features

Joan Solomon

Putting together ideas from the previous fifteen chapters which were written by those who knew from first hand experience, something valuable about autodidactism, has been an absorbing and often surprising exploration. I did not begin by speaking to the other authors about what I thought of the general topic, and even the complete title of this book was unknown until long after all the writing was finished. My understanding of the topic grew partly from my own experiences, but much more from reading and rereading their chapters, and trying to see patterns in them. The point of this whole procedure was to ensure that we did not engage in a semantic wrangle about the meanings of terms, or of chickens and eggs. Autodidactism is not a very graceful word at the best of times, and the contributors were all wise enough not to labour over producing yet more definitions of it when the real need was to show it in action. 'Showing' is a useful word, borrowed from the ancient art of rhetoric which abandoned logic and depended instead on the telling of stories (Billig 1987) for the purposes of persuasion – trying to get others to see things as you yourself do, as Jack Diamond remarked in the last chapter. Rhetoricians regard the logical approach as far more domineering and invasive than their own. For them rhetoric can be symbolised as an open hand, while logic is represented as an implacable tub-thumping closed fist which makes discussion almost impossible. Meanwhile the working definition provided at the beginning of Chapter 1 – of autodidacts as people who would rather not be taught, but do enjoy learning for themselves – will do us well enough.

So the authors have described people they knew, told stories about their own or other people's learning, and made useful comments from different points of view. Stories may not *prove* much, to use a non-postmodern word, but they do provide other advantages which may well be more valuable. Stories about one's experiences communicate far more than definitions do, and there is a good reason for this. Telling a story has the function of a narrative and, as the Soviet linguist Mihkael Bakhtin (1976) argued, narrative is essentially dialogical. This means that the language has to be expressive enough to seem to be directed towards the reader quite personally as part of an exchange of views, even a conversation. That sets the tone of the narrative some way along the path towards real dialogue, even if there can be no direct response from the reader. Out of these dialogues or stories some common features may emerge, although rather uncertainly and to different extents. We might expect variation because our quarry, the autodidacts, are most unlikely to be just one kind of people. In effect, as was commented in several chapters, we are all likely to possess some autodidactic features to some extent, and at some time in our lives.

In this chapter the common features will be collected together under four general headings.

- The emotions connected with learning
- Environmental effects
- The future perspective, and
- Space for independence and autonomy.

We might not have expected so much commonality. Even the vivid emotions involved, which were the first to strike me, did not seem to sit very easily with learning of any kind. Sometimes the common features of the autodidacts were just a display of enjoyment or exhilaration in learning, but at other times the emotional features could be anger, humour or distress. In some cases it seemed as if the environment itself was exerting an influence on the learners, encouraging the development of local skills which were at a far remove from any sort of aesthetic reaction. We shall also pick out some cases, in adult education, where this intense kind of learning is directed by what seems to be a personal mission to improve the world. Finally we shall begin the process of sorting out aspects of independence and autonomy which turn out to be both theoretical and diagrammatic, and yet readily understood.

Any theoretical explanations of these common features, which may be tentative and difficult, as well as explanations that are subject to fierce ongoing debate, will be left to the last chapter. Common features first.

The emotions connected with learning

In the first two chapters of this book, we were told that it was not just a question of autodidacts being those who were untaught because instruction was not available to them. In Boden's words autodidacts can be 'defiant' people, those who dislike, or sometimes even 'hate being taught,' as one recently told me, with attitude. In spite of this they want, sometimes very much, to learn.

Not all autodidacts display anger, sometimes the emotion is humour, as in Chapter 11, or pure elation. The chemist Humphrey Davy, it is reported, was so thrilled when he saw the first globules of potassium glistening in his electrolysis cell just as he had planned and hoped, that he literally danced round the laboratory and no one could get a word of sense out of him for a full half hour! One feature that these emotions – anger, humour and elation – have in common is that they all encourage the release of adrenaline, arguably the most precious and energy-extravagant hormone in our bodies. Its function is to enable us to withstand both immediate crises and also long term stress, by stimulating the whole of our sympathetic nervous system. We have been told about emotions that arise in the conflicts during project work in Roskilde University (Chapter 14), by returning learners at the Open University, in the impassioned letters written to museum curators, and overwhelmingly in the clients of genetic counsellors.

In the special schools of which Paul Howard writes in Chapter 4, pupils are said to have serious emotional and behavioural difficulties, and indeed it is their strong emotional reactions to being taught and usually against their teachers, which are often given as the reason for their potentially damaging exclusion from mainstream schooling. But to accept this, as Paul Howard cleverly tricks us into doing at the start, could be to stand deceived by our own labels. We may, and probably all do, behave this way at times. Howard warns us that if we treat autodidacts, or any other group of pupils, as a minority group with problems, we deny the essential value of their emotions and reject any similarity between them and us. In my experience previously troublesome and violent pupils quite regularly become almost model citizens once they have left school and gone out to work. They may simply but urgently have been calling for another kind of learning, probably arising from experience in another environment. Howard's quotations from the ancient writings of Lao-tse, such as, – 'If I keep from imposing on people, they become themselves' – highlight a dangerously muddled territory of cause and effect.

There are two chapters about children at play. None of the youngsters involved had any obvious behavioural difficulties. In Chapter 3 most of them move confidently towards their goal while playing in a non-directive Interactive Science Centre without written instructions. In Chapter 5 Robin Hodgkin's account is of two brothers avoiding family investigations which were 'too systematic' for them, and making instead a complicated game out of dripped-sand structures on the beach. Here the heightened emotion is a reaction to the threat of danger: the tide will soon come crashing down upon their artefacts and flush them away. That would be enough to produce a raised level of adrenaline which they might relish. Some people, like rock-climbers or bunjee jumpers, can become seriously addicted to this release of adrenaline. (One of these two boys playing on the beach was to become a mountaineer world-famous for his skill and courage.)

In Chapter 3 Aeron was the young boy at the Interactive Science Centre who reacted almost explosively to one of the shadows formed which turned out to be yellow, when the coloured lights producing it were red, green and blue. 'That's crazy!' he said. It disturbed his equilibrium (affective or cognitive, can we distinguish between them?) that such effects could take place at all. Questioning the 'sense' of what we observe in terms of causes and possible effects is the important first step towards investigation (see Figure 3.1 on page 38). Even a week later, now back at his own school talking to the researcher from the Centre, Aeron could hardly stem his stream of suggested explanations which, he seemed to be hoping, might return a topsy-turvy world to rights.

Arousal, energy, and boredom

Although we are not rich in theories of motivation that can be directly applied to human learning, the psychologist Berlyne (1960) developed a now well established descriptive account of the general arousal of interest and curiosity. His measurements of babies' reactions, based on the rate of sucking on a teat, or infant eye movements, yielded an 'arousal curve' which is illustrated in Figure 16.1. This can be seen either as a simple graphical description of arousal followed by a decline of interest, or as the operation of a safety device designed to prevent too great and damaging a flow of energy into the fragile brain. There is no arousal if the stimulus seems too complex, since complications for their own sake are not enjoyed by any of us and, perhaps, it becomes important to economise on the release of that potentially dangerous drug, adrenaline.

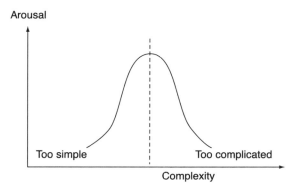

Figure 16.1 Arousel related to comprehension

On the other hand, 'Boring!' is the whingeing cry of the adolescent school student; older ones are more restrained but may feel much the same. It is also a reason commonly given by autodidacts for disliking being taught at all. Why should boredom be such a strong switch-off?

Berlyne conducted a wide range of experiments to pursue this question. The best known of these were on the effects produced by sensory deprivation, using student volunteers. He found that, despite how well he paid them, very few could bear to continue beyond one or two days in the non-arousal state of uniform diffused light, and no fluctuation of sound or temperature, however comfortable they might seem to be. They were experiencing none of the common modes of excitation – perceptual, cognitive or emotional – which seem to be essential in order to avoid what we call boredom. In another set of experiments Berlyne was able to locate an arousal region in the brain of a cat that could inhibit the functioning of the parasympathetic nervous system which controls our internal organs, unless it was stimulated to act normally by some adrenaline in the blood stream. Perhaps being unable to tolerate the absence of any sensory stimulation is a normal reaction due to abnormally low levels of adrenaline. Total boredom can be seriously bad for us.

The practical problem here is that what is a useful level of arousal for some pupils could be courting classroom chaos for others. We humans have varied reactions to adrenaline, because we all learn differently, as Paul Howard argued in Chapter 4.

A mixture of emotions, perceptions and cognition

What we need for thinking about the learning of autodidacts, and so for all learning, is an approach that allows the cognitive, perceptual and emotional to act together. Chapter 6 on genetic counselling is particularly valuable here. During the attempts of Brazilian doctors and researchers to lay down clear rules for trainee genetic counsellors on how to separate cognitive learning (providing knowledge of genetic probabilities) from the affective (comforting their clients and helping with practical advice), they found themselves faced by continual problems and defeats. It seemed that the affective and cognitive could not be kept apart. They had hoped to deal with one – the cognitive instruction – first, and then with the affective. However they found that emotions blocked out understanding of the genetic information.

Trying to explain how perception is tied to cognition has been made much simpler by the illustrations and explanations provided by Richard Gregory (1970, 1998). In addition to the illusionary drawings, like those that Hanson used (Chapter 6) Gregory shows from experiments, like those performed with inverting spectacles, that what we see is not simply a magnification of the retinal image, but a clever eye-and-brain joint interpretation of it. Thus after a few days of wearing such spectacles the subject sees the world the right way up again, only to see it inverted again for a few days when the glasses are finally removed. So perception includes, or is included by, cognition.

In Chapter 6 we read a short introduction to Tulving's three ways of remembering. The *semantic memory* relies on remembered abstract conceptual words that need to be applied in a new context. *Procedural memory* is remembered non-verbally in our bodies where it was first practised. Tulving's special new contribution was *episodic memory*. This is the familiar way in which we recall a whole incident complete with perceptions (including smells), cognition (if we were learning or experiencing) and emotional reactions which make up motivation (horror, delight, curiosity, etc.). Indeed it is often the case that only one of these needs to be retrieved from memory for the whole episode to be vividly recalled. An example might help. As I returned from school as a teenager on the London Underground I used to read up for my homework (was it always geography?), and the train had often reached Royal Oak station before I finally capitulated to hunger and faced the stale cheese sandwiches of those pre-cling film days. Now, if I ever go past Royal Oak station, I can recall the smell/taste of strong and hardened cheddar, as well as fragmentary maps of British coal fields, all triggered by a visual image of that dingy unchanged station. Emotion, perception and cognition seem to be linked together in our fluent complex brains.

Looked at in another way we may see that emotion and cognition are, after all, not so very different. As the philosopher Mary Midgley wrote, the heart, which some see as the seat of all emotion, seeks out what is 'the core of concern', while the mind, which may be the centre of cognition, thinks out possible reactions to it and begins to devise strategies. Together they make a very powerful collaborative system, ready to struggle with difficult ethical issues and providing a rich variety of feedback which can keep us informed when one kind of reaction gets out of step with another.

Susanne Langer may have been the first philosopher to discuss feeling as well as thinking in the context of learning. To her, feelings were similar to thoughts in that they were able to bring about powerful transformations of meanings. What before was just moderately interesting may become frightening. This was also one of the words that Boden used in discussing creativity in Chapter 2. The transformation of meanings lies at the very heart of creativity, of new thinking and so also of learning. If the process takes place through the medium of words it will be immersed in thinking and talking and so be discursive; if through music or art it will be non-discursive intelligence, but both forms, Langer insists, can equally well transform our feelings. A rather trivial example of this is the way in which a Gestalt switch in perception can make us believe that the drawing of a rabbit has become that of a stork without any 'real' change in it.

> Every object that emerges into the focus of attention has meaning beyond the 'fact' which it figures. It serves by turns, and sometimes even at once, for insight and theory and behaviour . . . that means that we respond to every new datum with *a complex of mental functions*. Our perception organises it, *non-discursive intelligence, reading emotive import into the concrete form*, meets it with purely sensitive appreciation; and even more promptly, the language habit . . . gives it a place in *discursive thought*.
>
> (Langer 1942: 285, original emphasis)

We shall return to this cluster of issues in the final chapter.

Effects of the environment

This feature could be related to the one before if the environment lends emotion to the memory of some episode, but it will be more useful to concentrate on the nature of a direct learning link to the environment. Some people who have a special delight in learning choose their learning environments with great care – the shed, the study, the woods. Tim Hunkin's complaint, while still a student engineer in training, was about being taught only what could be learnt while sitting still in a classroom, and the need he felt to be in a workshop. The illustrations he provided for this book, and others he has published, seem to confirm a two-way connection with the environment. His arresting picture of a giant android made from discarded electronic equipment set in waste land, which towers over him, effectively creates an argument about human effects on our environment. Learning environments can also be specially created for particular kinds of learning.

There have been several other examples of this. For example, we can see in Chapter 14 (Figure 14.1) how the founders of the university at Roskilde set their ideas about learning through group project work into the concrete fabric of the rooms where the learning projects were to be carried out. It was a special group learning environment. Or we could look to the boys at play on the beach who crouched down to bring their perspective to the same level as the sand architecture they were creating so that they could themselves take part in the environment.

We also know that modern museums work hard to create an environment which will be welcoming to visitors and, at the same time, stimulate them to learn. Paul Caro writes at the beginning of his impressive chapter (Chapter 10), 'Autodidactism is a very natural way of learning in a museum.' Some autodidacts may want to teach themselves at their own rate from the display, but others might need more coaxing and learn better from an exciting *mise-en-scène*. Caro seems to have more of a predilection for the solemn and historical, than for the jazzier 'son et lumière' complete with actions and actors. Clearly it is a matter of choice. Young visitors to the Natural History Museum in London seem to find the combination of its pseudo-Gothic hall with the reconstructed dinosaurs lifting their huge bony necks towards the distant ceiling, both awe-inspiring and wonderful. Caro complains from his wider perspective that any 'movement towards sensationalism' may do damage to the (adult) autodidactic effect.

Do we know how autodidacts respond to a constructed learning environment? Probably not, but we do have a suggestion from the work of Helen Brooke with young people having Down's Syndrome who visited our small Interactive Science Centre (see Chapter 3). There were no written instructions on the walls or labels. We just demonstrated how some of the simpler apparatus worked, and asked the youngsters to try to find out something for themselves – to 'make discoveries', 'like scientists do'. It was clearly a very new environment and a new experience for them: their teachers had told us that they expected their students to be too passive to respond to such demanding novelty. However even though we did not help them unless absolutely necessary, it seemed that they relished this freedom to make mistakes on their own. We quietly video-recorded the whole scene, and Brooke later analysed the students' behaviour every five minutes, to a tested code. She showed that significant gaps existed in the record of the students' patient and repeated attempts to learn from the equipment, and that these gaps almost always occurred when one of their teachers came over to help or instruct. Then the youngsters just looked out of the window and stopped trying until the teacher stopped speaking and left. There was no animosity between them and their teachers, just an understanding that the expectation of the learning environment was somehow being contravened. And when, at the end, we asked what they had 'discovered', all of them talked to us as best they could – with one simply pouring out loud babble and pointing because it was important, and she had not yet learned to speak.

There is another chapter of the book which describes how autodidacts respond to a quite different learning environment. That is in Anita Rampal's fascinating report on learning mathematics which begins with the methods and skills of Indian market women (in Chapter 12). From there she went on to describe a whole body of mathematical knowledge which was 'situated', a term used by Jean Lave (1988) in her study of mathematics in the supermarket. Here the mathematics was at work in some familiar part of the environment, and also used emotion, cognition and action.

Unlike most traditional cognitive theories that distance the learning mind from the learner's experience, situated learning does not separate thought, action and feeling. This not only makes it richer than the usually abstract school learning, but also provides the self-confidence that, as we have seen (Chapter 9), characterises this kind of knowing. Knowledge is always being constructed, retuned and transformed by autodidacts, as and when they need it for other processes.

To illustrate this Rampal begins by describing how an unschooled market trader teaches herself to multiply and divide using only the simplest addition and subtraction strategies, which she devises for herself to fit the problem. Then Rampal goes on to show how this mathematical autodidactism has penetrated into common rhythms, rhymes and riddles in different parts of India. Perhaps the most memorable way in which she shows the environmental impact of this old kind of mathematics is via its use of measurement. She explains that the realistic measurement of the area of a field cannot be additive in common-sense terms, because each piece of land may be of a slightly different quality. So a deeper familiarity with the environment is needed where the unit of measurement is the 'labour-time' required to work the soil and make it ready for sowing. Only then can the addition of pieces of a field be carried out with justice and the realism that such experiential knowledge always demands.

Living, dwelling and skill

To understand more about this connection between learning and the environment in which it takes place, we can go beyond the facile connections between environment and environmentalism, or between environment and primitive hunter-gatherers which most of us expect and remember from the work of anthropologists. Learning from the environment could have many goals. In Tim Ingold's (2000) perceptive book on this subject he explains why the objective is *not* learning to recognise the landscape or forming a map of any sort.

> Knowledge of the world is gained by moving around in it, exploring it, attending to it, ever alert to the signs by which it is revealed. Learning to see, then, is a matter not of acquiring schemata for mentally *constructing* the environment but of acquiring the skills for direct perceptual *engagement* with its constituents, human and non-human, animate and inanimate.
>
> (Ingold 2000: 55)

Ingold's phrases 'learning to see' and so 'acquiring skills' are reminiscent of informal experiential learning. For Ingold true 'dwelling' in an environment requires skills and perceptions which need to be learnt by being there. The examples we have given of environmental influences on learning could go some way towards matching Ingold's criteria. In most cases we can identify skills related to being in the environment. The two boys playing on the dangerous beach who have developed a language for describing their sand structures. The Indian women market traders, in Chapter 12, have taught themselves a mathematics which copes more directly than school learning with selling and giving change in the busy market. Even the young people with learning disabilities who used their own ways of learning through slow but important actions in the Inter-active Science Centre, are all dwelling to some extent in their learning environments.

Most of us now live in a concrete built-environment and learn to select food from the supermarket and commodities from a shopping arcade. Groups of Danish students at Roskilde University learn through group project work in buildings specially designed for this purpose. Nevertheless the concepts that Ingold develops still have explanatory power. Skilled living, dwelling, may involve reading the signs of unrest and avoiding violence in a troubled housing estate, just as much as reading different signs on the land does for native people living in the remote Australian outback.

Living does not always imply learning, but true dwelling makes possible a new sort of lived learning (see Chapter 1). Ingold claims that 'it is only because we live in an environment that we can think at all' (2000: 60). Places where we have been at home – Ingold calls this dwelling in an environment in a comforting, intimate sense – retain not just a good memory for us, but also a strong hold upon our perceptions of ourselves. The sociologist Anthony Giddens (1991) has an arresting phrase for the locality where the child first developed a sense of self identity separate from that of his or her carers. He calls it the 'archaic environment'. It might be a room, a house, or just the backyard to be explored on their own, and then remembered ever afterwards in their night-time dreams, or in their daytime plans for design and invention (Solomon 2000). At the end of Chapter 8 Stephen Lunn shows how the primary teacher and their class can form a learning community when together, in which they may share a common need for autonomy, engendered, at least in part, by walls embellished by the children's different pieces of imaginative work.

The future perspective

Planning one's learning, with an eye to the future, is probably more likely to be met in adults than in the young. Richard Edwards writes in Chapter 7 about choices of training and the kind of changes that adult workers might expect. He argues that the old kind of apprenticeship (the apprentices and the master) which was said to have given way to more autonomous lifelong learning where the workers choose their own learning courses, is now beginning to return. The continual threat of redundancy and dismissal focuses worker's eyes on preparing for more control over their future. In government jargon this might be called flexibility. At first it was seen by the government as a way to transform the training operation of firms and to provide the workers with chances to develop new skills. Now, sadly, there is another kind of flexibility in the working of firms, which translates into downsizing the workforce or putting parts of the work out to piecemeal tender.

Autodidactism has rarely been a part of the modern workplace. In earlier times it might have been a kind of learning by experience not unlike a loose form of apprenticeship. However, change comes so fast at the present time that from the impudent young hackers to the new generation of gifted programmers there are signs that the slow pace of traditional apprenticeship, with the gravely experienced master at its centre, are gone for ever. People would rather organise their own learning, as the scientists in Chapter 9 describe. In the tables of different approaches that Edwards usefully presents to us, it is made clear that more complex self-initiated learning could not easily have been started by the traditional methods of instruction. Learning can be both action-based and informal, and Edwards claims that those who succeed in learning from their own actions in this way 'are those most likely to adopt a lifelong autodidactic stance'. That would provide a valuable gift to the worker.

About the continuous informal learning which has always taken place in the workplace – the very kind which is said to produce the flexibility that employers and governments seem to want – Edwards warns that 'We may seek to harness and credentialise it, thereby undermining its informality and the powerful role such learning plays in peoples' lives' (page 83). Autonomy, with its promise of creative lifelong learning, cannot be commanded, as Boden (Chapter 2) would almost certainly agree, and its very existence is presently at stake. If workers feel that some other course of action may fulfil their plans for the future they might, for example, go into a training course in management hoping to open a business of their own, thereby building a more independent future. That would be unlikely to be supported by their employers.

Preparing for a life mission

The term 'life mission' has been examined recently by Kroth and Boverie (2000) to investigate how it impinges on adult learning. They claim that the sources of these purposeful missions can be spiritual or social, which makes them deeply personal and autonomous in a way that can also be illustrated by one of the teachers in Chapter 8. She was a primary teacher who claimed, in interview, that she had given up the job she loved as a pharmacology technician, to teach young children about caring for the environment.

> I felt if I could teach the next generation to put it right, to know what to do and at least to make them care so they do something about it, then I'd have perhaps put back a little bit of what my generation has done wrong. So I just sold everything, upped sticks and went. I did a four year BEd course and specialised in environmental science, and that's how I became a teacher.

In Chapter 15 the politician Lord Jack Diamond looks back to the time when he first thought of entering politics and provides a similar example. At the end it only needed a friend to trigger him with the comment 'With your views, I don't know why you don't join the Labour Party!' for him to act. Like the teacher quoted above he had a strong underlying motive, a life-mission. We can see this emerging in two stages – one a growing feeling of unease and the other a sudden personal decision for change, like the teacher.

> I had begun to realise that what I had been doing in the Boys' Club was dealing with effects, not causes, and that we must now move on and deal with causes . . . I had always felt strongly about poverty and inequality in the distribution of the good things of life. So I joined the Labour Party – just like that – in 1933.

Unlike the primary teacher, but similar to the scientists mentioned in Chapter 9, Diamond does not choose to enrol in any existing courses. He pursues his own path both as to the topics to be learnt and the method used. He goes straight into the social situation taking voluntary positions on the governing boards of a school in the East End and of a large hospital. Those are his learning places. The questions which this provokes is how and why people like these – the teacher, the politician and the scientists – were so sure about the direction in which they wanted to move, and also the learning method that they needed.

The scientists described in Chapter 9 were not really as free and autonomous as they seemed with respect to the direction of their research. When they had first entered on postgraduate studies, there was a moment (or even several) when they deliberated and exercised some choice about their research topic. Even here the shortage of funds is now so great that considerable pressure is often exerted to get promising students into a 'useful' line of research in terms of the laboratory's projected interests.

Yet, as Ziman points out:

> they are the sort of people who want to be in charge of what they do. They celebrate curiosity because it implies autonomy. It can only be exercised by someone who is free to look around them, reflect on what seems strange and inquire further into it. In other words by describing pure research as 'curiosity-driven' – even as 'unfettered' – they proclaim that it ought to be undertaken by researchers who formulate their own research problems and apply their own criteria to what counts as good science.
>
> (Ziman 2000: 23)

The scientists, even while still learning, mostly knew that they would be taking on a professional role. They would belong to a strong social system which only publishes their all-important papers if they conform to the appropriate norms of the community; and if the young scientists cannot publish they will sink. Yet there is another equally strong norm which insists that their work should be original. No wonder then that they have to be both self-confident and autonomous about learning any small extra skills, and yet also uncertain and rather fearful about changing their research field to another, even if they would find that one more interesting. There is plenty of anecdotal evidence that potential scientists know early what they want to be. It was probably while at school, or even earlier, that these potential scientists first felt the urge to take up science as a kind of life-mission.

Space for independence and autonomy

Space may mean, at one and the same time, a measurable volume of any size, and also an inviting largeness which may be empty. The cry for autonomy may be 'Give me space!' because the learner feels enclosed in a place, whether physical or metaphorical. In several of the chapters contributed to this book there are metaphors concerning space of some uncertain sort. Boden, writing about creativity, speaks of 'opening up new spaces' (Chapter 2). Then, in Chapter 5, we find a diagram by Hodgkin of what he calls 'potential space' which represents a region that is available to be explored by further learning encounters (see Figure 5.1, p. 59). The broad scope and nature of this metaphorical space is shown by Hodgkin's inclusion of toys, tools, language, music and social encounters.

It was to be expected that this general idea – gaining space, winning independence, or exerting autonomy – would emerge in most of the chapters, and so it did. It is, in one sense or another, the very kernel of autodidactism. The two words – independence and autonomy – are not quite the same in the context of learning. While being independent implies *not* being dependent on the authority of others, which would include teachers and regulations of many kinds, being autonomous means being free for the purpose of following one's own will. So while the first rejects the influence of other people, the second implies that the person has ideas or pathways that they wish to follow up. *Neither of these necessarily imply being solitary, or even working on one's own.* Both however are likely to reject any kind of compulsion in what they want to do, and this may well include teaching, although for a variety of reasons.

Kroth and Boverie name this second sort of learning – that we call autonomous, and which may exist in a private corner of any adults' life – emancipatory learning. It reminds us of the struggles to learn by members of the Chartist movement of the nineteenth century and all that followed from that into Third World education (Chapter 1). However autonomous learning is *not* synonymous with emancipatory learning, which is exclusively designed to regain and refurnish one's place in society by changing its social norms via a new political ideology. The Canadian philosopher Charles Taylor (1989) suggests that life-long autonomous learners are trying to answer questions like – 'What sort of person am I?' and 'What sort of person could I be?' that plague or tantalise us at every moment of choice. He then comments that 'We are only *ourselves* insofar as we move in a certain space of questions' bringing back the illusive but expressive space metaphor, which now describes a sort of freedom which, paradoxically, can itself be an implacable task-master.

Further questions relating to adult learning will be explored in the next chapter.

The autodidact in a group

Autonomous learners may sometimes find that social learning, in groups, can be very positive. Whereas the politician (Chapter 15) remarked how pleasant he found his first experience of social learning in the Left Book Club, both the Interactive Science Centre (Chapter 3) and the group project work at Roskilde University (Chapter 14) were found to be difficult and conflictual at times. A group may either be assembled to carry out a given task, or may gather together by happenstance, in some unselected environment, for observation, discussion or simply experience. In both cases the group members will need to talk together, taking turns, and performing all the routines necessary to a social situation. Collaborating at a young age requires a considerable measure of friendship if it is to succeed smoothly (see John and Grant at the Interactive Science Centre in Chapter 3). The situation is different if the task is strictly specified with each person having a role or specialism. That is what happens in collaborative groups and committees in business or politics, and they will usually run quite smoothly after practice, as the students at Roskilde came to learn. This is sometimes called working in teams, rather than just groups, to emphasise the differentiated specialised roles that the members usually take up.

People in groups are caught between two objectives: one is to help solve the problem, and the other is to maintain their 'social honour' in the eyes of the others, as the psychologist Rom Harré (1979) has put it. Can they join in the social exchanges to the extent of compromising their own values (cognitive or evaluative) in the name of collaboration, even if they are in disagreement with the others? For those who do not greatly care about the learning process or its outcome there is less difficulty. But for autodidacts whose values so prominently include learning to understand, the situation could even lead to break-up of the group.

This question, whether to compromise quietly or to engage in conflictual argument, is at the heart of the social problems with which Moscovici and Doise described in *Conflict and Consensus* (1992). The first author had previously established that a single 'plant' in the group, a person infiltrated into the group by the experimenters to take on an opposing view, can change the consensus to a surprising extent. On one occasion the plant suggested that one of two rods (of equal length) was clearly longer than the other. After a while almost all the members of the group began to show some agreement with him. It was only necessary that the minority influence be consistent, self-confident, and the focus of attention. Moscovici (1976) wrote that the explanation of this required an interactionist model of discussion rather than a static functional one.

> In the functionalist model minorities can have no influence . . . (but) 'interactionist' implies reciprocity of influence. . . . Deviance, which appeared as a disfunction in the previous (functionalist) model, can now contribute to social transformations.
>
> (1976: 107)

This shows group discussions as being naturally mobile affairs where all may have influence, although those who are most consistent and argumentative change more opinions. Some of the group work in Chapter 3 shows just this sort of interaction taking place, although it is reduced by the atmosphere of play which is voluntary, self initiated and, being without imposed objectives, provides an invaluable moratorium on failure.

Similarly Moscovici and Doise (1994) found that when a newcomer enters the group it is the intensity of his or her values which count most. There is, of course, a natural leaning towards agreement in the operation of any human group, but this could be produced either by compromise or by consensus. In practice:

the more one is personally involved, the less likely one is to change and act with others . . . extremist individuals who are generally more committed and more sure of their opinions stand firm on their position. Only moderate individuals, normally less involved and more uncertain, modify their opinion in order to draw closer to one another.

(Moscovici and Doise 1994: 103)

For our special topic this suggests that determined autonomous learners who find themselves in a group have a real chance to affect the final verdict, and that they may perceive this, and feel more comfortable and reassured than when subjected to the more remote teacher's unquestionable authority.

It sometimes seems that the need for autonomy grows stronger throughout life. We have several examples which suggest this from Scanlon's research into the students who enrol at the Open University, or to the varying reactions of Jack Diamond to learning at different phases in his life. In Chapter 8 we heard a teacher expressing a wish for professional autonomy which was not surprising, but to hear one admit that *despite enjoying science, I had a growing feeling of being "trapped"'*, is more interesting. He speaks about a time in the sixth form when he was always being told not to keep on asking questions. His subsequent defection from the teaching profession seems almost an inevitable outcome of his professionally heightened need for autonomy both for himself and for his students, especially in the present climate of teaching and testing to reach teacher imposed 'personal targets' (see the Epilogue on educational implications.)

This need for autonomy is sometimes associated with the release from the pressure of instruction which was discussed in Chapter 1 in relation to the research by Monique Boekarts. Hunkin's pictures in Chapter 11 have an impudence which seems specifically designed to protect his precious autonomy. His model of *The Nose-Picker* operated by a 2p coin, is an example of this will to do the things that he wants to, and he almost literally cocks a snook at the pretensions of the Fine Arts community. Later he found himself a more comfortable place in the community of the Useful Arts. For autodidacts working independently means keeping what attitude theorists call the locus of control well within their own hands. At the very least such learners want to be free to start or stop at will, which most school children may not do. Indeed, as pointed out in Chapter 1, within the field of school education, true independence rarely exists, and even autonomy – licence to follow up one's own ideas – is rare. But when it happens, autonomy makes the learner feel powerful. As one of the teachers in Chapter 8 remarked after taking a foundation-level evening class in catering, 'for the first time in my life' she felt 'like a leader'.

In Chapter 13 we hear the voice of a student at the Open University, who has learnt through taking a distance education course, and from that experience felt that she had gained the ability to follow up any of her life projects in the future. 'It's this precious tool of being able to go find out, that I never had . . . And now I know how to do it, . . . The OU has opened up every possibility.' The data Scanlon quotes shows more students giving 'sheer interest' for their entry into study, than for employment qualifications. Scanlon calls them 'self-regulated learners' because they have been taught the self-discipline required to find their way through distance education courses.

How does this relate to more autonomous learners who want to choose their method of learning as well as the topic? Scanlon reports in Chapter 13 that she is trying to help Open University students to go beyond the confines of self-regulation which is sometimes necessary for those who return to study under difficult conditions. The 'space of personal questions' about which Taylor wrote, demands an autonomous choice of learning, as well as a chance to express an independent voice of their own. Scanlon conveys some of the passion with which many students describe their experience of study, and she reports comments about being 'in charge of their own learning for the first time in their lives'. Some students, this argument suggests, after a previously rather disconnected and unhappy learning career at school, are only beginning to achieve a satisfying level of autonomy when adult.

Some people would jump on this sort of conclusion to renew their harsh criticism of schools and schooling. But this discussion of autodidactism opens up another line of thought. Students in a classroom have a range of arousal levels, toleration of boredom, and personal space of questions. Schools and their teachers 'are places where students learn and collectively struggle for . . . the social preconditions that make individual freedom and empowerment possible' as Giroux wrote in 1997. Where Bourdieu and Passeron (1977) and others have seen teachers as aggressive, oppressive or both, to Giroux they are, or can be, 'transformative intellectuals'. This picks up on both the term that Boden used to describe the highest category of creativity, and on the struggle for freedom that marks out the autodidact. Four of the five teachers in Chapter 8 are finding their way as best they can along the ambitious path towards transformation. One comments that she has taken to heart the belief that 'education is not the filling of a pail, but the lighting of a fire'. She sees her mission as finding and igniting this within every child, a metaphor that links with having space and scope.

Dionysian or Apollonian?

The frequently emotional, strongly autonomous, passionate, and future-orientated features of the autodidactic's approach to learning might perhaps be called Dionysian after the Greek god of ecstasy. That is opposed to the more sober, disciplined learning in the here of the classroom and the now of the present, sometimes including the qualifications needed for future employment, which might be called Apollonian. (These names seem to have been first used by the German philosopher Nietzsche but have turned up recently in Gerald Holton's (1978) critique of popular attitudes towards science.) My use of the terms is not to contrast scholarly study with a populist over-the-top reaction. Between these opposing categories there are no neat and sharp boundaries. Neither is well defined, both are almost undoubtedly multidimensional. The contrast between them concerns the emotions, but also to varying extents the environment, life missions, and attitudes towards change.

The world, like our society, is now pluralist in many ways and needs therefore to tolerate if not welcome some uncertainty. It is no longer as precisely structured as it once seemed to be either in the knowledge we learn nor in the manner of its learning. This is especially true of informal, experiential learning which may be totally ignored or a matter of great excitement, Apollonian or Dionysian. We may be Apollonian on some days for some contexts of learning, and then Dionysian on other days for other learning. At base this is a very old demarcation, a dialectic in Hegelian terms, which can by synthesis remove the harsh separation between thought and delight that has plagued all education, but especially science education, for so very long. It also brings out the more holistic features of autodidactism and suggests once again, that it is a general characteristic of all human learning, for young and old, and for those with outstanding ability, for others with special needs, and for all and anyone, old or young who need more time or more space in which to learn.

> Descartes' world-view did, of course, produce many triumphs. But it produced them largely by dividing things – mind from body, reason from feeling, and the human race from the rest of the physical universe. . . . For a long time our culture has tolerated this deprivation. But it has become a serious nuisance in many areas of knowledge. The problem of free-will (or autonomy) is incomprehensible to people who think of mind and body as radically separate. Similarly, it is impossible to understand human motivation (to learn) if one thinks of feeling as radically separate from thought.
>
> (Midgley 2001: 179, my additions in brackets)

References

Bakhtin, M. (1927, trans. 1976) *Freudianism: A Marxist Critique*. New York: Academic Press.

Berlyne, D. (1960) *Conflict, Arousal and Curiosity*. New York: McGraw-Hill.

Billig, M. (1987) *Arguing and Thinking*. Cambridge: Cambridge University Press.

Bourdieu, P. and Passeron, P.-C. (1977) *Reproduction in Education, Society and Culture*. London: Sage.

Giddens, A. (1991) *Modernity and Self-Identity*. Cambridge: Polity Press.

Giroux, H. (1997) *Pedagogy and the Politics of Hope*. Oxford: Westview.

Gregory, R. (1970) *The Intelligent Eye*. London: Weidenfeld and Nicolson.

Gregory, R. (1998) *Eye and Brain*. Oxford: Oxford University Press.

Harrér, R. (1979) *Social Being*. Oxford: Basil Blackwell.

Holton, G. (1978) *The Scientific Imagination*. Cambridge: Cambridge University Press.

Ingold, T. (2000) *The Perception of the Environment*. London: Routledge.

Kroth, M. and Boverie, P. (2000) 'Life Mission and Adult Learning', *Adult Learning Quarterly* 50(2): 134–149.

Langer, S. (1942) *Philosophy in a New Key*. Cambridge: Harvard University Press.

Lave, J. (1988) *Cognition in Practice*. Cambridge: Cambridge University Press.

Merton, R. (1942) 'Science and technology in a Democratic Order', *Journal of Legal and Political Sociology* 1: 115–126.

Midgley, M. (1981) *Heart and Mind. The Varieties of Moral Experience*. London: Methuen.

Midgley, M. (2001) *Science and Poetry*. London: Routledge.

Moscovici, S. (1976) *Social Influence and Social Change*. London: Academic Press.

Moscovici, S. and Doise, W. (1994) *Conflict and Consensus*. London: Sage.

Solomon, J. (2000) 'Learning to be inventive: design, evaluation, and selection in primary school science', in J. Ziman (ed.) *Technological Innovation as an Evolutionary Process*. Cambridge: Cambridge University Press, 190–203.

Taylor, C. (1989) *Sources of the Self*. Cambridge: Cambridge University Press.

Tulving, E. (1984) 'How many memory systems are there?' *American Psychologist* 40(4): 385–398.

Ziman, S. (1978) *Reliable Knowledge*. Cambridge: Cambridge University Press.

Ziman, J. (2000) *Real Science*. Cambridge: Cambridge University Press.

Chapter 17

Useful theories, great and small

Joan Solomon

In common usage the word 'theory' has something uncertain and tenuous about it. It is thought to be the product of speculation, but not totally disconnected from practice. Theory is based on accepted work, or on empirical results and observation going beyond just picking out common features, as celebrated in the last chapter. The theory attempts to explain the process even though it is bound to fail in the long run. Sooner or later a better theory will supplant the present one. (I used to worry about this and tried to explain the insecurity of theories to my students, but not many of them let it trouble them a lot!)

The theories discussed here will not be directly about education, that is for the Epilogue. As Rosalind Driver (1977) argued in one of her last publications, educational theories may be normative and goal-directed, but theories about the processes of learning are not. They are semantic, concerned with understanding, and lie in the domain of social science. Goal-directed theories are positivist since the method employed is self-validating. All students, including those who may prefer autonomous methods of learning, should be able to profit from the semantic results of our explorations.

The theories introduced in this chapter are far from secure. Some are very new, some controversial, and at least one is little more than a metaphor. Nevertheless theoretical explanations are always important because they make some attempt to mend a worrying gap in our consciousness of the world where our understanding is incomplete. They are temporary explanations, offered in a hesitant, 'the-best-we-can-do-now' way. But if the gap seems to be repaired, enough to keep out the draughts of doubt for a while, then what we have noticed becomes much more richly satisfying.

First part: the complex thinking of autodidacts

During the course of previous chapters there has been an emphasis on the emotional reactions of learners, which seem stronger than average for autodidacts, for whom learning is so important. To explain this we need a theory that allows the cognitive, perceptual and emotional to act together. From Chapter 6, for example, we could see that the attempts of Brazilian genetic counsellors and researchers to separate cognitive learning from the justifiably emotional reactions of their clients brought nothing but problems and defeat. Then Tulving's theory of the chunky nature of episodic memory, was used to suggest that perceptions of various different kinds were involved, together with emotions and cognition. They might all be knotted together so firmly that to have an episode from the past triggered by one aspect, was to be flooded by almost total recall of the others.

Richard Gregory's work on perception, mostly visual, is invaluable here. The brain, he showed, is so busy interpreting what we see that our visual perceptions are created as much in the brain as in the retinal system. Little wonder then that the memory of perceptions acts in a similar way to the memory of cognitions. As Midgley (2001) implied in the quotation used at the end of the last chapter, the emotions involved may be so similar to cognitions as to be indistinguishable from them in their transits through parts of the brain. So it is likely that the different regions of the nervous system of the brain handle different sorts of message – emotive, cognitive, and sensory – as if they were of much the same kind.

The learning and remembering brain is certainly *complicated* but is it also *complex* in the way that systems complying with the requirements of complexity theory have to be? Finding out enough about complexity to understand its implications is rewarding because the pay-back is likely to be rich in terms of understanding learning.

What is a complex system?

As the structure of the brain is extremely intricate and still far from well understood, it is best to begin learning about complex systems in a couple of more familiar contexts. There are a lot of these to choose from. We could pick out Darwinian evolution or economic systems, a gas enclosed in a cylinder or global financial dealings, a settled woodland area or a rotating shoal of small fish, the body's immune system or the origins of life itself. The notion of complexity is now widely applied and does not depend on the actual nature of the system's substance and components so long as they fulfil certain general conditions.

> The system must be open to a flow of energy going through it: it is never just an inert web or net.
>
> It should be composed of items of some sort that are coupled together: strongly or weakly – this coupling is the agency by which energy moves through.

It must be complicated enough to ensure that accurate prediction about what kind of change will take place, *is impossible*.

That last point is the most surprising. Scientists have always seemed very keen on making predictions based on theories: you could almost say that it was in the very nature of science to do so. Indeed the eighteenth century French mathematician P.-S. Laplace once wrote that if an intelligent being could completely understand the situation at one instant in time, it could use the simple laws of science to predict what the situation would be like at any other time. (Rather like firing a snooker ball into the triangular array of red balls – difficult and laborious calculations to make, but possible.) For this new kind of complex system that possibility has gone.

Example 1

Our first example concerns the model of a gas that we all learnt about in school. We assume that the molecules of a gas are like tiny hard balls, and that as they move they can carry energy with them (Figure 17.1) from 'hot' to 'cool'. If only a few molecules are involved they may, one after another, bounce happily off the wall at the far end which may be cooler, and then come back to the warmer end. This train of gas molecules passes the first test about flow of energy. However they are not interacting with each other; they are not colliding or coupled together in any way, so the system has not passed the second test, nor for that matter the third.

On the other hand if we squash millions of little molecules into the container they will collide with the others from all directions, sometimes being reduced almost to rest for a tiny fraction of a second, until hit from the side or back by other molecules. They are all interacting, but there is

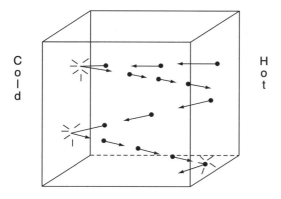

Figure 17.1 Uncoupled molecules, energy flow.

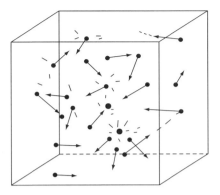

Figure 17.2 Interacting molecules, no energy flow.

not a flow of heat across the gas. The second test has been passed (Figure 17.2), but not the first.

How can we be so sure that the third test is passed? No one is going to set up a long list of calculations in order to prove that they cannot be used successfully. All we can do is to work out the probability of a molecule being in a certain region and having a certain amount of energy. (This was not what Laplace wanted to be able to calculate.) How fast a molecule is moving translates into how hot the gas will be at that spot. So we could, in principle, calculate the probability of the gas, at any point, being either at the boiling point or freezing point of water. We cannot predict the temperature itself, only these probabilities.

In some ways this is a terrible example. It is useless and old fashioned, stemming as it does from the causal certainties of the nineteenth century; but it has one big advantage. Figure 17.3 shows the system with a kind of order – a bunch of hot molecules or cold molecules spinning in a vortex within the tea. So it illustrates a phenomenon which has come to be known as 'order at the edge of chaos', or more simply as 'an emergence' of some new and quite unpredictable event. This is a marvellous and surprising effect, one that only truly complex systems can show, and will be very useful for considering our learning brains as complex systems.

Example 2

The second example concerns the beginnings of ecology, takes place mostly in the twentieth century, and is illustrated by the work of Charles Elton. While researching invertebrate populations in Spitzbergen, and still a student, he read about fluctuations in the populations of the arctic fox and the snowshoe rabbit in northern Canada. The records of furs brought in by the trappers of the Hudson's Bay Company went back

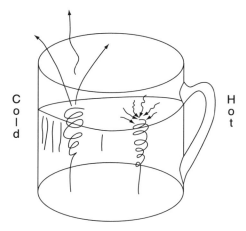

C
o
l
d

H
o
t

Figure 17.3 The unlikely complex cup of tea.

some two hundred years also showing regular fluctuations in the animal populations, like arctic lynxes and hares, which were repeated every ten years. Elton was most intrigued by this, and also by the more irregular and suicidal migration of lemmings. Later he worked for the Hudson's Bay Company using their records for his research.

In the terms of the complexity theory, we could say that the population of predators was coupled with that of its prey. So any increase in, say, lynx numbers was followed by a decrease in the hare population, and vice versa – see Figure 17.4.

Hares feed on grass which photosynthesises energy from the sun, so clearly there was an energy flow through the wider system. The coupling is very weak because the animal populations are small and scattered in this cold, inhospitable environment. Other climate variations may also affect the outcome, but the interaction clearly exists. (Eating each other is a very strong form of coupling!) But is the third condition for complexity also met? Is the system sufficiently complicated for predictions about its future to be impossible? Elton certainly tried to predict the system's fluctuations in terms of the sunspot cycle, but the period, eleven years for sunspots, was wrong for the populations. This suggests that the animal numbers might be too small for real complexity.

Elton (1927) continued to believe that 'some climatic oscillation . . . must be postulated to *explain* the phenomenon'. The emphasis added is mine. Elton was looking for cause and effect, as all pre-complexity researchers, as well as modern ones in other situations, would have done. His main research was carried out on a far more complicated animal population in Wytham Wood near Oxford. He wrote:

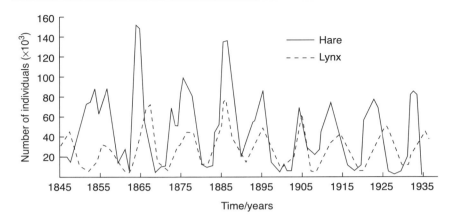

Figure 17.4 Complexity theory.

The earth is a unique natural park of life, whirling through an otherwise lifeless space. In this natural park, separating in various proportions from the *common stream of materials and energy*, are over a million forms of life, evolved into *an unstable and highly complex network of communities* . . . From a wider point of view they form inside the ecosystem of the whole world and surrounding universe, complex capillaries through which flow streams of matter and energy, subject to *laws that are still almost unformulated*.

(Elton 1936, my emphasis added)

As before Elton found events which were unpredictable. There were times when the population of one species' population crashed drastically and a new species – virus, bacterium or rodent – increased and re-established order. Elton tried out ideas of stress caused by over-crowding, but without much success. (In Complexity Theory this phenomena is now called 'self re-organisation' or 'autopoesis'.)

Neither James Clerk Maxwell (for gases), nor Charles Elton (for ecology), could see precisely how their complex systems should be understood. Maxwell thought that increase of knowledge on a molecular scale (Maxwell's Demon) would influence the distribution of gas velocities and so change the temperature distribution in the cup of tea. Elton tried to test several ideas about population crashes, but failed. Nevertheless the complex woodland population with its unknown feedback processes was to form the basis of modern ecology. Both men rightly saw that the complexity of the system they studied was likely to require a whole new science for its understanding.

The consciousness of learning

The human brain is the mother of all 'neural networks', indeed the term is now used metaphorically for quite different complex systems. The brain contains about 100 billion neurons and hundreds of trillions of synaptic connections! All parts of it must be open to energy flow, which is largely provided by the bloodstream with all its dissolved substances, because of the need for continual input of energy to keep the brain working. Deprive brains of energy and they die. An interruption of only four minutes is enough to bring about permanent brain damage. So it seems that all three of the conditions for complexity to operate – energy flow, coupling between the items (neurons and their synaptic links), and the multiplicity of these – are present. It is a complex system, or rather a set of complex systems in different brain regions.

We should not expect to be able to predict how any particular brain will learn: that would be antisocial but also irrelevant because the feedback from any learning induces yet greater plasticity (more connected synapses) in the brain. Learning constructs yet more potential learning. The most famous case of this is the experienced London taxi driver, where the learnt knowledge of roads etc., is being so constantly used that the size and weight of the region where these extra memories are stored can be shown to have increased in weight. Nevertheless the all-over cause and effect that Laplace had so much valued for making predictions about objects, is just not possible for this or any other complex system. So we can expect to see some of the general outcomes of complexity theory.

Brain scans have produced some fascinating new findings. During first-time learning a greater than usual input of energy is needed, and the increased network activity seems located in some metastable structures, in one or several distinct parts of the brain. These areas of activity can be made to show up by special techniques; positron emission tomography (PET), or functional magnetic resonance imaging (fMRI).

> One now sees the brain not as an orderly fixed pattern of cells and their connections, but in constant dynamic flux, with different areas 'lighting up' at different times depending on the mental challenges being faced. No-one can see such patterns, illuminated as they are by computer enhancement, false colour and all the tricks of the imaging trade, without being entranced and awestruck by the beauty and complexity they reveal.
>
> (Rose 1999: 10)

After about two minutes the power consumption in these regions falls back to nearer its usual level, but the centres of activity continue to exist and even migrate to other locations (this fits astonishingly well with the findings of Biggs, Chapter 1, page 10). It also seems that the brain can reorganise itself without our help or knowledge. What is worse, we do not know how to think or talk about our own thinking. Almost everyone speaks in the vernacular about learning difficult ideas 'making my brain hurt' or 'giving me a head ache' so they may think they have located learning in some general sense. We may even be conscious of having learnt something new, but cannot find the corresponding engine of consciousness in the substance of our brain. Learning is a deeply subjective experience; we may be able to test its *outcomes* (as our present student population knows only too well) but that is quite different from being conscious of making the new synaptic junctions, or even of learning having taken place.

Some people, mostly philosophers, worry about using different languages to describe the internal process and the external function of learning. PET scans of the brain are material things produced when we switch on the apparatus, and the other is the *consciousness of thinking* that we cannot stop, start, or set out deliberately to explore. That sort of argument is as old as Plato, but was restarted recently by John Searle (1995). We might ask basic questions which are quite impossible to answer. Where is consciousness located in the brain? Of what neural substance is consciousness constructed? Is it legitimate to use different domains of explanation for describing the same effect? Does talking about consciousness require us to move into a completely different kind of thinking, like metaphysics, or does it imply using different perspectives on a matter which everyone, from artists to map-makers, usually welcomes?

Searle's argument is completely right in one sense. If we cannot talk easily about our deep learning processes then they cannot acquire the social and personal reality which is the product of exchanging meanings. Most of the mental processes involved in learning or reflecting on it, do not even have concept names, so constructive exchanges of views remain beyond reach. But complexity theory can help us a little along the way when the two new idea-words we have just encountered in complexity theory – emergence, and autopoesis – are applied to our learning.

Emergence, the apparently spontaneous appearance of a new region of order 'on the edge of chaos' is defined in the *Oxford English Dictionary* as 'An effect produced by a combination of several causes, but *not* capable of being regarded as the sum of their individual effects. Opposed to resultant' (attributed to G. H. Lewis 1874).

Autonomous learners who have a great investment in the consciousness of their own learning, may have memories of what are sometimes colloquially called 'eureka events', or 'a-ha' moments! If we turn to Chapter 5 we can find Robin Hodgkin's useful extracts about two well-known cases of emergence. The first comes from the story of the deaf-blind child Helen Keller on the day when she first understood that things have names. Her teacher poured water over her hand and then drew with her finger the letters of its name in the palm of her hand. Suddenly an emergence occurred and Helen was exhilarated. She brought all kinds of objects to her teacher, wanting to have the name of each traced out for her.

The second of Hodgkin's examples was Michael Polanyi's description of how, while still a young medical student, he learned to interpret an X-ray photograph. At first he said he could neither see the different parts of the photograph, nor understand the explanations the lecturer was giving. Then, out of this total perplexity, an emergence occurred. At one and the same moment, he could both see what was being pointed out, and make sense of what the lecturer was saying.

Then if we turn to Chapter 15 for Jack Diamond's story of learning we find that it contains the description of what might have been a similar moment of personal illumination, and also an assertion that such moments had recurred several times in his life.

> I can still remember how thrilled I was . . . This was one of the occasions when the future seemed to open out. That has happened on two or three occasions in my life. I don't understand it, but each time I have known quite clearly that there was going to be a new turn in my life.
>
> (Chapter 15 page 159)

His assertion that he 'does not understand it' is also central to the argument about thinking about one's own consciousness. Emergences arise without warning and defy both prediction and understanding in the normal senses of these words.

There has been relatively little recent discussion of the nature of understanding in the educational literature, although a few modern educationalists, like Nickerson (1985), do sometimes refer to Ausubel et al.'s (1968) theory of an interconnective structure for meaningful knowledge in the mind of the learner (see Chapter 1). Most educationalists draw back from the whole field because of the lack of definition of what understanding might mean in terms of consciousness. They assume that we could say absolutely nothing relevant about the mechanism of understanding if we did not understand how it works. But the common words and metaphors we use about our thinking, and about other wonderful but not fully understood events, can have the recognition of life-world meanings built into them. Some of these, like 'it makes my brain hurt' or 'it gives me a headache' were used in Chapter 1 without a qualm. It would be strange indeed if the experience of successful learning, which can be so very exhilarating, could not be communicated between friends.

A starting point for such exploration was Janet Burns' investigation into what her Year 13 chemistry students understood by 'understanding'. This qualitative work, based on careful interviews that focused on the students' personal meaning for understanding and then the distinguishing features of it, showed much the same sudden emergence as Polanyi, Helen Keller and possibly Jack Diamond had experienced: '. . . everything fits into place; it all interlocks: it clicks' (quoted in Burns *et al.* 1991: 280). It is also possible to see this process as self-reorganisation (autopoesis) when existing parts of a problem which was defeating us, come together without our conscious help.

We have quantitative evidence from laboratory experiments (Stickgold *et al.* 2001) that lists of words, learnt in the morning and only partially remembered at night time, can be restored by the next morning after sleep. Most of us have experienced waking up with a solution or memory that we could not reach on the previous night. This self-reorganisation is reminiscent of Macbeth's incantation 'sleep that knits up the ravelled sleeve of care . . . balm of hurt minds'. It is also recognised in the wisdom of the everyday advice to 'sleep on it'. Much of Jungian psychotherapy might also be based on this recapture of memory traces, lost or suppressed, which may become manifest in our dreams.

Neurobiologists are almost sure that the healing process of autopoesis takes place during dreaming. We have known for some time that dreaming is important to our mental health, so that if subjects are woken up whenever the rapid movement of their eyelids shows the onset of dreaming, for several nights in succession, they seem to suffer from dream deprivation. When finally allowed uninterrupted sleep they go through a veritable orgy of dreams, as if to make up for its deprivation. Michel Jouvet (1999) describes how he and his colleagues explored the nature of dreams in humans, cats and other animals over some four decades. First they showed that it was a phase of deep sleep but with the activity of a waking brain, accompanied by a drop in body temperature, and almost complete paralysis of the body's muscles. (This is horribly reminiscent of nightmares when one was being chased by monsters and struggling against paralysis, and trying desperately to wake up!) Only the eyelids in humans, and the tip of the tail in cats, continue to move. Many researchers (see LeDoux 2002: 107) now believe that memory consolidation occurs during sleep when the information acquired during the day and stored in the hyppocanthus is carefully interleaved into the cortex while the animal is asleep.

No complex systems can accommodate linear relations like those which link cause and effect – 'if x then y' – because of the multitude of interconnections between any two effects. (Breaking one link, or several, does not prevent all communication between the two effects – see Figures 17.5 and 17.6.)

When research tries to find the correlation between students' scores on motivation and on achievement the results are very low, between 0 and

Cause

Effect

Figure 17.5 Cause and effect – linear relations. One path from cause to effect.

Cause   Effect

Figure 17.6 Cause and effect – non-linear relations. Several paths from cause to effect.

0.4 despite our common-sense expectations of cause and effect. This may arise from this lack of causal pathways. Paul Gardener, in his meta-analysis of all the international research on students' interests uncovered this perplexing situation in 1975. It was not easy, at that time, to think about these two linked concepts in terms of complexity. Now we can see that the motivation, emotion, cognition, sensory perception and achievement, are so complexly interlinked that searching for cause and effect may be entirely ineffectual. Complex systems are like that: they avoid causal analysis just as much as they do prediction.

The second theoretical problem: social or personal learning?

Many of the objectives of teaching are social every bit as much as cognitive, so it is discouraging to find that the very term autodidact is sometimes misunderstood as learning on one's own and refusing to take part in any group activities. It is true that there are some examples in this book which seem to support this. Group work at the Interactive Science Centre may fall apart (see Jim and Aeron in Chapter 3) and the project groups at Roskilde University may lead to conflict, especially near the beginning of the course. On the other hand, it is clear that some autonomous learners positively need social contacts with others to accelerate their learning. The brothers in Chapter 5, the primary teacher Linda who was inspired by taking part in an evening class in Chapter 7, and the cohort of younger students at the Open University to be described in the next section of this chapter, all show how much some autodidacts value the social aspects of learning.

Both ways of learning, the personal and the social, are available to almost all of us. Both can be valuable or the reverse. To be very weak in social learning may, at worst, mean having the kind of 'mind blindness' which is the condition of autism. Yet to be weak in personal learning is to become an unthinking follower of the majority view. Some examples of the latter are to be found in Moscovici's (1976) accounts of group consensus being won over by pressure from a single individual 'plant'.

The self and its identities

This is the site of a great deal of controversy, since social learning is *not* the same as sociable learning, and personal learning does *not* exclude sharing with others. The fundamental question is what could be meant by a concept of a totally independent 'self', which is especially important for autodidacts.

A recent series of BBC television programmes entitled *The Century of the Self* (April 2002) made the claim that the twentieth century, beginning with the ideas of Freud, has been almost obsessed by the concept of self. Go back three or more centuries before that and even the painted images of different people in a crowd were represented as very like each other, as if they were no more than fragments of a uniform social whole. A recent book subtitled *'How glass changed the world'* Macfarlane and Martin (2002) suggests that it was the development of mirrors as well as the rise of autobiographical writing, that stimulated a renaissance of individualism which encouraged portraiture, especially in Holland and Italy. The Enlightenment had re-emphasised this trend, but some two centuries later the work of G. H. Mead began a movement back in the opposite direction, which produced a strongly social view of the self.

> The *self* arises in the process of social experience and activity, that is it develops in the given individual as a result of his relations to that process as a whole and to other individuals within that process.
>
> (Mead 1934)

At about the same time early psychotherapists were working out the multiple concepts of selfhood. Jung (1933) had written about consciousness of self as beginning when children first have a continuing memory of their activities. Later it becomes stronger as the memory becomes richer. One of Jung's colleagues remarked, 'people were drawn to his work by . . . the *space* it provided for describing the individuality of different patients'. (The word *space* has the same importance here as in the last chapter.) For these Jungian psychologists individuality included many sub-personalities and what Redfearn (1985) wonderfully describes as 'a migratory feeling of "I"'. At the end of the last century another psychiatrist, Lifton (1993), was to use this same space to describe the damaged notion of self held by Chinese and Americans who had suffered from thought-reform programmes during the Korean war. He claimed that the ever-changing protean self is maturing in response to the very forces of change and ambiguity of life that make all our lives so difficult to steer. The increasing consciousness of self when produced in this way may be internal and personal like an autobiography which we continually reconstruct throughout life (Harré 1983). This line of thought draws out a continuity from Jung's early ideas to the present day.

However the concept of the social self is still very strong. It has influenced some postmodernists to deny the very possibility of autonomous selfhood – individuals who are self aware and act on their own coherent point of view. Such authors refer only to a social self, imposed by a wide range of global, local and institutional forces. Advertising certainly does influence what we buy, eat, wear and think, from canned music, to the machinery of public relations operating in every corner of the industrial democracy. We are rarely alone, our selves are continually manipulated, and most of us dance to the same tune. Post-modern sociologists refer to the result as the 'de-centred self', or the 'de-centred subject' stripping off all that might be too personal and liberal, like the individualistic hero of the Enlightenment. It could be added that solitary confinement which denies us the comfort of social conformation, severely damages our sense of self.

There are some signs that the tide may be turning. The anxiety, stress, lawlessness and anomie of our present society may be a response to the pressures of having to be free and flexible enough to make up our own minds about how to lead our lives in the bewildering 'flows' (Giddens 1991) of this world. The fall of communism in Europe brought about a consensual verdict from citizens in many countries that reflected their continuing individualism and scepticism about forms of government.

On a smaller scale the traditional social categories of family, community and gender are no longer secure. Beck and Beck-Gersheim refers to them as *'zombie categories'*, 'the living dead' having little to offer those who long for social solidarity. Being a follower of fashion provides reassurance of being 'in the crowd', and brand marks ensure that no choices need be made. But there is a limit to how much social pressure people can accept. They rarely want to dress exactly alike. Edwards's comments that our 'sensibilities are attuned to the pleasure of new experiences, part of a constant making and remaking of a life-style' (1997: 17). But, as Beck (2001) wrote, individual views continue to show up in all kinds of social statistics as irritating, incalculable errors.

A mixture of selves

It might seem that we now have two almost irreconcilable views of the self. However Edwards (1997) argues that even in a postmodern world people do not live such controlled lives as the image of a completely de-centred self would suggest. Others hold that it is naïve to believe that a completely autonomous self could exist in the complex modern world, far too liberal and individualised for the essentially social beings that we are. The practice of freedom in our thinking demands self organisation and self awareness of a very high order, and it needs to be geared to appropriate action. In most cases, some argue, it is only by means of group consciousness that this can be achieved.

Layder (1997) believes that such opposing views on selfhood can co-exist. Being a member of society is reflexive. Individuals will inevitably be influenced by social forces, such as the global forces of commercialism, as well as by cultural trends (Giddens 1991). Some may stand out against peer group influence more than others, or they may have some private atypical interests. But they are not likely to wait for the next election to record their passionate disagreement with some aspect of policy, nor do they. Beck calls them 'freedom's children' who suffer stress from being free to make decisions (Beck and Beck-Gernsheim 2001). The philosopher Richard Rorty (1991) discriminates between the social and personal, between 'solidarity with others' by embracing a social life style, and 'solidarity with an idea', by following an internalised personal value. He seems to assert that each of us belongs to either one tribe or to the other. But the aversion of post-structuralists towards such over-arching 'meta-narratives' without local context, should disapprove such a broad distinction.

The objectivity of an individual, and the subjectivity of a group do not include all the possibilities. Those in any working group will need to share an intersubjective view if they are to function effectively. This quality is neither simply objective nor entirely subjective; it is communally built on shared perceptual and linguistic meanings which make the views of participants coherent and consistent – at least to some extent and whilst they are working together. The process produces as realistic a description of the external world as any kind of agreement could, despite being local, and provisional.

Liberation education and the 'ownership of self'

This is a third perspective on the 'self and others' question. It is certainly closer to our previous discussion of autodidactism, being passionate in its concern with learning, and more practical in its recommendations than the sociological considerations in the last section. Libertarian education exists, as it were, on the far left of a continuum where the personal self inhabits the centre, and the de-centred social self is on the right. Libertarian education searches for freedom for all learners – children or adults. Children are rarely given the freedom to avoid schooling altogether, but there are home schooling regulations which make it just possible within unusually devoted families. The freedom that they want is not to wander around entirely by themselves in an untouched and empty 'natural' environment, as J.-J. Rousseau wanted for Emile in his book on education. (This is the 'negative education' that Paul Caro mentions in Chapter 10.) The freedom that later libertarians wanted was more realistic. It aimed to protect the learners from the insidious and continuing effects of dogmatic teaching. The libertarians wanted to give children freedom from intruding views at an age when the plasticity of the brain is high and memories persistent. That implied an indoctrination which could last a lifetime. An obstinate autodidact might refuse blandishments from the commercial world, but who could avoid corrupting ideas if they had already been implanted in their neural networks?

Rousseau's ideas were always sketchy and eccentric. He himself was not only a Dionysian autodidact of a high order, teaching himself almost everything from books, but had also 'suffered' a climactic emergence at the age of thirty-seven. Rousseau (1968) was a champion of liberty in ways other than education. His most famous and influential book was about democracy – *The Social Contract* – which has been influential in France up until the present day. Perhaps the best example of a libertarian educator is the nineteenth century German ideological school teacher Max Stirner, who even attacked his former mentor Karl Marx for the lack of freedom he had been allowed. He argued that people must be in control of their own learning processes if they are going to 'own their selves'. This is the nub of libertarian education. Stirner (in Spring 1998: 38) was fond of declaiming 'Man, your head is haunted. You have wheels in your head!' (I imagine this as what a science fiction writer might have called being an android.)

In libertarian education we can expect to find little uniformity in educational practices, but a great deal of commitment to one method or another. Stirner wrote about the lack of equality in the modern state, and the overbearing powers of the church, which he blamed for the shortcomings in education. Others like Fransico Ferrer in Spain and A. S. Neill in England tried to create model schools to provide a 'free' education, but found their efforts partially blocked by the indoctrination already incorporated in most books. The Kibbutz movement in Israel blamed families, and Paulo Freire's efforts to educate the peasants of Brazil blamed colonialisation. He focused on helping the oppressed to create a new awareness of self and society. He called it 'naming the world' and 'speaking their name'. Here was another powerful reference to self. These men and others, criticised and theorised society, Bourdieu and Illich arguing strongly against the influence of schools and teachers, and Giroux wrote about giving the students a voice. And yet the world has not changed much. Perhaps this is because we long so much to guide our own children for ourselves.

Third theoretical problem: adult education for autodidacts?

Lifelong education, wrote John Field (2000) at the beginning of his book on this topic, 'is a beautifully simple idea'. This may be because he saw it in terms of adults who learn naturally, or in terms of the new training plans made by industry. But simple it is not.

Even Chapter 13, which is confined to science courses at the Open University, shows a constant tension between the teaching of science, and science being taken up by an audience of 'grazers' or 'knob-twiddlers'. Those terms seem patronising, suggesting shallow short term learning. Certainly these learners do not enrol on courses, choosing instead to protect their silent autonomy; so we know rather little about them. Nevertheless they may be as strenuous in their search for knowledge as any of the workers in Chapter 7 who react to threats of redundancy. Or they may learn as Jack Diamond did, by searching for critical political knowledge in the poorer sections of society. Or they may join with friends to follow up a practical interest or hobby. Or they may endlessly seek out books, and read them on crowded London Underground journeys, or more secretly at night while the busy household sleeps. To those of us who are caught up in the investigation of learning this is all part of a variety that is certainly not simple – although it may seem to be so to those in government whose vocabulary seems confined to terms like flexibility and skills.

Of one thing we can be certain. Those who put their energies into learning far away from institutions like schools or colleges or training programmes, are autodidacts by definition since there is now so much provision for teaching they do not choose to take it up, preferring to learn on their own.

Research on age and gender

A recent study by Gardner (2000), apparently unconnected with auto-didactism, looked at the reactions of a new cohort of Open University who are younger than any previously taught, and found them having great difficulties. The imposition of tuition fees for higher education has encouraged some school-leavers to take their degree course part-time, while working. On the whole the results have been disappointing with a larger than usual drop-out rate. The most common reason for dissatisfaction given by this cohort aged 18 to 21 years, was that the process was 'too solitary'. At school, living and learning is an intensely social activity. But older 'drop outs' rarely mention lack of company as their excuse. Do adults grow more autonomous with age?

Substantial new research about the development of adults' learning is generally sparse and usually inconclusive. Fortunately, however, there is a classic longitudinal case study of an American post graduate medical school by Howard Becker et al. (1961), published in 1961. Immersed in this are some curious and valuable insights. While the students often started the course with a very idealistic approach, the researchers found that it soon plummeted to a kind of medical cynicism, although some years later, after graduation and starting practise, the idealism might return. Becker viewed this as 'a major process of personal development' for which the triggers reside in the situation. The elation at entry to the course may be similar to the adoption of a life-mission, the dejection which follows is often blamed on their enforced lack of responsibility for patients. The third phase may point to a greater maturity, when the doctor recaptures his autonomy and commitment at one and the same time.

An equally well-known four year American longitudinal study, this time of college humanities students by William Perry (1970), showed how difficult they found coping with the existence of two or more alternative interpretative possibilities of text or theory. This ambiguity, which the lecturer would not resolve for them, often led to discontented relativism, and general disenchantment. Later it seemed that a new depth of understanding was produced when a personal commitment to one or other interpretation was seen to be essential to learning, and regenerated the students' engagement. Perry saw this final stage of *commitment* to one or other interpretation as a development of autonomy, and thus also as an expression of self-identity.

In gender studies it has been shown that women's development of autonomous decision-making may follow a route somewhat different from that of men. Gilligan's (1982) brilliant interview study of young women in an abortion clinic during the early 1980s began with them having to decide, amid all the emotional reactions of parents and boy friends, whether or not to terminate their pregnancies. Characteristically they took into account their responsibilities towards the feelings of others, almost to the exclusion of their own feelings. Gilligan not only showed that the moral stance of these women differed from those of the young men, but also how much the women grew in autonomy and self confidence during the five years that followed their first decision.

> Since the reality of *connection* is experienced by women as given rather than as freely contracted, they arrive at an understanding of life that reflects their *limits of autonomy and control*. As a result, women's development delineates the path not only to a less violent life but also to a maturity realised through *interdependence*.
>
> (Gilligan 1982, my emphases)

The 'less violent life' that Gilligan hypothesised might suggest that a calmer spirit established after maturity had brought them more autonomy, self-confidence and sometimes interdependence within a group. Another possibility is that the need for autonomy could lead to a series of stressful and embattled situations as the women put right the earlier dependency decision (like the two female teachers in Chapter 8). Some extracts from interviews with mature entrants to a university course who were having a second chance at studying science provide illustrations of reflection on this earlier decision.

> 'I should have taken it then, but I funked it. Now I have *got* to succeed.'
> 'I wanted to do it when I left school, but I didn't have the get up and go.'
> 'I did the teenage rebellious thing . . . and then when I got to 21 I thought "Oh no, what have I done?"'
> 'This one (study course) is for my daughter. . . . No it's not, it is for *me*.'

The last extract was from an interview with a single mother (Solomon 1997). All demonstrate the same consciousness of a previous lack of autonomy and forethought, and the intention to fulfil their potential this time round.

Recent feminist approaches to adult learning come to rather similar conclusions. Both Benkenly *et al.* (1986) and Wingfield and Haste (1987) have pointed in more detail to the 'connectedness' of women's ways of knowing. Their analyses include 'listening to others' and 'received ways of knowing' as well as 'personal and intuitive ways of knowing'. All of these traits imply relying on others to some extent, and could extend to a denial of self amounting to a lack of autonomy. More recently Hughes (2001) has added that taking on responsibilities can even seem quite 'despotic', as can autonomy itself, if it competes against women's natural sense of care and connection with others. But Hughes concludes that although taking responsibility for one's own learning shows an independence and maturity of thought, it should take care not to overthrow a woman's gift of caring, and a well-balanced feeling of responsibility towards others. Such a balance is hard to achieve and a process of maturation may account for the length of time it takes some young women to reach a stable attitude towards adult education, especially when domestic duties make study time itself a kind of battlefield.

All these examples may have been indicating a maturing sense of autonomy which may increase with age, or with experience. There is no certainty in the interpretation of these messages. It was the same in the cases of medical and humanities students where we can see immaturity as a struggle against the ambiguity or pluralism of knowledge.

What kind of adult learning?

If would-be learners enrol for more education at an institution, the chances are that they will be met with offers of 'Study Guides', with titles like *How to Learn* or *Back to Study*, although the route into adult learning might well have been expected to be forward. Such Self-Regulated Learning (SRL) produces a growth industry turning out huge numbers of publications aimed at anxious or vacillating students. The books are full of prescriptions, and sound advice, but there is some evidence that they are not much used by adult students (see quotations below). Regulation of any kind is clearly the antithesis of autodidactism, both of the secret and defiant kinds. But when SRL succeeds, as Scanlon (Chapter 13) claims that it does at the Open University, its results are impressive. The last two quotations in Scanlon's chapter show – first a learner who speaks of the OU helping her to find out the answers to any questions, and then a more emotional autodidact who said he felt like crying 'inside' when he realised how hard his schooling had been.

The two categories of self-regulated student and autodidact are not enough to describe the wonderful richness of adult students' attitudes. There is great variation in their views about the way they want to study. The following extracts come from letters to a single issue of the OU monthly magazine, *Sesame*, (issue 208).

'The little brown envelope, especially if it contains notice of a high grade, is all the "recognition for success" that's reasonable or necessary.'

'Last year I stopped sending in TMA (assignments) because of the constant requirement to detail my study problems. . . . As I only study to keep my brain active . . .'

'I stuck at my revision, kept writing until the bell went and achieved 42% in the exam. I was thrilled to scrape a pass.'

'I returned to study on my retirement in order to update myself, and found I was required to sit the examination, although it had little relevance to my reasons for taking the course.'

'Would it be possible to have some residential weeks set aside in the summer for short research projects? . . . Some of us choose to explore our potential later in life. This doesn't make our ideas any less valid.'

Two important books about the nature of adult learning were published in 1997. One, by Robin Usher and two colleagues (1997) took a post-modern approach to both the social decentred self and to the ambiguity of knowledge. But to these was added personal autonomy, a sense of self awareness that was at odds with the more usual social self of the post-modernists, and a broader knowledge of the world than younger students would have. The authors drew out this contrast as though the humanist individual self who was opposed by overbearing influences from society. The adult's experience of the world can be used to reflect upon and produce knowledge of various sorts. Conversely the experience is itself produced or enhanced by the reflection. Experiential adult learning is thus less certain and fixed, more shifting and ambiguous.

The three authors drew out these continua of variation from the poles of adaptation to autonomy, and from application to expression and labelled what they called the 'sites of struggle', as different ways of learning from experience.

Application involves a goal for action. The goal of *personal autonomy* may drive any of the four quadrants, as also may expressive learning and the

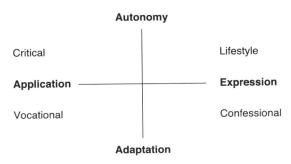

Figure 17.7 The poles of adaptation and autonomy and of application and expression.

intention to adapt knowledge to new situations. So although the matrix is clearly useful as a starting point, its boundaries cannot be sharp and the separation distances are variable and ambiguous.

The other book, by Richard Edwards (1997) published in the same year discriminated between the 'field of adult education' and the 'moorland of adult learning'. This double metaphor began as a way of framing the differences between taught courses bounded by hedges, and a moorland over whose unbounded stretches of learning a more autonomous learner may wander at will. But still adults' learning remains curiously difficult to compartmentalise because it can only be identified by private emotional and cognitive perceptions. Moorland knowledge may be dismissed as 'learner-centred rather than supply-driven' (Field 2000) in those sectors of society where the usefulness and accreditation of knowledge in Lyotard's terms its 'performativity' (1984), is the all-important feature of learning. By contrast moorland learning may be more highly prized by committed autodidacts because it can be picked up informally through reading and television, and, being context dependent, it is often helpfully couched in life-world terms. But these theoretical approaches all show that autodidacts, as claimed at the beginning of this book, are not a sharply bounded group of people to be labelled as such, but a continuum of learning attributes.

This postmodern approach, a promising step towards a pluralist system of knowing, has been welcomed by Ziman from the other side of the modern/postmodern, humanist/scientific divide.

> Post-academic science is not merely transdisciplinary. It is defiantly postmodern in its pluralism. It welcomes wide definitions of knowledge and decentred diversity, without fear of possible inconsistencies. The 'context of application' inevitably introduces 'trans-epistemic' factors such as human values and social interests.
>
> (Ziman 2000: 210)

So we finish with more of a melée of metaphors than a controversy of theories. The difficulty of making the contradictions in adult education explicit enough to distinguish between them, and yet not impose boundaries upon its deeply ambiguous goals, are the features that makes its study intrinsically postmodern, as Edwards and Usher (2001) have recently argued. This ambiguity was foreshadowed by the work of Becker *et al.*, and Perry, and is also to be found in the new concept of citizenship within a civil society which both welcomes diversity, and insists upon civil structure. It touches on all the different senses of self to which auto-didactism may appeal – the development of values, the rejection of both consumerist indoctrination and ideological fundamentalism, and yet accepts the inconsistencies inherent in learning about and for a society with pluralistic social order.

References

Ausubel, D., Novak, J. and Hanesian, H. (1968) *Educational Psychology: a Cognitive View*. New York: Holt Rinehart and Winston.

Baron-Cohen, S. (1990) 'Autism: a specific cognitive disorder of "mind blindness"', *International Review of Psychiatry* 2: 81–90.

Beck, U. and Beck-Gernsheim (2001) *Individualisation*. London, Sage.

Becker, H., Geer, B., Hughes, E., and Strauss, A. (1961) *Boys in White*. Chicago, IL: Chicago University Press.

Benkenly, M., Clinchy, B., Goldberger, N. and Tarule, J. (1986) *Women's Way of Knowing: the Development of Self, Voice and Mind*. New York: Basic Books.

Bourdieu, P. and Passeron, P.-C. (1977) *Reproduction in Education Society and Culture*. London: Sage.

Burns, J., Clift, J. and Duncan, J. (1991) 'Understanding of Understanding: implications for learning and teaching', *British Journal of Educational Psychology* 61: 276–289.

Crowcroft, P. (1991) *Elton's Ecologists. A history of the Bureau of Animal Population*. Chicago, IL: University of Chicago Press.

Davis, A. (2002) *Public Relations Democracy*. Manchester: Manchester University Press.

Driver, R. (1977) 'The application of science education theories: a reply to Stephen Norris and Tone Kvernbekk', *Journal of Research in Science Teaching* 34(10): 1007–1018.

Edwards, R. (1997) *Changing Places*. London, Routledge.

Edwards, R. and Usher, R. (2001) 'Lifelong learning: a postmodern condition of education?', *Adult Education Quarterly* 51(4): 273–287.

Elton, C. (1927) *Animal Ecology*. London: Sidgwick and Jackson.

Elton, C. (1936) *Bureau of Animal Population, Annual Report*. Oxford: Alden Press.

Field, J. (2000) *Lifelong Learning and the New Educational Order*. Stoke on Trent: Trentham Books.

Freire, P. (1970) *Pedagogy of the Oppressed*. London: Penguin.

Gardener, P. (1975) 'Attitudes to science: a review', *Studies in Science Education* 2: 1–41.

Gardner, J. (2000) 'Young students in distance higher education', Oxford Brookes University, unpublished M.Sc. thesis.

Giddens, A. (1991) *Modernity and Self-Identity*. Cambridge: Polity Press.

Gilligan, C. (1982) *In a Different Voice*. Cambridge, Mass.: Harvard University Press.

Giroux, H. (1997) *Pedagogy and the Politics of Hope*. Oxford: Westview.

Harré, R. (1983) *Personal Being*. Oxford: Blackwell.

Hughes, C. (2001) 'Developing a sense of literacy in lifelong learning research: a case of responsibility', *British Educational Research Journal* 27(5): 601–614.

Illich, I. (1963) 'The deschooled society', in P. Buckman (ed.) *Education Without Schools*. London: Souvenir Press.

Jouvet, M. (1999) *The Paradox of Sleep*. Cambridge, Mass.: MIT Press.

Jung, C. G. (1933) *Modern Man in Search of a Soul.* London: Kegan Paul, Trench, Trubner & Co.

Layder, D. (1997) *Modern Social Theory: Key Debates and New Directions.* London: UCL Press.

LeDoux, J. (2002) *Synaptic Self.* New York: Viking.

Lifton, R. (1993) *The Protean Self.* Chicago, IL: University of Chicago Press.

Lyotard, J.-F. (1984 (trans)) *The Postmodern Condition: A Report on Knowledge.* Manchester: Manchester University Press.

Macfarlane, A. and Martin, G. (2002) *The Glass Bathyscope.* London: Profile Books.

Maturana, H. (1970) 'Biology of cognition', in H. Maturana and F. Varela (eds) *Autopoiesis and Cognition.* Dordrecht: D. Reidal.

Mead, G. H. (1934) *Mind, Self, and Society.* Chicago, IL: University of Chicago Press.

Midgley, M. (2001) *Science and Poetry.* London: Routledge.

Moscovici, S. (1976) *Social Influence and Social Change.* London: Academic Press.

Nickerson, R. (1985) 'Understanding understanding', *American Journal of Education* 92(2): 203–239.

Perry, W. (1970) *Forms of Intellectual and Ethical Development in the College Years.* New York: Holt, Reinhart and Winston.

Redfearn, J. W. T. (1985) *My Self, My Many Selves.* London: Academic Press.

Rorty, R. (1991) *Objectivity, Relativism, and Truth.* Cambridge: Cambridge University Press.

Rose, S. (1999) 'Brains, Minds and the World', in S. Rose (ed.) *From Brains to Consciousness?* London: Penguin, 1–17.

Rousseau, J. J. (1968) *The Social Contract.* London: Penguin.

Searle, J. (1995) *The Construction of Social Reality.* London: Allen Lane.

Solomon, J. (1997) 'Girls' science education: choice, solidarity and culture', *International Journal of Science Education* 19(4): 407–417.

Spring, J. (1998) *A Primer of Libertarian Education.* Montreal: Black Rose Books.

Stickgold, R., Hobson, J., Fosse, R. and Fosse, M. (2001) 'Sleep learning and dreams: off-line memory reprocessing', *Science* 294: 1052–1057.

Usher, R., Bryant, I. and Johnston, R. (1997) *Adult Education and the Postmodern Challenge.* London: Routledge.

Wingfield, L. and Haste, H. (1987) 'Connectedness and separateness: cognitive style or moral orientation?', *Journal of Moral Education* 16: 214–225.

Ziman, J. (2000) *Real Science.* Cambridge: Cambridge University Press.

Epilogue

Joan Solomon

Making provision for the better education of autodidacts in the light of what we have learnt about them is bound to be difficult. Autodidacts, as we have seen, do not like being taught; the more teaching and formal instruction they get, the more angry and defiant they may become. But we are all autodidactic to some extent, and if there are ways of improving the learning situation, then we should at least be able to recognise which they are by a species of extended empathy.

Boredom

In Chapter 16 a little was written about the physiological basis of boredom, in terms of Berlyne's experiments with students subjected to an absence of sensory stimuli. The conclusion reached was that boredom is seriously bad for our psyche. So how can we avoid it in the classroom when each person's boredom threshold is bound to be different from that of the others? Tim Brighouse, the busy and charismatic Chief Education Officer of Oxfordshire while I was teaching there, once arranged to spend a few days shadowing a group of pupils through school when his three day trip to New York was cancelled at the last moment. A little later he told us all how excruciatingly boring he had found it. 'Well, of course it would be for *him*' you might say. 'He was a clever adult; he already knew it all.'

But that would be to miss the important point. The cause of his boredom was much more likely to have been a fault in the presentation. Teachers want so much to keep the students quiet so that they can listen and learn. We have found that learning is a conglomerate of sensory, emotional, and cognitive signals; our input to lessons should be the same. To see what one such a classroom might be like we need only turn to Paul Howard's description in the opening to Chapter 4, to see so rich an assortment of inputs that the casual observer might have thought it quite out of control. Each student was able to choose how he or she wanted to learn. A friend of mine who taught in a 'difficult' school near a very troubled and deprived housing estate, had a somewhat similar method of coping with the threat of boredom. He would stop following the school scheme of work and give the class an exciting challenge. The lesson would be less cognitive but more sensory, like 'Make a Balloon-Burster', designed to take up the whole of the next lesson. After such a remedial bout of sensory excitement, the pupils found the normal cognitive fare much more palatable.

The expression of emotions

There are circumstances when learning in too emotional a setting becomes just as difficult as when it is too cognitive. Chapter 6, about training genetic counsellors, showed very clearly how emotion clouded their learning. Something a little like this happened when soldiers, like my father, returned shell-shocked after the First World War, to university and found sitting in a largely silent lecture-hall impossible to endure, unless they were near enough to the door to be able to escape at will to a richer environment. To learn well, we all need a better balance of cognitive, sensory and emotional inputs.

When there is too little emotional input, how could we increase it? This whole subject is deeply affected by national culture. In a Portuguese classroom I have watched a female teacher explaining to an eleven-year-old boy about the difference between mass and weight, while gently and affectionately ruffling his hair to hold his attention. In a Japanese classroom, along with some ten other foreign observers, I have watched a nine-year-old boy admitting publicly to a list of the shortcomings in his learning and achievement. Neither of those two events could have happened in England.

We English have begun to kiss each other in public without embarrassment, but in the classroom there are now less rather than more expressions of affection and care. Much of this is due to fear of paedophilia, but we need to ensure that the rare and horrible does not exclude the everyday and comforting which is essential to learning and to living. If even the little ones in our primary schools, at age four or five, can no longer be held gently by their teacher while the pain of a bad fall passes, then we may need to question our whole approach to the displaying of emotion.

Less controlling teaching

The relationship between a teacher and members of her class is difficult and even unnatural. When, for example, a primary teacher asks a question, the 'right' response is not an answer at all, but to sit in silence and raise a hand and wave it frantically in the air! The teacher's judgement on the rightness of knowledge or behaviour is not to be questioned.

Controlling behaviour and assessing learning are teacherly activities which run contrary to usual human relationships. Both can become oppressive and 'controlling' to the students, be they child or adult, and a source of resentment to the more autodidactic (see Boekaerts 1993, Chapter 1). Data from that study showed that increasing the amount of teaching actually decreased pupils' achievement by raising the levels of anxiety and irritation. That suggests teachers need to reduce their controlling behaviour and the continual commentary of assessment about the students' work. The first of these may be done by using strategies that do not require the presence or intervention of a teacher, such as project work.

Some classes of GNVQ students whom I monitored in 1994 gave a sad indication of the legacy of an oppressive teacher/student relationship that they carried over from pre-16 education. On being asked (Solomon 1995) 'How do you cope when you find the work difficult?' the students were more likely to answer 'ask a friend' than either of the other options supplied – 'look it up in a book', or 'ask the teacher'. Significantly, it was the third option which was *least* often picked.

Assessment is the second problem area for autodidacts. We have seen in the last chapter (pages 202–3) how averse some adult learners are to either assignments or examinations. To whom will they grant the task of pronouncing on the quality of their work? Paul Black, a leader in the field of formative assessment once wrote that 'Formative assessment involves a close relationship between teacher and pupils . . . to modify the work in order to make it more effective.' (1993: 49). In the old BTEC system, as in GNVQ which has supplanted it, action planning – very like formative assessment – involved quite long sessions between student and teacher identifying characteristic faults and how they might be emended in future work. Very helpful, of course, except to the touchy autodidacts who could well find it similar to the public confessions to faults in learning described above for the young Japanese boy. Can we let them keep their precious self-esteem? It is far more effective for autodidacts to evaluate their own work, with the teacher only commenting afterwards, than to muscle in with the first point in a list of faults. Ecclestone (2002) in her study of learning autonomy that seems to have the potential to improve motivation, commented that she could see little evidence for the transformative effects that Mezirow (1990) and others had been expecting from it.

The learning environment

Different parts of the school environment – the classroom, gym, workshop, playing field, and the laboratory – are settings redolent of different kinds of learning. Class teachers may have a chance to see how these different learning environments and their teachers produce different effects on the learning of the students. The combination of the teacher's personality, and the subject skills related to the subject, can be enough to make the student's work quite different in one place from another. This is another example of skills being connected to the environment.

One way in which environment can certainly be used to help estranged and occasionally truanting learners is by removing the class and teacher to an entirely new situation. I learnt this from a secondary biology teacher who regularly took groups of children from his school in a poor area in north London to walk some miles along the hilly south coast from Brighton to Eastbourne. He also took with him a mixed bunch of teachers, which often included me. As we all struggled up and over the steep grassy slopes and ate our picnics, new friendships seemed to form, irrespective of the discomfort. The memory of these walks and the jokes made during them, almost always improved relationships later in the classroom, and made learning possible where previously it had been very strained.

Most primary schools make an attempt to vary the learning environment of the classroom so that it is different in different corners. There is carpet to sit on for story-time, free seating for discussions, and a home corner for cooking. This usually works well. Brit Lindahl (2001), who has been researching the vexed question of why girls feel so inhibited from studying physics, has evidence that many secondary girl students find the decor and lighting of the physics laboratory dark and uninviting. For a description of the intricate ways in which groups of secondary adolescent students use the territory of the teaching laboratory to gain or maintain 'social honour' in the eyes of their teacher, see Solomon (1989).

Another chance?

As teachers know, examinations fail many students, as well as rewarding others.

> The knowledge-based revolution of the twenty first century will be built on investment in the intellect and creativity of people . . . by transforming inventions into new wealth, just as we did a hundred years ago. But unlike then, *everyone* must have the opportunity to innovate and gain rewards.
>
> (DfEE 1998)

Despite such egalitarian rhetoric, opportunities seem different to different students at different times in their lives. When the stakes are high, failure in tests leaves severe scars on the defeated who, in some cases, later turn against society in anger. The most difficult task of teachers and lecturers is *to help learners survive failure.* Put baldly like that it seems a poor goal, and it certainly is difficult. But for the peace of society and the lives of those who may be excluded from employment, it is paramount. The Open University was founded as the 'University of the Second Chance', and the enthusiasm quoted by Scanlon in Chapter 13 was often a rejoicing in success after failure.

The pain of failure needs time to heal. Below are extracts from two students who failed their physics examination (Solomon 1995) the previous year and are preparing to retake in GNVQ. The first is that of a young man retaking it while the failure was still strong in his mind. The second is a young woman returning to study at college after some years at work, the reactions are not gender specific.

> 'I failed my physics (at GCSE). I was dreadfully upset. I just fell apart at the exam. I found it quite difficult so I've sort of got this fear of physics now.'

> 'Now this year, . . . Like I said, if I am stuck I'll get help. So I try to work it out for myself, but if I can't I ask for help . . . When I was at school I did give up and I have learnt from my mistakes. I left, I started working, and I got my confidence back. And then I thought "Well I am capable, so I am going to go back and, you know, get there".'

The results of these two failures were very different. The first student dropped out before taking any examinations. But the second student, who had understood her failure without losing a sense of autonomy, passed the examination. What can teachers do to help? Once again every case is different. Jarvis (1995: 113) in his account of autonomy in adults quoted in Boud and Bridge (1974) to the effect that student's essential freedoms were 'pace, method, content and assessment'.

Truanting

Do our children still enjoy school? In the 1970s and early 1980s it was common for city children to wait eagerly for the date of going back to school at the end of the summer holidays. Often they had enjoyed little in the way of trips away from home, even for a day, and poured back into the classroom in September full of talk and new games. If there is now too much pressure to learn, and too much revision in order to 'do well' in the tests, the same children may dread going back to school. The more autodidactic of our pupils may well be the ones to feel it most.

Our students truant from school when the pressure increases too much, and for them our streets may be dangerous places. To 'solve' this, the government encourages the police round-up of truants and the public even applauds as they are returned reluctantly to school. Under the head-line 'Teaching truants the value of schooling' the following comment, made by the local Police Superintendent, was printed in a well-respected newspaper.

> We . . . are extremely proud of our innovative schools programme. Indeed its success is recognised by the Home Office and is currently being spread nationwide *as part of the anti-street crime initiative*. We are also proud of the excellent working relationships we have with local schools.
>
> (*Oxford Times* 31 May 2002, my emphasis)

If it takes a police round-up to teach students the value of schooling one can only wonder what this value might be.

There are two main messages for teachers from this Epilogue: first that learning should be autonomous and enjoyable; second that we should reduce failure lest students lose heart. This is *not* another argument like the fabricated 'All shall have prizes'. Autodidacts are rarely competitive. Instead of failure learners can choose alternative learning. For example, to pass from level 3 to 4 in literacy pupils have to be able to do joined-up writing. But is that essential for a lifelong interest in reading and writing? Too much pressure on such a mechanical skill rather than, for example, allowing them to write their own books, could move our children even further away from a delight in literature.

Adults learn lifelong, sometimes through open access courses, but mostly via the autonomous experiences of living (like the politician in Chapter 15). Cutting down on school tests would reduce the pressure to teach and revise endlessly, and avoid the psychic damage of student failure, all without lessening the opportunities for lifelong learning. To those with a strong autodidactic passion to learn it would undoubtedly be a particular blessing, and an advantage to us all.

References

Black, P. (1993) 'Formative and summative assessment by teachers', *Studies in Science Education* 21: 49–97.

Boekaerts, M. (1993) *Motivation in education.* Vernon-Wall Lecture. Series editors P. Kutnich and P. Sutherland. London: British Psychological Society.

Boud, D. and Bridge, W. (1974) *Keller Plan: a case study in individualised learning.* Institute of Educational Technology, University of Surrey.

DfEE (1998) *The Learning Age: a Renaissance for a New Britain.* Sheffield: Department of Education and Employment, 9–10.

Ecclestone, K. (2002) *Learning Autonomy in Post-16 Education.* London: Routledge Falmer.

Entwistle, N. and Ramsden, P. (1983) *Understanding Student Learning*. London: Croom Helm.

Jarvis, P. (1995) *Adult and Continuing Education*. London: RoutledgeFalmer.

Lindahl, B. (2001) *A Feeling for Science?* Thessaloniki, Greece: Third International Conference of the European Science Education Research Association.

Mezirow, J. (1990) *Transformative Dimensions of Adult Learning*. San Francisco: Jossey-Bass.

Solomon, J. (1989) 'A study of behaviour in the teaching laboratory', *International Journal of Science Education* 11(3): 317–326.

Solomon, J. (1995) 'GNVQ Science at Advanced level: motivation and self-esteem', *Physics Education* 30(4): 223–227.

Index